WANDSWORTH PUBLIC LIBRARIES
M.S.C.

...rough of Wandsworth.

...PUBLIC LIBRARY WANDSWORTH,
LONDON S.W.18

£ 20.75
nett

KV-614-448

100 837 508 00

REWRITING HISTORY

The Original and Revised World War II Diaries of Curt Prüfer, Nazi Diplomat

REWRITING HISTORY

The Original and Revised World War II Diaries of Curt Prüfer, Nazi Diplomat

Edited and with an Introduction by
Donald M. McKale

Translated by
Judith M. Melton

THE KENT STATE UNIVERSITY PRESS
Kent, Ohio, and London, England

©1988 by The Kent State University Press, Kent, Ohio 44242
All rights reserved
Library of Congress Catalog Card Number 88-12034
ISBN 0-87338-364-8
Manufactured in the United States of America

940.532443 PRUF

100837508

1 ac

M.S.C.

WANDSWORTH PUBLIC LIBRARIES

2443

Library of Congress Cataloging-in-Publication Data

Prüfer, Curt Max, b. 1881.
  Rewriting history : the original and revised World War II diaries
of Curt Prüfer, Nazi diplomat / edited and with an introduction by
Donald M. McKale ; translated by Judith M. Melton.
      p.   cm.
  Bibliography: p.
  Includes index.
  ISBN 0-87338-364-8 (alk. paper)
  1. Prüfer, Curt Max, b. 1881—Diaries. 2. Diplomats—Germany—
Diaries. 3. Germany—Politics and government—1933-1945. 4. World
War, 1939-1945—Diplomatic history. I. McKale, Donald M., 1943- .
  II. Title.
DD247.P73A3   1988
  943.086′092′4—dc19   88-12034
                                                            CIP

British Library Cataloging-in-Publication data are available

Contents

Editor's Introduction

Two Versions of the Same Diary: Their Origins and Significance

"Today," Curt Max Prüfer wrote to himself on 3 September 1946, "I concluded the manuscript that I have labored over for nearly a year. The heart of the work is a diary, which was written in the months from October 1942 to September 1943, during the time I lived in Germany in the war."[1] The former German diplomat, whose long and distinguished career is chronicled elsewhere, was living with little economic means in Switzerland and seethed with anger and bitterness at Germany's defeat in World War II and the subsequent prosecution of the Nazi war criminals at Nuremberg. He had just completed his apologia and intended it to explain the German catastrophe that had resulted from Adolf Hitler's regime.[2]

---

1. See Prüfer's diary notes, "Schweizer und Indisches Tagebuch vom 13.III.46−2.2.51," entry for 3 Sept. 1946, Olaf Prufer Collection/Kent, Ohio (hereafter OPC/KO). For a discussion of this and Prüfer's other postwar diaries referred to in this essay, see Donald M. McKale, *Curt Prüfer: German Diplomat from the Kaiser to Hitler* (Kent, Ohio: Kent State University Press, 1987), p. 193 n. 1. These diaries, along with the other personal papers and materials of Prüfer in OPC/KO, will be placed for public use in the Hoover Institution on War, Revolution and Peace at Stanford University.

2. For a discussion of the apologia as a type of diary, note Thomas Mallon, *A Book of One's Own: People and Their Diaries* (New York: Ticknor & Fields, 1984), pp. 166−206. Prüfer's biographer is McKale, *Curt Prüfer.*

However, the diaries from 1942 and 1943, which Prüfer incorporated into the manuscript and which he intended to publish as a book, had been heavily edited. A comparison of the diaries with Prüfer's original ones from those years reveals that during 1945–46 he substantially changed portions of the 1942–43 diaries. Both versions of these diaries are presented here: the original in Part One and the rewritten or revised version in Part Two.

The handwritten original diaries, kept between the time Prüfer returned to Germany in the fall of 1942—after serving as Reich ambassador to Brazil—and September 1943, when he began a leave acquired from the German Foreign Ministry (*Auswärtiges Amt,* or AA) to live in neutral Switzerland, showed him supporting overwhelmingly the nationalism, dictatorship, and anti-Semitism of the Nazi government and despising the Anglo-American and Russian enemies. The revised diaries, on the other hand, which Prüfer claimed to have written during 1942–43 but which he wrote after Germany's defeat and occupation by the Allies, portrayed the reverse: Prüfer and the Germans appeared therein as anti-Hitler and anti-Nazi, sympathetic to the Jews, and much less hostile towards the Reich's conquerors.

The diaries' significance does not stem from a lack of such intimate writings by Germans during the Third Reich. Numerous diaries exist, with at least one "reconstructed" after World War II by its author from notes, private papers, and recollections.[3] Nor do the Prüfer diaries provide much new information regarding Nazi foreign policy. What makes them valuable historical records is that, with the exception of the daily journals kept by Hilter's minister of propaganda, Joseph Goebbels, similar writings of such German officials as Prüfer, who supported the Nazi regime, are almost nonexistent.

Of special interest, furthermore, is the fact that Prüfer left two sets, one the original, of his 1942–43 diaries.[4] This is most unique because historians studying the Nazi era have often found the original manuscripts of diaries

---

3. See Ursula von Karsdorff, *Berliner Aufzeichnungen 1942–1945* (Munich: Deutscher Taschenbuch Verlag, 1982), p. 5. The recently published diary of Marie Vassiltchikov, *Berlin Diaries, 1940–1945* (New York: Knopf, 1987), was retyped and corrected by its author shortly before her death in 1978. Neither Karsdorff nor Vassiltchikov, however, was a Nazi follower.
4. To my knowledge, the only comparable example that has been published is the Civil War journal of Mary Chestnut, the wife of a United States senator and general in the Confederate army, and the version of the journal that she wrote two decades after the war. Note C. Vann Woodward, ed., *Mary Chestnut's Civil War* (New Haven: Yale University Press, 1981); and C. Vann Woodward and Elisabeth Muhlenfeld, eds., *The Private Mary Chestnut: The Unpublished Civil War Diaries* (New York: Oxford University Press, 1984). Chestnut did not seek to falsify the record, however. For a discussion of the different versions of memoirs written by

from the period unavailable or inaccessible. A comparison of the original and revised versions of Prüfer's diaries should caution scholars anew against accepting diary accounts of Nazi leaders that cannot be verified as originals.[5] On the other hand, portions of what Prüfer added to the revised diaries were not simply fabrications, but additional facts and observations recalled by him from memory and based partially on documents and conversations with others. Thus, some of the revised entries possess the value of a memoir; the revision was not solely an apologia, but in its own way a source of information.

These two versions of the same diary show with a stunning and almost unrivaled clarity how a member of official and upper middle-class Germany, having served Hitler from 1933 to 1945, tried after World War II to protect himself and his people from the condemnation of history by insisting on their innocence during the Nazi regime. "The book," Prüfer noted privately when he began the manuscript containing the revised diaries, "should support the thesis that the German people were not to be blamed for the outbreak of the war, but that it had instead been prepared systematically and with every premeditation by a clique of German warmongers."[6]

Prüfer's typewritten manuscript, which opened with an autobiographical discussion through which the author introduced the altered diaries, remained unpublished. Although he had hoped in 1946 to receive badly needed money from sale of the volume, it is unclear whether he actually submitted it to a publisher. While writing it he declared on one occasion that "I suspect [it] will never appear; who would print something like it? It is also too boring and not sensational enough for today." Moreover, he feared that because the work denounced his former boss, Foreign Minister Joachim von Ribbentrop, as part of the Nazi gang responsible for the German debacle, it might be used by the Allies to prosecute the minister at

---

Ernst Freiherr von Weizsäcker, the secretary of state in the AA from 1938 to 1943, and how they have contributed to the controversy among historians regarding Weizsäcker's actions, see Leonidas E. Hill, "The Genesis and Interpretation of the Memoirs of Ernst von Weizsäcker," *German Studies Review*, 10(1987): 443–80. A blatant instance in German history of a person seeking to alter personal papers for the sake of self-justification is explained in Isabel V. Hull's review of Hans Wilhelm Burmeister, *Prince Philipp Eulenburg-Hertefeld, 1847–1921: His Influence on Kaiser Wilhelm II and His Role in the German Government, 1888–1902* (Wiesbaden: Steiner, 1981), in *American Historical Review*, 88(1983):130–31.

5. As they have tended to do, for example, with Rudolf Semmler, *Goebbels—The Man Next to Hitler* (London: Westhouse, 1947); and Wilfred von Oven, *Mit Goebbels bis zum Ende*, 2 vols. (Buenos Aires: Dürer-Verlag, 1949–50).

6. See one of the several volumes of diary notes Prüfer kept during and after World War II, "Tägliche Notizen 7.9.44 bis 21.4.46" (hereafter "Notizen," III), entry for 10 July 1945, OPC/KO.

Nuremberg. Prüfer admitted that, despite the animosity he harbored as a career diplomat against Ribbentrop, whom he considered a Nazi intruder in the AA, "it would be very difficult for me, a German, . . . to put someone such as Ribbentrop on the block, even though he was so unpleasant to me."[7]

That the autobiography resembled a propaganda tract also probably lessened its chances for publication. Riddled with distortions and omissions and written in a polemical tone reminiscent of the numerous memoirs published after World War II by former German diplomats, it provided little information on Prüfer's career. It focused instead on defending the Reich's policy during the era of both World Wars. Prüfer mentioned nothing of his birth in Berlin in 1881, his early life in Imperial Germany, and the influence of that background on his political and social attitudes. After noting his entry into the Foreign Service in 1907, he dismissed in a few pages his work as German consul general in Tiflis (1925–27), minister to Ethiopia (1928–30), deputy director of the AA's Anglo-American and Middle Eastern Division (1930–36), head of the ministry's Personnel and Budget Division (1936–39), ambassador to Brazil (1939–42), and ambassador for special duties in the AA's Middle Eastern section (1942–43). He also omitted how he had welcomed Hitler to power in 1933, collaborated with the Nazis in their penetration of the Foreign Ministry, and joined the Nazi party (*Nationalsozialistische Deutsche Arbeiterpartei*, abbreviated NSDAP) in 1938.[8]

Although unable to publish the autobiography, Prüfer retained copies of the manuscript—which included the revised version of the diaries—when he gave the bulk of his private papers to the Foreign Ministry of the German Federal Republic in Bonn.[9] The manuscript, he had decided, would be his legacy to his family:

To satisfy myself, I at least wish to leave behind for my descendants a coherent portrayal of what I experienced in this 'great era' and what—modest—role I played in it. It is an apologia, a defense of myself, and not only that, it is an explanation for the behavior of many of my friends and colleagues who stood in service to the Hitler government and believed they were acting in the best interests of Germany.[10]

---

7. Ibid.; and Prüfer, "Schweizer und Indisches Tagebuch," entry for 26 June 1946, OPC/KO.

8. See Prüfer autobiography manuscript, esp. pp. 10–18, 29–36, 76–79, OPC/KO. His career is detailed in McKale, *Curt Prüfer*.

9. The records were given to the AA following Prüfer's death in 1959 by his wife, Anneliese; see the ministry to A. Prüfer, 7 Jan. 1960, OPC/KO.

10. Prüfer, "Schweizer und Indisches Tagebuch," entry for 26 June 1946, OPC/KO.

He kept the original version of the diaries, however, and following his death in 1959, the materials passed to his wife and then to his son, Olaf, the latter living in the United States. The son, who opposed his father's political views and prejudices, eventually made both the revised and original sets of diaries available for publication.

Comparing the Original and Revised Diaries

Prüfer introduced the revised version of his 1942–43 diaries by declaring in his autobiography: "Now I will let my diary speak, whose text I have in no way changed."[11] A comparison of the revised diary with the original, however, quickly reveals the falsity of his claim. In some instances Prüfer had changed the original only slightly, merely altering in the revised diaries a sentence or a few words in a paragraph. But such modifications usually changed the content of the original version significantly. More often he fabricated substantial material in the revised diaries; the major example was his invention of all the entries for October 1942, for which no original diaries existed.[12] Also in the revised version he used long and convoluted sentences. These reflected not only his turgid writing style, but also his bitter emotional turmoil after the war and his efforts to conceal his true feelings. He hid behind the length and detail of what he wrote, a practice not uncommon among Nazi bureaucrats, who had frequently manipulated language during the war to camouflage their activities.[13]

Prüfer's attempt to rewrite history in such a fashion had two goals: to absolve the Germans and himself of all responsibility for the Hitler regime's policies of aggressive war and annihilation of the Jews; and to persuade the world that his people did not deserve postwar foreign occupation or de-Nazification. What he did also provides considerable insight into his personality. As his biography has shown, except for his education, his talent as a linguist and diplomat, and his nearly thirty-eight years of uninterrupted service to German governments, there was little to admire about Prüfer. A product of the narrow and illiberal culture of Imperial Germany, he worshipped the German state and held exceedingly arrogant and prejudiced

---

11. Prüfer autobiography ms., p. 79, OPC/KO.

12. For an explanation, see chap. 12, n. 1.

13. Just as the bureaucrats involved had repressed the psychological effects of the killing operations carried out by the Nazi Elite Guard (*Schutzstaffel*, SS) against the Jews and others during World War II; Raul Hilberg, *The Destruction of the European Jews* (Chicago: Quadrangle, 1967), p. 216.

views towards non-Germans, particularly Jews, and persons of lower social standing.[14]

These traits (especially his contempt for other peoples), which he tried to soften in the revised diaries, possibly explain why Prüfer never came close in that version to respecting the Latin meaning of *diarium* and its lack of knowledge of the future. As the reader will note, little surprised Prüfer in the revised diaries. He portrayed himself as anti-Nazi and able to foresee many political and military events from this crucial period in the war, when key battles in Russia and North Africa turned the tide in favor of the Allies and against the Axis. The reader will also observe that Prüfer insisted in the revised diaries that the Allied policy, adopted at the Casablanca Conference in January 1943, of fighting until the "unconditional surrender" of the Axis, undermined peace. He mentioned nothing of this, however, in the original version.[15] In addition, although the original diary indicates that he knew several key figures of the German anti-Hitler resistance, the diplomat apparently had no knowledge of their conspiratorial activities.[16]

Prüfer's portrait of himself in the altered diaries as hostile to Nazism also resulted from the influence of the Nuremberg trials, which began as he made the changes. He detested the Allied tribunal and erroneously accused it of holding the Germans "collectively guilty" for war crimes.[17] Prüfer apparently believed—at least for a time—that his "revelations" could help

---

14. McKale, *Curt Prüfer.*

15. Contrast the revised and original diaries, entries for 19 July 1943. The typewritten revised diaries (hereafter RD) are included in the Prüfer autobiography ms., OPC/KO. The handwritten original diaries (hereafter OD) are Prüfer, "Tägliche Notizen 11.11.42 bis 7.1.44," OPC/KO. Also, in this connection, Prüfer referred in the revised version to Germany's alleged brutal fate at the hands of the allies if the Reich surrendered; such discussion was omitted from the original. Compare the entries for 11 Nov. 1942; 7 Jan.; 30 Apr. 1943.

16. His acquaintances, in this regard, included Friedrich Werner Count von der Schulenburg and his kinsman, Fritz-Dietlof Count von der Schulenburg; Ulrich von Hassell; Adam von Trott zu Solz; Erwin Planck; Axel Freiherr von dem Bussche; Erwin von Witzleben; and possibly Hans Oster. See, for example, OD, entries for 19 Nov. 1942; 11, 18, 20, 21 Jan., 8, 9 Feb., 10 Apr. 1943. On occasion Prüfer observed their unhappiness. His generally reserved reaction to the bomb plot that nearly killed Hitler on 20 July 1944 is in the diplomat's diary, "Tägliche Notizen 10.1.44 bis 6.9.44," entry for 21 July 1944, OPC/KO.

17. The rejection by Germans of what they perceived to be the charge of "collective guilt" is in the studies conducted by the American government immediately after World War II, the so-called OMGUS (Office of Military Government for Germany, United States) surveys, in Anna J. and Richard L. Merritt, eds., *Public Opinion in Occupied Germany: The OMGUS Surveys, 1945–1949* (Urbana: University of Illinois Press, 1970), esp. pp. 121–22, 149. Shortly after the trials started in Oct. 1945, Prüfer wrote in his diary: "The bloody farce in N. [Nuremberg] has begun." See Prüfer, "Notizen," III, entry for 20 Nov. 1945, OPC/KO.

refute the mountain of evidence produced at the trials against the former Nazi leaders in the dock.[18]

Several examples of the differences between the diaries should alert the reader to their author's deception. Following the successful Anglo-American landings at Casablanca, Oran, and Algiers on 7-8 November 1942, Prüfer acknowledged in the original diaries that the Allies "had their first great success" in North Africa, "and the Jews are rejoicing." A few days later, he complained about German policy: "Again, as in the first war, the Orient and Mediterranean are being neglected."[19] The revised diaries, however, excluded the reference to the Jews and attacked the Italians for failing to use their fleet to halt the enemy in the Mediterranean. Prüfer also used the occasion to portray the German people as longing for peace and ready to overthrow the Nazi regime, adding an extensive section in the revised diaries for 11 November condemning the enemy for allegedly wanting "the destruction not only of Hitler, but of everything German."[20]

When the shocking news arrived on 1 February 1943 that German forces had surrendered at Stalingrad, Prüfer appeared relatively unconcerned in the original diaries. Only on 23 February did he indicate an awareness of the serious situation in the East, as he recorded how an officer and friend serving in Russia had reported the "disaster" there and blamed Hitler.[21] Nevertheless, when Goebbels addressed the leaders of the Reich government two weeks later and demanded that they (in Prüfer's words) "desist from all criticism" and "stop grumbling," instead striving to "encourage our coworkers by setting a good example," Prüfer applauded in the original diaries: "That is exactly what I would have said."[22] In the altered version, however, he provided an opposite picture, even holding Hitler responsible for the Stalingrad debacle.[23]

Prüfer worried much more in the original diaries about the steady collapse of the German position in Tunisia, the last position of the Axis in North Africa, and the Allied bombings of the Reich. His bitter invective

---

18. The best survey of the quantity and quality of Nazi records produced at Nuremberg is John Mendelsohn, ed., *The Holocaust*, 18 vols. (New York: Garland Publishing, 1982).

19. See OD, entries for 11, 14 Nov. 1942.

20. RD, entries for 11, 14 Nov. 1942.

21. OD, entries for 1, 23 Feb. 1943. Possibly illustrating Prüfer's nationalism and reluctance to assess his people and other government officials with part of the responsibility for what was occurring, this and other comments in the original diaries on negative or unpleasant subjects were often not made in German but in a foreign language. Note, for instance, OD, entries for 22 Nov. 1942 and 22 Feb. 1943.

22. OD, entry for 15 Feb. 1943.

23. See RD, entry for 1 Feb. 1943.

against the bombings resulted in part from his firsthand experience with them when he lost much of his property in Berlin during a raid on 16 January 1943.[24] The original diaries also show that, by the summer of 1943, he hoped there was substance to one of the many peace rumors circulating in the press and diplomatic circles and that the war would end soon.[25]

When that did not occur, his fear and disillusionment mounted; the original diaries record that he intensified efforts begun in November 1942 to acquire a leave from the AA and settle with his family in the safety of neighboring Switzerland. His personal problems also multiplied. Tensions with his wife increased, exacerbated by their declining health and his drinking and repeated philandering. Such problems formed a dominant theme in the original version.[26] Despite his relatively comfortable and secure lifestyle as he moved between Berlin and his residence in Baden-Baden, he was full of self-pity and a snobbish disdain for the "black marketeers" and suffering of the lower classes.

In the original version, moreover, bitterness consumed him as he observed the political world he had known for nearly forty years coming apart at the seams. He despised how he and the other career officials in the AA had been stripped by Ribbentrop of even the remnants of influence in the Reich's foreign policy. In this regard, he differed little from other civil servants in Nazi Germany when the regime did not deliver the rewards and status the bureaucrats had expected from it.[27]

Prüfer spent considerable time in the original diaries vilifying the younger officials in the AA who dominated key positions, owed their careers to membership in the Nazi party, and sought to avoid service at the front by staffing the many new divisions and committees created by Ribbentrop. Prüfer especially resented the *Abteilung Deutschland*, the Division for Internal German Affairs in the AA, which was responsible for liaison with the NSDAP and its Elite Guard (*Schutzstaffel*, or SS). He disliked the Abteilung not because it helped arrange for the AA's participation in the Nazi extermination of the Jews, but because it included numerous interlopers in the AA from the party.

When the intrigue perpetrated against Ribbentrop by Abteilung leader

---

24. OD, entry for 16 Jan. 1943.

25. OD, entries for 18, 24 May and 1, 4, 9, 10 July 1943.

26. Examples are in OD, entries for 16 Nov. 1942 and 19 Jan., 2 Mar., 22 Mar., 8 Apr. 1943. See also, McKale, *Curt Prüfer*, p. 174.

27. A survey of the attitudes of the civil service in Bavaria can be found in Ian Kershaw, *Popular Opinion and Political Dissent in the Third Reich: Bavaria, 1933–1945* (New York: Clarendon Press-Oxford, 1983), pp. 323-26.

Martin Luther misfired in December 1942, Prüfer eagerly cooperated in an investigation ordered by the minister to help remove Luther.[28] Raging against such outsiders on 21 January 1943, Prüfer denounced in the original diaries "the inappropriately proliferating 'bureaucracy' in our Fatherland." However, indicating his powerful attachment to Hitler, he closed the diary entry on a note of hope: "If only there were someone who would quite openly tell the Führer about all these loathsome things!"[29] Also worthy of note is the fact that no matter how furiously Prüfer denounced Ribbentrop in the revised diaries, portraying him as the scapegoat for the corruption and demoralization in the AA, Prüfer's help in removing Luther had contributed to the survival in office of the minister, a man condemned and hanged at Nuremberg for war crimes.

In addition, Prüfer had become mired in the petty jealousies and conflicts separating the major Arab leaders allied with the Axis during the war: Haj Amin al-Husayni, the Grand Mufti (*Grossmufti*) of Jerusalem, and Rashid Ali al-Gailani, the former prime minister of Iraq, as well as their respective supporters in the AA's Middle Eastern section, Erwin Ettel and Fritz Grobba. Both Arab nationalists tried unsuccessfully to obtain from the Axis a declaration of Arab independence, partly because Hitler feared alienating Germany's ally, Italy, and collaborator, Vichy France, both of which hoped to use the war to expand their imperial holdings in the Middle East. The Mufti and Gailani rivaled each other for influence with Berlin and Rome and recognition from the Axis as the official spokesman for the Arab world. Prüfer, however, rarely mentioned in the revised diaries either his involvement in the quarrel or his support of the Mufti, possibly because the Allies sought Husayni following the war as an accessory to the Nazi annihilation of the Jews and other peoples.[30]

---

28. OD, entries for 14, 15, 19, 30 Dec. 1942 and 7, 20-1, 22, 23 Jan., 11, 16 Feb., 9, 19 July 1943. The best discussion of the new layer of bureaucracy in the AA and conflicts between the older generation of careerists in the ministry and the group of NSDAP appointees is Christopher R. Browning, "The Government Experts," in Henry Friedlander and Sybil Milton, eds., *The Holocaust: Ideology, Bureaucracy, and Genocide* (Millwood, N.Y.: Kraus, 1980), pp. 183—98.

29. See OD, entry for 21 Jan. 1943.

30. Both Yugoslavia and Britain sought the Mufti as a war criminal. The Yugoslavians wanted him "for inciting brutalities and for pro-German activities among the Bosnian Moslems." See J. C. Hurewitz, *The Struggle for Palestine* (New York: Greenwood Press, 1968; first pub. 1950), pp. 234—35, 251—52; and Lukasz Hirszowicz, *The Third Reich and the Arab East* (London: Routledge & Kegan Paul, 1966), p. 313. Had Husayni had his way, he would doubtless have exterminated the Jewish population in Palestine; Prüfer recorded after a discussion with the Mufti in July 1943 that the latter "kept insisting on 'getting rid of the Jewish settlements in Palestine.' " Note OD entry for 17 July 1943.

As the original diaries also indicate, Prüfer's attitude towards the Nazi regime and the war during the summer of 1943 paralleled that of other nationalists and conservatives who had supported Hitler. Like them, Prüfer's frustration and disappointment intensified, particularly with the overthrow of Benito Mussolini in Italy and the massive Allied bombings of Hamburg and the cities along the Rhine and Ruhr rivers. Nevertheless, in his attempts to analyze what had gone wrong, Prüfer showed his admiration for Hitler by refusing to blame the dictator.[31] Those responsible for Germany's recent setbacks, he suggested on 19 July, included the Nazi officials who had replaced the professional bureaucrats like Prüfer in positions of authority.[32] Three years later, however, when he rewrote the entry for inclusion in his postwar apologia, Prüfer reversed its content by excluding the praise of Hitler and Nazism.

Furthermore, he fabricated a sentence alleging the sympathy of the German population for the Jews.[33] His lack of concern for the Jews and

---

31. In the wake of Mussolini's removal, for instance, there were apparently numerous feelings of sympathy among Germans for Hitler, as some pardoned the Führer by maintaining that he had been dealt a bitter disappointment by his circle of closest friends. See "SD-Berichte zu Inlandsfragen von 29. July 1943," Heinz Boberach, ed., *Meldungen aus dem Reich: Die geheimen Lageberichte des Sicherheitsdienstes der SS 1938–1945*, 17 vols. (Herrsching: Pawlak Verlag, 1984), XIV:5540–43; and Marlis G. Steinert, *Hitler's War and the Germans: Public Mood and Attitude during the Second World War*, ed. and tr. Thomas E. J. DeWitt (Athens, Ohio: Ohio University Press, 1977), pp. 215–18. This contradicts the assertion by Max Domarus, ed., *Hitler. Reden und Proklamationen 1932–1945* (Munich: Süddeutscher Verlag, 1965), II:2024, that the event led the majority of Germans to hope that "Hitler and his regime would soon be shoved aside."

32. OD, entry for 19 July 1943. His only negative remark towards Hitler in OD, which Prüfer attributed to another German official and wrote in Arabic, was in the entry for 23 Feb. 1943.

33. Contrast RD, entry for 19 July 1943, with the original version. The judgment of historians remains divided regarding the important issue that Prüfer raised here, i.e., the degree of anti-Semitism among the German population and the potency of the sentiment in contributing to the people's relationship to the Nazi regime. The following are part of the vast literature on the problem: Kershaw, chap. 9; Sarah Gordon, *Hitler, Germans and the "Jewish Question"* (Princeton: Princeton University Press, 1984), pp. 186–97; Otto Dov Kulka, "Die Nürnberger Rassengesetze und die Deutsche Bevölkerung im Lichte geheimer NS-Lage-und Stimmungsberichte," *Vierteljahrshefte für Zeitgeschichte*, 32(1984): 582–623; Gerhard L. Weinberg, *The Foreign Policy of Hitler's Germany*, vol. 1, *Diplomatic Revolution in Europe, 1933–36* (Chicago: University of Chicago Press, 1970), I:23–24; Michael H. Kater's review of Kershaw, *Popular Opinion*, in "How Popular Was the Third Reich?" *Simon Wiesenthal Center Annual*, 2(1985): 213-20; Wolfgang Scheffler, "Wege zur 'Endlösung,' " in Herbert A. Strauss and Norbert Kampe, eds., *Antisemitismus. Von der Judenfeindschaft zum Holocaust* (Frankfurt/Main: Campus Verlag, 1985), pp. 186–214; William S. Allen, *The Nazi Seizure of Power: The Experience of a Single German Town, 1922–1945*, rev. ed. (New York: Franklin Watts, 1984), p. 291; and Norman Rich, *Hitler's War Aims*, vol. 1, *Ideology, the Nazi State, and the Course of Expansion* (New York: Norton, 1973), I: xxxix.

their fate, which is revealed in the original diaries, could be traced to his rabid, long-held anti-Semitic views.[34] He excluded from the revised diaries the numerous anti-Jewish references in the originals.[35] He thus appeared determined to hide his anti-Semitism and the fact that both he and his friends, particularly in the upper and upper-middle classes to whom he belonged, possessed information about the destruction of the Jews. At the beginning of the revised diaries, he stated in the entry for 16 October 1942 that on his return home from Brazil, he had "heard for the first time about the mass deportation of Jews." He also observed that while in Brazil, "rumors about these deportations had reached us from Germany as well as from enemy sources; however, they seemed to us to be so dreadful that we held them to be 'atrocity stories,' or at the very least exaggerated, like so many other reports of enemy propaganda that had proved to be incorrect."[36]

Because no original diary notes are available for that entry, it is impossible to check its truthfulness. However, based on Prüfer's well-documented anti-Semitism and on the radical changes in the rest of the revised diaries aimed at concealing his support for the Nazi regime, one suspects that he knew more in Brazil about the fate of the Jews and even accepted that the "rumors" were true. Information regarding the murder of the Jews, coming primarily from Polish and Jewish sources through Switzerland, had spread throughout Western capitals by autumn of 1942.[37] Numerous leading officials in the AA, including Secretary of State Ernst Freiherr von Weizsäcker, had read and initialled reports since 1941 from the SS killing squads (*Einsatzgruppen*), each referring to many thousands of Jews slaughtered. There are indications that even in remote German legations abroad—including Uruguay—some diplomats knew. Much information also passed orally inside the AA and apparently even more often outside, through friends or members of families.[38]

---

34. As examples, see McKale, *Curt Prüfer*, pp. 41, 59–63, 94–97, 100–101, 103–9, 134, 174–76, 180–81, 182.

35. His mention of Jews in OD is in the entries for 11, 22 Nov. 1942 and 26 Feb., 9, 14, 30 Apr., 14, 17 May, 16–17 July, 11 Aug. 1943; these should be compared to the same dates for RD. On other occasions, Prüfer fabricated pro-Jewish comments in RD, e.g., entries for 12 May, 3 June, 4, 19 July 1943.

36. RD, entry for 16 Oct. 1942.

37. According to Martin Gilbert, *Auschwitz and the Allies* (New York: Holt, Rinehart and Winston, 1981), p. 87: "There was no longer any reason for anyone in the west to live in a 'fool's paradise.' Publication of the terrible facts had become an almost daily event."

38. See Walter Laqueur, *The Terrible Secret: Suppression of the Truth about Hitler's 'Final Solution'* (Boston: Little, Brown and Co., 1980), pp. 25-27; Christopher R. Browning, *The Final Solution and the German Foreign Office: A Study of Referat D III of Abteilung Deutschland, 1940–43* (New York: Holmes and Meier, 1978), pp. 72–75; and Donald L. Sing-

What strengthens the belief that Prüfer sought to obscure what he knew in Brazil are the significant differences on the subject between the entry for 22 November 1942 in the original diaries and that for 21 November in the altered version. In the original, he recorded hearing "horrible stories" about Jews being "slaughtered in large numbers by poison-gas or by machine guns" and observed: "Today every child knows this in the smallest detail." In the revised version, however, before noting that his "sources confirm that all this is true," Prüfer cast doubt on the statement by fabricating several sentences: "It appears that it has finally come hereabouts to grave Jewish persecutions. . . . They are all said to have been . . . exterminated—men, women, and children—by gas or machine guns. If these stories really correspond to the facts, only hatred can result from this, which will never die and will cause us unspeakable harm."[39]

Prüfer closed the revised diaries with the entry for 7 September 1943, the day he arrived with his family in Switzerland following Ribbentrop's approval of his leave from the AA. It was unlikely that his exiting Germany represented a final act of indifference on his part towards the catastrophic policies of his government. It is more plausible that, in the face of what he knew about such policies, his departure resulted from a wish to escape the consequences of his failure to oppose those policies.

Ribbentrop justified the leave by accepting Prüfer's proposal that he carry out a special mission, code-named "Rosita," in which Prüfer would gather information on the Middle East by contacting Arab exiles in Switzerland. The leave, however, represented a prelude to his official retirement from the ministry on 1 April 1945, shortly before the end of the war in Europe.[40] Posing in his revised diaries as sympathetic to democracy and Western liberalism and fearful of the German Secret Police (*Gestapo*) and Security Service (*Sicherheitsdienst*, or SD), he recorded in the entry on 7

er, "German Diplomats at Nuremberg: A Study of the Foreign Office Defendants of the Ministries Case," unpublished Ph.D. dissertation, American University, 1980, especially pp. 269–70. Leonidas E. Hill, ed., *Die Weizsäcker Papiere 1933–1950* (Berlin: Propyläen, 1974), asserted that Weizsäcker did not know what was happening to the Jews.

39. Contrast OD, entry for 22 Nov. 1942, with RD, entry for 21 Nov. 1942. These entries are also in Hans-Jürgen Döscher, *Das Auswärtige Amt in Dritten Reich. Diplomatie im Schatten der "Endlösung"* (Berlin: Siedler Verlag, 1987), pp. 252–54. O. Prufer published the original diary entry in a brief letter to the editor in *Der Spiegel*, No. 10, 5 Mar. 1979, and added in the note: "I was twelve years old at that time [22 Nov. 1942]. In the Jungvolk and Hitler Youth in Baden-Baden, where I lived then, expressions like 'If you do not obey, you will land in a concentration camp and be gassed' were absolutely a daily occurrence." The *Jungvolk* was a division of the Hitler Youth for boys aged ten to fourteen.

40. The details are in McKale, *Curt Prüfer*, pp. 177, 179.

September 1943: "Today for the first time in a year, we can breathe, think, and talk freely."[41]

Prüfer made it clear in several postwar diaries that he did not mean such words and instead remained after World War II full of hatred for the Jews and for those who had defeated Germany.[42] Such views augment the few studies of public opinion in postwar Germany. To my knowledge, no other diaries or similar private records exist from that period that could reveal the innermost thoughts of Germans. Opinion polls, however, such as those conducted between 1945 and 1949 by the American military government (OMGUS) in its zone of occupation suggest that Prüfer differed little from his countrymen in their immediate postwar attitudes towards National Socialism and the Allied treatment of Germany and its former leaders.[43]

Thus, Prüfer's example, albeit limited, offers a further justification for the Allied de-Nazification campaign, whose effectiveness was plagued by several problems.[44] Prüfer's revised and original diaries provide a rare glimpse into how deeply the Nazi philosophy had been embedded in at least one German, how he remained loyal to it after the war, and how he thought of concealing it from the world. He died in 1959 in Baden-Baden, at the age of seventy-seven.[45]

Editorial Note

Both versions of the Prüfer diaries are published here in their entirety—the original in Part One and the revised in Part Two. Accompanying the text are numerous biographical and explanatory notes, made nec-

---

41. RD, entry for 7 Sept. 1943. Although he mentioned the Gestapo and SD in the diaries, except for occasionally recording in a foreign language unpleasant or negative thoughts, little in Prüfer's OD suggests that he feared or resented police suppression.

42. See, for instance, Prüfer, "Schweizer und Indisches Tagebuch," entries for 17 Oct. 1946 and 21 May 1948, OPC/KO; and the other virulent passages from his postwar diaries quoted in McKale, *Curt Prüfer*, chap. 12.

43. Merritt and Merritt, pp. 31–32, 51, 146, 239–40, 304; Elisabeth Noelle and Erich Peter Neumann, eds., *The Germans: Public Opinion Polls, 1947–1966*, tr. Gerard Finan (Allensbach and Bonn: Verlag für Demoskopie, 1967), pp. 188-89, 193, 203; and Lutz Niethammer, *Entnazifizierung in Bayern. Säuberung und Rehabilitierung unter amerikanischer Besatzung* (Frankfurt/Main: S. Fischer, 1972), p. 486.

44. These are discussed in Niethammer, pp. 15–17, 483–86, 531; John Gimbel, *The American Occupation of Germany: Politics and the Military, 1945–1949* (Stanford: Stanford University Press, 1968), especially pp. 101–10, 158–62, 246–52; Merritt and Merritt, p. 36; and W. Friedman, *The Allied Military Government of Germany* (London: Stevens, 1947), p. 332.

45. McKale, *Curt Prüfer*, p. 185.

essary by the many persons, historical events, abbreviations, and code words mentioned by Prüfer. There is also a descriptive appendix (Appendix I) of persons who appear often in the text. The names Prüfer consistently misspelled and his frequently long sentences add to the difficulty in reading the diaries. Names spelled incorrectly are noted in the text, except for Prüfer's repeated misspelling of his wife's name, Anneliese.

Also complicating the study of the original diaries is the fact that Prüfer later added comments, some in pencil, in the margin and elsewhere in the manuscript. In addition, he struck through (i.e., marked for deletion) a few passages. It is evident that he made some of the alterations as part of his writing of the revised diaries. Such changes are not incorporated in the text of the original version, except those of a substantive nature, which are presented in the notes. For ease of reading, many (although not all) code words and abbreviations are identified in the text instead of in notes. Some abbreviations, including those Prüfer used for his wife, (A.) Anneliese, and son, (O.) Olaf, are only identified the first time they appear in a chapter. The full names of other acronymns, particularly those he used for more than one person, are given each time they appear. A list of the most basic and frequently employed abbreviations is provided in Appendix II.

Prüfer, presumably after the war, also pencilled in many identifications in the original version of the diaries, most of which are not cited here as his; Olaf, his son, provided the editor with others. Historical sources and other bibliographic data are not cited in the notes. Readers will find most of the materials used to annotate the diaries in the extensive list of sources in the editor's biography of the diplomat.[46] Finally, the Arabic, Latin, Italian, and French words or phrases used by Prüfer have been retained in the text; the notes identify when he wrote in English. Translations are provided for the Arabic in the notes, but only when necessary for the other foreign passages. The only exceptions are Prüfer's occasional use of Arabic script; these are translated in the text.

Many people helped move the Prüfer diaries from manuscript to print. Most of them are acknowledged in the editor's previous study of Prüfer, just cited. Another who provided valuable assistance in editing this book and should be thanked is Judith M. Melton. As noted previously, a special debt of gratitude is owed to Olaf H. Prufer of Kent, Ohio. However, whatever errors of judgment, interpretation, or fact appear in the introduction to and annotation of the diaries are the editor's responsibility.

---

46. Ibid., pp. 243–61.

part one

The Original Diaries, November 1942 to September 1943

one

November 1942

11 November 1942

On 11 November I arrived in Berlin again, in fact accompanied by Ingrid v. Langenn-Steinkeller, who had gone with me to Baden-Baden two weeks before, in order to help A. with the great amount of work brought on by re-opening our house.[1] All of us underestimated the technical difficulties that the smallest building or manual change presents in these times. Thus my first long-awaited vacation in Baden-Baden was nowhere near as enjoyable as I had imagined. All building materials were lacking, and above all [there were no] workers, and it was no pleasure doing business with the few specialists who were available, since they were always in a bad mood because of overwork and frayed tempers.

---

1. "A" is Prüfer's abbreviation for Anneliese Fehrmann Prüfer, his second wife, whom he had married in 1927. For reasons that are unclear, he often misspelled her name in the diaries as "Annelies." On his relationship with her, see p. xiv. "Ingrid v. Langenn-Steinkeller" was the daughter of an aristocrat and estate owner near Bellin, Helmut von Langenn-Steinkeller, a former officer in the Imperial German army and friend of Prüfer's since World War I. Prüfer had an affair with Ingrid until 1943, when she married Maj. Hans-Ulrich von Oertzen, who was implicated in and arrested for the attempt of 20 July 1944 on Hitler's life; he later committed suicide. The Gestapo arrested many in the Langenn family. Prüfer had returned to Germany from Rio de Janeiro about the middle of Oct. 1942. He had served as the Reich's ambassador in Brazil from Sept. 1939 until the Rio government broke diplomatic relations with Germany in Jan. 1942 and, following the sinking of several Brazilian merchant ships by German submarines, declared war on Germany in August. Until his return to Berlin on 11 Nov. 1942, Prüfer and his family vacationed at their residence in Baden-Baden.

During my stay in B.B., Littmann from Tübingen visited me.[2] He has only aged outwardly and is still full of jokes and stories that he tells, unconcerned about his listeners, in a loud voice, even if they are rather coarse, or perhaps precisely because they are. Also Max Krüger and Glock visited us.[3] The first vigorously helped arrange furniture.

The last two days in B.B. were especially ruined for us because of the news from the new front in French North Africa.[4] It appears that reconnaissance and the intelligence services of the Axis failed completely, otherwise the surprise attacks of the English and Americans could not have been possible in so many places in Algeria and Morocco simultaneously. In any case, the result is a bad situation for the already hard-pressed Rommel,[5] and it is a further weakening of Italian strategic and moral positions. Today, in order to defend the coast ourselves, we invaded previously unoccupied Southern France. It is also planned to occupy Corsica before the Allies do. They have had their first great success, and the Jews are rejoicing.

The mood here in Berlin appears to be even a shade worse than in Baden, although this is not meant to imply that it is very good there, either. Particularly noticeable here are the edginess of the people and the impoliteness, even rudeness, in the way they behave towards one another. This lack of patience and friendliness is particularly noticeable among the personnel at the hotel. The tone in the Hotel Adlon defies description, it is so vulgar and odious. Although the prices are extremely high, the guests are treated by the waiters as if they were beggars. The only person well-served is the black marketeer who appears at the table with numerous boxes, tin cans, and tiny packages, full of rare foodstuffs. From this illicit wealth the waiter hopes for some leftovers and scraps for himself. In contrast, I was badly treated today by the maitre d'hotel, an overfed "gentleman" in a black jacket, who had me wait, with unmistakable contempt, until a table was free. This, although I am an ambassador and live in the hotel. To be sure, the sleeves of

---

2. Enno Littmann, professor of Arabic at the University of Tübingen and virulent Jew-hater.

3. Gustav Glock was an AA official and former staff member of Prüfer's at the German Embassy in Brazil. Krüger was a senior civil servant who had been employed in the German Embassy in Moscow and became a secretary at the Consulate General in Tiflis while Prüfer served there in 1927.

4. On 8 Nov. 1942, Anglo-American troops initiated "Operation Torch" in North Africa, landing successfully at Casablanca, Oran, and Algiers. Although the Germans had received the cooperation of Vichy France since June 1940, the Allied invasion was aided by Vichy forces led by Adm. Jean Darlan. In response, the German army rushed troops into Tunisia in an attempt to shore up Axis units against the enemy. The Germans also occupied southern France. The landings in North Africa shocked both the German leadership and population.

5. Gen. Erwin Rommel, commander of the German Africa corps.

my coat have taken on a questionable sheen, which is not to be found on the clothes of the black marketeers. After half an hour, when I again modestly asked the man in the black jacket for a place, I still had no luck.[6]

We are again on the surest road to disaster because of internal decay, hoarders, black marketeers, and grumblers.[7]

---

12 November 1942

A long, rather fruitless conversation with Grobba.[8] He is probably often right in the details about Ettel,[9] who is a dilettante and busybody, but generally his [Grobba's] viewpoint is false because he deviates from the stated political line in the *Schark al Adna* in favor of his own political power base.[10] Without doubt, Grobba is intriguing with his relative of another sort and is availing himself of rather underhanded methods, suppression of news about his own officials, withholding letters, etc.[11] He cannot accept

---

6. Prüfer wrote later in the bottom margin of this entry: "These comments were written in the first flush of anger. It turned out later that the Adlon personnel were considerably better. They suffered because of the black marketeers just like the respectable guests."

7. This and Prüfer's same statement in RD, entry for 11 Nov. 1942, show that he still believed in the so-called "stab-in-the-back" legend, which was popular among Germans after World War I. The myth claimed erroneously that the German socialists, Communists, Jews, and other alleged "anti-German" elements, not the Allies, had defeated the Imperial German army with the revolution in November 1918.

8. Original in Arabic script. Fritz Grobba was the German minister (*Gesandter*, a diplomatic rank in the AA and not to be confused with the Reich foreign minister) in Iraq until 1939 and subsequently on special assignments in the AA. These included heading the so-called Arab committee in Pol. VII (the Middle Eastern section of the AA's Political Division) and administering the principal Arab leaders allied with the Axis during the war—Rashid Ali al-Gailani, a former prime minister of Iraq ousted from power in 1941 by the British, and Haj Amin al-Husayni, the Mufti of Jerusalem. See p. xv.

9. Original of "Ettel" in Arabic script. Erwin Ettel was Germany's former minister in Iran. When differences had arisen between the Mufti and Grobba, German Foreign Minister Joachim von Ribbentrop ordered on 30 June 1942 that Ettel should replace Grobba as the AA's liaison to Husayni. The appointment had produced a rivalry between Grobba and Ettel, which was fueled by the conflict between their respective Arab cohorts, Gailani and the Mufti. See p. xv.

10. Original "busybody" in English; *Schark al Adna* translates as "Middle East."

11. Original "Grobba" in Arabic script. The "relative of another sort" is Gen. Helmuth Felmy, Grobba's cousin and a commander of German forces in Greece. Such troops included the German-Arab training division (*Deutsche-Arabische Lehrabteilung*, or DAL), a small unit comprised of Arab followers of the Mufti and Gailani and originally headquartered at Cape Sounion near Athens. Felmy supported Grobba and Gailani in their feud with Ettel and Husayni.

that we must be junior partners when he hopes to have full authority.[12]

In the evening I was visited by an acquaintance from Rio, who described the same disturbing conditions and popular attitudes in the Rhineland that I have observed here. There the background is more Catholic. The total picture is very unpleasant.

---

13 November 1942

Conference in the A.A. in Woermann's office with Erdmannsdorff, Ettel, and Schnurre, regarding the subject of the "Arab training division."[13] These troops, which amount to only 3 companies, comprising mostly men from the Maghreb, and of which 40 men are from the Mufti and still fewer from Gailani, have been sent to the Caucasus (!), naturally at the instigation of Grobba and his supporters, in order to deprive the Mufti of his followers. Now the Mufti's people are again supposed to be placed at his disposal. A pretty picture of German unity![14]

---

12. Original "junior partners" here in English. As for Grobba's deceptions, by the fall of 1942, when Prüfer returned from Brazil, the Mufti-Gailani conflict had deepened the clash between their respective backers, Ettel and Grobba. The Mufti and Ettel set forth to undermine Grobba's position in the AA by accusing him of waging a campaign of political intrigue to poison the relations between the Arab leaders. Although Ribbentrop and his secretary of state in the AA, Ernst Freiherr von Weizsäcker, resisted becoming involved in the dispute, believing that both Arab leaders could provide valuable service to Nazi propaganda, they quietly favored the Mufti because of the prestige and influence he exerted as a religious leader in the Arab world. The conflict finally escalated to where Ribbentrop dispatched Ettel to Rome to verify the existence of a secret Arab organization which the Mufti claimed to head. Naturally the choice of Husayni's supporter, Ettel, prejudiced the outcome of the inquiry.

13. Ernst Woermann was director of the Political Division in the AA and held the title of undersecretary of state. Karl Schnurre was a leading official in the ministry's Economic Policy Division. Otto von Erdmannsdorff was deputy director of the AA's Political Division and former German ambassador in Hungary.

14. Regarding the German-Arab training division (DAL), see n. 11. Beyond personalities and politics, military considerations also aggravated the Mufti-Gailani clash. The main issue involved the basic composition, eventual deployment, and ultimate authority over the DAL. The German army, along with Felmy, Grobba, and Gailani, wished to use the small unit (roughly 130 men in May 1942) in the southern sector of the Russian front, from which it would play a significant role in the German thrust from the Caucasus into the Arab lands and particularly Iraq. The Mufti and Ettel, however, opposed such a plan because Husayni was much more of a Pan Arab nationalist and because it placed the DAL under the control of the rival faction. When the high command of the German Armed Forces (*Oberkommando der*

Spent the evening with Becker and his wife.[15] Subdued mood.

---

14 November 1942

The news from the Mediterranean sounds increasingly unfavorable. Tobruk has been evacuated. Derna is the next assembling point. We hold Tunisia with weak forces. The Yanks have all of Algeria and Morocco well in hand. 150,000 men are supposed to have landed. 220 transports passed Gibraltar. How was that possible? Weber[16] told me that there was even a warning concerning the American intentions in Algiers that came through him from Lisbon. Musso has taken steps for a separate peace with the U.S.S.R.[17] The Italian fleet was allegedly not deployed, because it has no oil. I can only ask, why does it have no oil? Again, as in the first war, the Orient and Mediterranean are being neglected. *Germania non discet.*

---

16 November 1942

A first letter from A., written on the 14th! And all this because I protested that she criticized me a bit too much. Is that such a grievous insult? All the more so since it really is the truth. We are all very nervous now which, of course, is completely understandable. Apples from Bärwalde. In this city, where no fruits can be obtained, that is a wonderful present, particularly for me, because I like fruits so much. Reprehensible carryings on about medals in the A.A., where R.[18] was earmarked for a decoration.

Wehrmacht, or OKW) transferred the DAL to Stalino in the Caucasus on 20 Aug. 1942, the Mufti protested bitterly and the Syrian and Palestinian elements in the unit expressed their unhappiness. On 5 November, Ribbentrop ordered that officials from the AA discuss the question of the DAL with the OKW.

15. Karl Walther Becker of the AA's Economic Policy Division. He had been on Prüfer's staff at the German Embassy in Rio.

16. An official in the German Embassy in Portugal.

17. The Italians and Mussolini ("Musso") knew that the Allied action in North Africa would doubtless intensify the threat to Italy. On 6 Nov. 1942 Mussolini had told Gen. Enno von Rintelen, the German military attaché in Rome, that the Axis "must make a separate peace with Russia as soon as possible."

18. Joachim von Ribbentrop, German foreign minister since 1938.

17 November 1942

Lunch at Weizsäcker's[19] in the [Hotel] Adlon with Dino Alfieri, Woermann, Melchers, Siegfried, and Prunas, a member of the non-European affairs section in the It. A.A.[20] According to the latter, Sola has resigned from the Service.[21] I put in a good word for him. My impression about the handling of Oriental affairs in the A.A. became worse after a conversation with Rühle, who works in the broadcasting office.[22] Infighting and the worst dilettantism.

18 November 1942

Lunch with the Bohnys and Beckers at Borchardt's.[23] Everywhere the same picture: swindlers and gluttons. Fabricius came to visit in the evening.[24] *Un minaret engrossi.*

19 November 1942

This morning I had an interesting visitor, the Alsatian doctor, Professor Schrumpf, who practiced in Cairo for 18 years and therefore has dabbled in Islamic and general Oriental affairs with obvious success. He knows all Orientals of consequence, is angry with Grobba, and very much pro-Hentig. For the time being he is working for Roller[25] in Sofia. Despite

19. Ernst Freiherr von Weizsäcker was secretary of state in the AA from 1938 to 1943.

20. The Italian Foreign Ministry. Renato Prunas was the specialist on European affairs in the Italian ministry. Herbert Siegfried was leader of the personal staff of the AA's secretary of state (Weizsäcker) from 1937 to 1943. Wilhelm Melchers was head of the AA's Pol. VII. Dino Alfieri served as Italian ambassador in Germany from 1940 to 1943.

21. Until 1942, Ugo Sola had been Italian ambassador in Brazil, where Prüfer knew him.

22. Gerhard Rühle was head of the radio section and deputy director of the AA's Cultural Policy Division.

23. Borchardt's was a noted Berlin restaurant. Capt. Hermann Bohny served as assistant naval attaché in the German Embassy in Rio, where he worked with Prüfer as an Abwehr (Military Intelligence and Counterintelligence of the OKW) contact until 1942.

24. Presumably Wilhelm Fabricius, German minister in Rumania from 1936 to 1941.

25. A code name for the OKW. Werner Otto von Hentig was a Middle Eastern expert on special assignment in the AA. Peter Schrumpf-Pierron was a rabid racist and Jew-hater whose

a rather eccentric appearance (curly locks and beard),[26] he does not make a bad impression. In his opinion, the Balkan Muslims and the Destour movement in Tunisia will have to be mobilized. He is terribly concerned about North Africa, and I think he is entirely right. Even Shekib has written to Max in this vein.[27]

For lunch I was with Schulenburg-Filehne at Horcher's.[28] He has very reasonable views. His head has become redder, which possibly goes back, in part, to his participation in the Polish campaign.

Ernst Wilhelm, whom I visited today, talked to me exhaustively about the case of R. H. who, according to him, almost ended his career—which might have been good.[29] He was very bitter toward Jochen [Ribbentrop].

The squabble between the fishwives [Grobba and Ettel] has taken on proportions that are almost unbelievable. This afternoon in the presence of Schnurre, I struggled in vain for over two hours with two men from Roller's office as to whether or not the Ar. [Arab] training division should return to the Mufti a few men he had made available to the division. The hidden

---

claim that the Mufti was a Circassian and "hence not an 'Arab' " resembled Hitler's similar racist approval of Husayni. Schrumpf was the Mufti's personal physician and a collaborator of the Abwehr in 1942.

26. *Rosenkranz und Fusssäcke*, literally "prayer beads and footmuffs." According to O. Prufer, however, these terms were used by his father to indicate a humorous and disdainful physical description of Schrumpf.

27. Baron Max von Oppenheim was an elderly archaelogist and director of the Tell Halaf Museum as well as a foundation in Berlin named for him. Shekib Arslan was a Syrian nationalist and publicist exiled in Switzerland. Arslan had written Oppenheim a letter on 18 June 1942, expressing concern that German policy appeared to favor Gailani over the Mufti. Prüfer had a long association with each, stretching back before World War I with Oppenheim. The Destour movement was a local nationalist party in Tunisia, comprised of Maghrebian Arabs. Muslims in Bosnia and Herzegovina were later enrolled in the SS in 1943 to help the Nazis combat the partisans of Yugoslavia, most of whom were Christian Serbs.

28. A restaurant in Berlin. Fritz-Deitlof Count von der Schulenburg was vice-president of the Berlin police and kinsman of Germany's former ambassador to Russia, Friedrich Werner Count von der Schulenburg. At the war's beginning, Schulenburg had served as the German government representative (*Regierungspräsident*) in Silesia and joined an infantry regiment in 1940. He was already a member of the opposition to Hitler.

29. This refers to the flight on 10 May 1941 of Rudolf Hess, the deputy Führer of the NSDAP, on a self-appointed, wholly unofficial peace mission to Britain, only a few weeks before the German invasion of the Soviet Union. Hess bailed out of his plane in Scotland and, much to his surprise, he was imprisoned, treated as a prisoner of war, and tried as a war criminal at Nuremberg. Hitler and the Nazi press declared Hess "insane." Ernst Wilhelm Bohle was a Nazi party *Gauleiter* and head of the party's Foreign Organization (*Auslands-Organisation*, or AO), which administered party groups in foreign countries. Prüfer had a close association with Bohle since the beginning of Hitler's regime. For an explanation of how the Hess affair presumably involved Bohle, see RD, entry for 19 Nov. 1942.

reason for the opposition is, of course, the notorious family affairs, which have spread to other comrades.[30] In this connection, it is of interest that Professor Sch., whom I mentioned earlier, observed this morning that Fritz [Grobba] is suffering from incipient paralysis. He claims to have recognized this from a disorder in his pupil reflexes and from a pathological increase in his self-assurance and energy. I believe that Molly[31] bears the main responsibility.

---

20 November 1942

    The boss [Ribbentrop] rejected my suggestion. I am supposed to work with the fishwives [Grobba and Ettel].[32] Meanwhile we lost Bengasi because of sheer Oriental expertise. Yesterday evening Langenn[33] arrived and ate with me in the hotel until 3:15 in the morning. He is the same good, decent man, but quite aged. Ingrid prepared a Christmas package for me of grapes, bread, and a folder for food stamps. She is truly an unusual, dear girl. Late at night we called Annelies, whose arrival on the 28th I am eagerly awaiting.

---

21 November 1942

    Lunch at Uncle Max's [Oppenheim]; a jocose, and very lively, skeleton. Extremely interested in all questions regarding the Orient, drinks wine, schnapps, coffee, and smokes despite his 82 years and bladder and

---

    30. The "family affairs" refer to Grobba and his cousin, Felmy. Prüfer and Schnurre had met with representatives from the OKW and failed to persuade them to agree to the Mufti's demand that the DAL be transferred from the Caucasus to the battle against the British in Egypt, Palestine, or Syria.

    31. Grobba's wife, Hilda.

    32. Ribbentrop presumably refused Prüfer's request for a leave from the AA to visit Arab exiles in Switzerland, including Shekib Arslan and the ex-Khedive of Egypt, Abbas Hilmi, to gather information from them on the Middle East (note p. xiv). Because of the bitter strife between Grobba, Ettel and their Arab cohorts, the foreign minister had agreed on 23 Oct. 1942 to Ettel's request that Prüfer replace Grobba as the AA's special commissioner for Arab affairs. On that basis, Prüfer was apparently ordered on 20 Nov. to remain in Berlin to deal with "the fishwives."

    33. Helmut von Langenn-Steinkeller; see this chapter, n. 1.

prostate irritations. Tania visited me in the afternoon, displeased with Germany. She looked unkempt, like many women in Germany now. One has the feeling that she smells bad, without it perhaps being so. She longs for Turkey. She scarcely spoke of Gos.[34] The love affair could not have been very deep.

I spent the evening with the Tiller and Langenn, talking about the price of geese, butter, and eggs, and about how you can get these foods in the most advantageous way, legally or illegally. You can despair when you see how need is ruining character and how it stimulates the forces of greed in man. Cuesta is coming through here on the trip to Rome.[35]

---

22 November 1942

On m'a raconté ce matin des histoires affreuses sur le traitement des Persans. Ils ont été massacres, hommes, femmes et enfants du grand nombre par des gas asphysiants ou par la mitrailleuse. La haine qui, forcément, doit en surgir ne sera jamais étainte.[36] Today every child knows this in the smallest detail. Spent the evening with Nanny and Bärbel at their mother's.[37]

---

23 November 1942

Today was more replete with experiences of the worst kind than any day since my return to Germany. It already started off badly before lunch in a discussion with Gr. [Grobba]. This man is absolutely unreasonable. He

---

34. Prüfer later pencilled in the name "Siems," but did not identify the person. For his association with Tania, see RD, entry for 21 Nov. 1942.

35. Raimundo Fernández-Cuesta y Merelo, Spanish ambassador in Brazil. At the bottom of the diary page, Prüfer had later observed about Cuesta y Merelo's scheduled visit: "Never came." Tiller, like Langenn, was one of Prüfer's longtime associates and officer friends from World War I.

36. "This morning, they told me horrible stories concerning the treatment of the Persians. Men, women, and children have been slaughtered in large numbers by poison-gas or by machine guns. The hatred which inevitably must arise from that will never be appeased." Prüfer added in a footnote to this passage that "Persians" was a "Kurfürstendamm expression for Jews." He wrote "Jews" in Arabic script.

37. Prüfer's sisters-in-law, Nanny Engelhardt and Barbara Fehrmann.

does not see the forest for the trees, is mired in details, and does not notice that he is no longer following any political line at all; he only sees his own present sphere of operations in exaggerated terms and is always hoping to play an ever greater role. To reach this less than praiseworthy objective goal, he has found a number of good and bad supporters, particularly in military circles, who are devoted to him, especially his completely stupid, but just as ambitious, cousin-in-law, F. [Felmy]. He [Grobba] can no longer see that we are supposed to make German policy as a whole. He is blinded by vanity and ambition. I received a letter from Paula[38] in Adana, which Gr. [Grobba] apparently knew about, although it was addressed to me and was sent to me sealed via some police office (!) This letter described the situation in the Ar. [Arab] countries fairly correctly, especially the role of the Mu. [Mufti], whom Paula also considers more important than his opponent. A further blow for me was the reunion with my old Turkish friend H.E.,[39] with whom I had a *tête-à-tête* over lunch, during which he candidly spoke his mind about the situation in his country and the political currents there. According to him, Inönü[40] is very cautious, does not want a war, but is basically convinced of our defeat. For that reason, no one knows what Turkey will do with increasing American pressure. If America penetrates further into North Africa and threatens Turkey with the loss of the Dardanelles, it is very uncertain what Ismet would do. The country is terribly poor, and bad inflation prevails. The provisioning of the mobilized army costs more than the whole military budget. German policies are frequently clumsy, specifically in the economic-political sphere, where the brother-in-law and his friend Vivebien, who perhaps were good businessmen, have been very poor diplomats. The tiny Silesian has little to say, and no one believes the boss because he talks too amicably: but his actions are not congruent with his words.[41] Anyway, he talks too much.

In the afternoon Bärbel and I went to the movies, where we saw the

---

38. Paula Koch, a female Abwehr agent in Turkey.

39. Habib Edib-Törelan, a special correspondent for the Anatolian news agency.

40. Ismet Inönü, general and president of the Turkish republic. The principal architect of Turkish neutrality in the war, he appeared to favor neither the Axis nor the Allies. He especially used his country's chrome supplies as a bargaining tool with each side.

41. The "boss" is Franz von Papen, German ambassador in Turkey since 1939. "Vivebien" refers to Lebrecht, director of the German Orientbank and economic adviser to the German Embassy in Ankara. The "tiny Silesian" was Hans Kroll, a counselor and specialist in economic affairs at the Embassy. The "brother-in-law" was Albert Jenke, Ribbentrop's in-law and a former businessman who had held the rank of consul general at the embassy in Turkey since 1939.

Jannings picture, *The Resignation*. A rather good film, definitely slanted against William II and the camarilla around him, without showing sarcasm towards the monarchy. W. II has a downright glaring similarity—not in appearance, but in bearing and speech—with Ziethen.[42] Afterwards we ate in a restaurant on the Kurfürstendamm, where I frequently used to meet Cons. Gen. St.[43] In this restaurant, previously very elegant, but now falling on hard times, the waiters look the best; the poor guests unpack sandwiches and apples from paper wrappings. When we wanted to leave, the manager recognized me and immediately began to sing a dire song about the situation in general and his in particular. I tried to give him some courage, without much success, I believe, and told him that the crew of a ship in danger could not complain to each other, but rather had to work together in order to avert the danger. Moaning would only hasten the sinking. If the man tells all his guests such things—he did not recognize me by name—as he told me this evening, then our propaganda and its successes are in bad shape. I fear that toughness and optimism and, let us be candid, courage in adversity, are not the virtues of our bourgeois middle class. We are also more materialistic than we ourselves and others would like to believe. The prattle about food is simply insufferable and totally undignified, particularly coming from the well-off and the well-educated. Precisely these classes should take pains to bear their petty deprivations with more good grace. Women show much more heroism and greatness, though not all, of course. Undoubtedly life today is very difficult for them, because without even considering the deprivations, they still have to bear the daily trials and indignities of shopping and doing the difficult housework. A woman who today can remain calm and confident is truly a good woman. It seems to me that there are a lot of good women these days. Certaintly different from the last war.

---

42. Prüfer later added in Arabic script that this was a code word for Ribbentrop. The film, *Die Entlassung*, was the second of two German movies from the beginning of the war on Bismarck's career. It anchored Hitler's war of conquest in Prussian history, alleging that the Nazi dictator had realized Bismarck's policies. The strangest episode of the film occurred during Bismarck's dismissal, in which Wilhelm II was shown as a homosexual making coy advances towards a piano-playing friend, oblivious to the fall of his father's greatest statesman. This could have been why Prüfer compared the figure of the Kaiser in the film to that of Ribbentrop; he almost always denounced as "homosexuals" persons whom he disliked.

43. Hans Steffen, a retired German major, international arms dealer, and former honorary consul general for Ethiopia in Berlin. Prüfer's close ties to him reached back to World War I.

24 November 1942

Wretched, tedious meeting of about 30 people concerning the methods and purposes of our propaganda. Results exactly zero. I honestly do not know what the people were talking about. A *soviet* of the worst sort, but without Stalin. I was at Bohny's in the evening. A splendid man.

25 November 1942

The situation in North Africa is deteriorating, and we are experiencing the results everywhere: the Russians are on the attack along the whole front and have severely damaged our lines southwest of Stalingrad; the Turks are vacillating more and more, and indeed our old enemy, Tewfik Rüshdi, has appeared on the scene as an open partisan of the English; Italy is coming apart everywhere. Milan and Turin have been evacuated. This evening I was with Melchers at Ghulam Siddiq's.[44] He too believes our situation to be rather threatened. Naturally he also condemns our Oriental policy.

26 November 1942

Lunch with Neitzel. He is the same as before, inwardly and outwardly. Later I had a conversation with a descendant of the great astronomer K. He did not inherit the great intelligence and extreme precision of his ancestor.[45] A. is coming tomorrow morning.

---

44. A former ambassador from Afghanistan in Germany, who had lived since 1932 as an exile in Berlin. Tewfik Rüshdi Aras was Turkish Ambassador in Britain.

45. Wilhelm Keppler, secretary of state for special duties in the AA, in charge mainly of affairs regarding India. Prüfer's dislike of Keppler probably resulted from the latter's opposition to the Mufti and Ettel and from Keppler's longtime background in the NSDAP. Neitzel was an acquaintance whom Prüfer met while serving as German minister in Ethiopia from 1928 to 1930.

27 November 1942

Visit in the *Banco alemão* [Deutsche Reichsbank] at Seeger's. A. arrived. We occupied Toulon. Letter of the Führer to Pétain.[46]

28 November 1942

Sigrid and Manfred had lunch with us.[47] M. is also very depressed. The waiter and the chauffeur begged from me without shame. *Perduta gente.* In the evening we were with the same people, along with Helmut and Ingrid. Long night. The news gets worse and worse. Dakar is lost, therefore the shortest route is open from the U.S.A. to Africa.

29 November 1942

Reunion with all the old friends! This time Arnim and his wife.[48] He has become a major. *Toujours le même.* He experienced the war in the West and the East and is now occupied with petroleum in Hannover, where Heiley is helping him. Again with Helmut and Ingrid in the evening.

30 November 1942

The Langenns left. Schröder visited me in the afternoon. Bad scandal. The nephew of my old boss from *Masr*, M., has behaved very, very

---

46. With many Vichy French officers in Tunisia electing to fight for the Allies and with the French having rejected Hitler's belated offer of an alliance, the Nazi leader followed his occupation of southern France on 11 Nov. 1942 with the seizure of the harbor at Toulon and with the order to dissolve the Vichy army on 27 November. Hitler informed Marshal Philippe Pétain, the Vichy chief of state, that Germany could no longer "trust French admirals and generals."

47. The von Richthofens were friends of Prüfer. Manfred was an estate owner in Eastern Germany and member of the famous aristocratic family. Sigrid was an opera singer.

48. Adolf-Oswald von Arnim, one of Prüfer's friends from World War I, and his wife, Heiley.

badly and will have to pay the penalty for it.[49] A disgrace for us all. Unthinkable. In Japan the whole cast would probably commit hara-kari. I also have the feeling that we[50] should do something similar. It is comforting that he is not of German ancestry. Levetzow was with me for lunch. He too is alienated, but carries his forced leisure *otium cum dignitate*, completely different than Don Martinho, whose self-importance, resulting from his stupidity, bursts forth in anger about the snub—according to him—that he suffered in the A.[51]

---

49. *Masr* translates as "Egypt." The "boss" was Hans von Miquel, Prüfer's superior at the German Consulate General in Cairo before World War I. Miquel should not be confused with his kinsman, Johannes von Miquel, the National Liberal party leader and Prussian minister of finance during the Imperial era. The nephew was Rudolf von Scheliha, a Silesian noble and official in the AA engaged since 1938 in espionage for the Soviet Union. He was a member of the Red Orchestra (*Rote Kapelle*), a group of roughly 100 pro-Soviet Germans who had established a widespread espionage system for Moscow inside Germany. The organization was uncovered, and Scheliha was arrested by the Gestapo on the night of 29–30 Oct. 1942, as he returned to Germany from Switzerland. Hans Schröder was director of the Personnel and Budget Division in the AA.

50. Prüfer later added *mutatis mutandi*, "as things change, they change."

51. *Amt*, or "office," referring to the AA. "Don Martinho" refers to Martin Schlimpert, one of Prüfer's former embassy officials in Rio, whom the ambassador disliked because of his alleged homosexuality. Werner von Levetzow was Prüfer's former embassy counselor in Brazil and rumored to have been impotent and also homosexual. During 1941 Levetzow was sent first to Uruguay, when local Germans were arrested on charges of "fifth column" activities and the German minister there, Otto Langmann, was declared *persona non grata*, and then to Paraguay, to replace the German minister in Asunción, who had died.

two

December 1942

1 December 1942

Annelies went to Neu Ruppin and is supposed to return tomorrow. Gaus confirmed the view as to the behavior of Atrak, a view which we had adopted on the basis of an official report, exactly as Kr. [Kroll] had presented it to me. He was visibly impressed when I voiced a different opinion. Willy Hahn died yesterday.[1] Certain circles reckon with the loss of North Africa. Then Hannibal stands *ante portas Romae*. Meanwhile Grobba and Ettel keep on squabbling about their "court Arabs."

2 December 1942

Annelies is coming back today before noon. This evening we were with Sigrid [Richthofen]. M. [Manfred] was away because of *amours*.

---

1. Hahn was a former Berlin judicial counselor and Prüfer's friend; he had close connections with Jewish circles in the capital. "Atrak" was a code name for Turkey. Friedrich Gaus was director of the Legal Division in the AA with the title of undersecretary of state.

3 December 1942

Once again Don Martinho [Schlimpert] cut up and talked about "honor," which has been violated. Actually he meant his own honor.

4 December 1942

Hentig and Idris were with me, likewise Kiram. All were complaining about the same thing. *Trop de zèle et d'organisation.* With Habib Edib in the evening. (The divorced Frau Furtwängler—a Dane, Frau Schwörbel,[2] and a couple of Turks.)

5 December 1942

Annelies left this evening. I was with Frau Best this afternoon. I cannot move into the new house until around Christmas.[3]

6 December 1942

With Manfred and Sigrid for lunch. Reconciliation of the two, *sans phrase.* Boring afternoon and evening.

---

2. The wife of Heribert Schwörbel, a specialist in Oriental affairs in the AA and former German minister to Afghanistan. Kiram was a minor functionary, presumably in the AA or another ministry. Professor Alimdjan Idris, an official in Pol. VII of the ministry, spoke Turkish, Persian, Russian, and Arabic fluently.

3. Prüfer rented a house in Dahlem from Werner Best, a senior SS police official who after Nov. 1942 had become Nazi commissioner in Denmark. Best was charged after the war with complicity in the murder of Jews and Poles in occupied Poland.

7 December 1942

Many orders from the boss [Ribbentrop], who is here incognito. I have not seen him, although I have reported [to his staff] over and over again. Once more I have had a long conversation with E. [Ettel] from Persia. Again he has refused any cooperation with G. [Grobba], for whom he has nothing but the harshest accusations. The Turkish question stands in the foreground of all written and oral discussions. Pessimism is more and more predominant. This evening I was with E. W. B. [Bohle] at the [Hotel] Kaiserhof; in addition to me, there was only Schr. [Schröder] from the A.A. Much praise and many high-sounding speeches. I fell flat with my praise of the A.O. people in Braz. [Brazil]. Especially v. C.[4] is in disgrace, which certainly must be unjustified.

8 December 1942

Luncheon with Köpchen and someone from the firm of O.W.[5] who, in earlier times, undoubtedly belonged anonymously to our concern [AA]. A conversation full of unpleasantness. Disappointed as they are, these people can accept their monetary benefits, but not the loss of social prestige, following their departure from the A.A. Unfortunately they had a lot of partially correct, but important, information about the present situation. K. was very bitter towards J. [Ribbentrop]. Despite careful reservations on my part, he judged him to be a destructive, although dynamic, and ambitious fool who egocentrically sees everything directed only at him and lacks the ability to make objective judgments. I contradicted this terrible condemnation, for in the last analysis every politician identifies himself with the center of his power and thus becomes egocentric. Napoleon was France and Frederick II was Prussia.

This evening with Nannie. A very successful evening, although poor

---

4. Hans-Henning von Cossel, the former country group leader (*Landesgruppenleiter*) of the NSDAP in Brazil, who presumably earned Bohle's displeasure because of Cossel's inability to reestablish or expand the party after the Brazilian government banned it in 1938.

5. Otto Wolff, one of the major German iron and steel firms. "Köpchen" referred to Gerhard Köpke, director of the West European Division (Abt. II) in the AA from 1923 (and from 1929 deputy secretary of state) until the Nazis forced his retirement from the ministry in 1936 because he had a Jewish grandmother and had expressed strong doubts about Nazi policies and Ribbentrop. After 1936 Köpke joined a wire service agency in Berlin.

Hans[6] had been quite afraid of all kinds of injuries from things falling when he picked me up during the blackout.

---

9 December 1942

Discussion in the office of the Marinierten with a man from the A. [Abwehr] and Reedersohn about the newest offers and requests from the Jerusalemer.[7] Once again he would like an official document which should delineate our policies in the Maghreb.[8] Although our assurances to Pétain force us to oppose this, I am nevertheless of the opinion that we should give him a vague general document, in which we recognize the rights of the Destour party. The French, after all, have also played a double game with us, and if we had not been so strong with him, Pétain would have gone over to the side of Giraud, Darlan, etc. a long time ago.[9] Militarily things are going better in Tunisia. We have been able to bring in important reinforcements and have air superiority.

Becker, who visited me in the evening, has already found something to quibble about in his new job [in the economic division]. Everywhere there is over-bureaucratization and overcrowding. This became apparent in a bizarre discussion of section chiefs of the Pol. Div., which I attended this afternoon. No less than 30 persons were present and reported about already well-known incidents in their domains. No solutions or directives, no new suggestions or perspectives pertaining to the situation came up in those

---

6. The husband of Nanny Engelhardt, one of Prüfer's sisters-in-law.

7. The "Jerusalemer" is the Mufti, who had just returned to Berlin from Rome and urged the Germans to cultivate the support of the Maghrebian Arabs in Tunisia. Husayni suggested that the Axis issue a declaration expressing its sympathy for the Arabs and promising to recognize the legal and political position of the Bey of Tunis and the Destour party. His ideas appealed to the Abwehr and OKW, which had a serious shortage of manpower in Tunisia, as well as to the AA; both Hitler and Rudolf Rahn (the AA's civilian administrator in Tunisia) opposed the Mufti's proposals because they feared alienating Italy, France, and Spain, each of which had imperial interests in the region. The Reedersohn, the "shipping magnate's son," was Woermann. The Marinierten, the "sailor," referred to Weizsäcker and his service as a naval officer in World War I.

8. Original in Arabic script.

9. Prüfer later added Charles de Gaulle, the head of the anti-Nazi Free French movement. Darlan had collaborated in the Allied landings in North Africa (see chap. 1, n. 4), and after Pétain dismissed him, the Americans made him political chief of the French administration in the region. Gen. Henri Giraud later succeeded Darlan, who was assassinated on 24 Dec. 1942, as French high commissioner in Africa.

discussions. The whole thing was only a debating club whose members buttered up to each other.

---

10 December 1942

Uneventful day. Lunch with Uncle Max [Oppenheim]. Telephoned A. in the evening; she appears to be rather despondent.

---

11 December 1942

Lunch with I. G. (Frank-Fahle, Oberhof).[10] These gentlemen were very interested in the case of Fenthol, to whom the company had actually granted only the well-known orders regarding the Hungarian petroleum concession of Standard Oil. It is true that F. [Fenthol] has a Jewish wife.[11] The Soederstroms[12] visited until after midnight. Unchanged, the same "good people."

---

12 December 1942

Herbert and Rosine had breakfast with me. Both of them have become old, but they are basically the same. In spite of their questionable situation, they conduct themselves well. Evening with Hilva[13] and her husband.

---

10. Frank-Fahle and Oberhof were officials of the foreign operations division of I.G. Farben Corporation, the largest German industrial combine.

11. Fenthol, whom Prüfer had known in Brazil, was a lawyer for I.G. Farben and an official of the Nazi Four-Year Plan, Hitler's program begun in 1936 to prepare Germany for war by making it economically self-sufficient. The AA and Farben were presumably displeased with Fenthol's role in the unsuccessful efforts during 1942 by a German consortium, which included I.G. Farben, to take over the majority of the shares of the Hungarian-American Oil Corporation. It is curious that Fenthol's Jewish wife entered the discussion; both Prüfer and Frank-Fahle possessed knowledge of the Nazi annihilation of the Jews in the East, according to the former German diplomat, Ulrich von Hassell.

12. A Swede, Karl Axel Soederstrom, and his wife, Clärenore. She was the daughter of the wealthy German industrialist, Hugo Stinnes, and schoolfriend of Anneliese Prüfer.

13. Hilva von Boroevich-Heemskerck, a member of the family of one of Prüfer's commanders in World War I, Hans-Eduard von Heemskerck. Herbert von Richthofen was a

13 December 1942

Boring Sunday like never before. Ingrid [Langenn] came to visit me in the evening.

14 December 1942

With R. [Ribbentrop]. I have a new assignment: I am supposed to investigate the status of an Information Office (set up by Martin). Something seems to be rotten in this organization, just as in the Mundus G.m.b.H., the official literary propaganda office.[14] In the evening, I went with Ingrid to the theater (a comedy with labored punch lines and starring Ida Wüst).

15 December 1942

Futile attempts to talk with Don M. L. [Luther].

16 December 1942

Hans [Schröder] tells many tales as to J.'s [Ribbentrop] standing with the chief [Hitler] regarding [Mussolini's] impending visit. His position

---

longtime colleague of Prüfer's in the AA's Middle Eastern section and former German minister in Denmark and Belgium.

14. Martin Luther, an ambitious protégé of Ribbentrop's, had become estranged from the minister by 1942 and plotted to oust him. Prüfer was commissioned by Ribbentrop to investigate Luther's burgeoning propaganda network, which included front organizations such as the Mundus Corporation and German Information Office (*Deutsche Informationsstelle,* or DIS), inside the Abt. Deutschland (see pp. xiv–xv). The inquiry resulted when Luther alienated Ribbentrop's wife, Annelies, and Gustav Adolf Steengracht von Moyland, a member of the minister's personal staff. Steengracht disapproved of Luther's attempted seizure of bookstores owned by Karl Buchholz in Berlin, Rumania, and Portugal. Luther also opposed Frau Ribbentrop's plans to have the bookstores entrusted with the legal representation of her family lawyer, Oskar Moehrung, thereby providing him with an extra income.

is said to be badly shaken. He is not supposed to be present during the visit. Stohrer has been recalled and is going into private business in Zurich. Moltke will be his successor.[15] I am traveling to the East early in the morning.

---

17 December 1942

Departure with the *Westfalen*. Ettel, Ritter, Braun-Stumm, and the others were on the train.[16] I was with the boss [Ribbentrop] during the afternoon. He has ordered the dismissal of Gr. [Grobba]. He expressed very reasonable views about exporting party propaganda. Ettel and I got off the train in Thorn and traveled back to Berlin in the cold night. Musso, Laval, and acolytes are expected tomorrow. Ingrid left.

---

18 December 1942

Arrival in Berlin. I gave Gr. [Grobba] the bad news, which he appears to have accepted quietly. I fear that he will continue to intrigue. At noon the Baltic Russian, Eylstein, together with another Russian, sidled up to me for lunch. Extremely bad impression. A slimy person in a German lieutenant's uniform. I met Eylstein again this evening. He introduced me to a Belgian count, who takes care of Belgian prisoners of war.[17] I contradicted

---

15. Hans Adolf von Moltke had been German ambassador in Poland from 1931 to 1939. Eberhard von Stohrer had served as German ambassador in Spain. The military crisis in Russia and worsening of the Axis position in the Mediterranean forced Hitler to call a summit meeting with Mussolini. From 18 to 20 Dec. 1942, the Italian foreign minister, Count Galeazzo Ciano, representing the ill and absent Mussolini, met with Hitler at Rastenburg in East Prussia. Pierre Laval, the Vichy prime minister, arrived for the final discussions. Hitler rejected Italian proposals for an Axis political settlement with Russia, and the meeting resulted in the decision to hold North Africa at all costs.

16. Braun-Stumm was deputy director of the AA's News and Press Division. Karl Ritter had been German ambassador in Brazil during 1937–38; from 1939 he was ambassador for special duties in the AA in charge of economic and military affairs. The *Westfalen* was Ribbentrop's personal train and traveling headquarters.

17. The "Belgian Count" is Count T'Serclaes. Prüfer informed Grobba of Ribbentrop's directive that Grobba be transferred from the AA's Pol. VII to a remote position in the German Embassy in Paris.

him when he gave the Belgian bad information or misinformation about our war situation. I fear that E. is an agent, certainly a babbler and drunkard.

---

19 December 1942

Long talk with M. L. [Luther] about the case of the Inf. Office. I have the impression that, perhaps apart from a burgeoning bureaucracy, this is not a serious matter. Kl.[18] does not make a bad impression. Bairam was a success.[19] Ettel was very pleased. Gailani unfortunately had gone to Dresden. In the evening I packed with Fräulein R. Esterl arrived.[20]

---

20 December 1942

Helmut [Langenn] is arriving this evening, but he already has plans, so I cannot see him. I am spending the evening with the Beckers.

---

21 December 1942

In addition to Stohrer, Ott is also supposed to be recalled. Sthamer [*sic*] from Nanking is taking his place.[21] According to the increasingly more vocal reports from Turkey, things are not going well for us there. Papen is painting a rosy picture. Everything will depend on events in North Africa. Helmut is coming this evening. He is given to tears and is grieving over the loss of his wife. Reproaches Ingrid, because she is not as grieved as he is.

---

18. Werner Klatten, the director of the section in Abt. Deutschland (D IV) responsible for the production and distribution of literature in and to foreign countries. In this role he also headed the DIS (see n. 14).

19. Bairam was a Muslim festival, celebrated in Berlin by the Mufti in connection with his opening of the Central Islamic Institute in the capital. Grobba and Gailani had bitterly opposed Husayni's leadership of the festivities.

20. Joseph Esterl was Prüfer's former valet in Brazil. "Fräulein R." referred to Martha Rohde, Prüfer's secretary and mistress.

21. Heinrich Georg Stahmer was a protégé of Ribbentrop. Eugen Ott was a major general and German ambassador in Japan.

22 December 1942

Helmut left. I am leaving for B.B. this evening.

23 December 1942

Arrived in B.B., where [I found] everything satisfactory.

24 December 1942

Christmas eve. A little melancholic.

25-26 December 1942

Packing books and household chores. Sleepless nights for incomprehensible reasons.

27 December 1942

Wrote letters. Visited Saur.[22] Darlan murdered.

28 December 1942

Air raid alert in the morning; weather beautiful. Afternoon with Annelies at the movies, a rather foolish French film, *Her First Rendezvous*. Returning home we found Olaf tired and feverish.[23]

---

22. A heart specialist treating Prüfer.

23. Olaf Herbert Hermann Carl Prufer, the son of Curt Max Prüfer, was born in Berlin in 1930. He spent his childhood and adolescence in Germany, Brazil, and Switzerland. After World War II he lived for a number of years in India, where he became interested in archaeology. He moved to the United States in 1954, where he earned the B.A. (1956), M.A. (1958),

29 December 1942

Olaf has a temperature of 40 degrees. Drs. Müller and Rossi have no clear picture. Pneumonia has not been ruled out. It is snowing. Baron Emil O.[24] and his wife were here this afternoon. Levetzow arrived.

30 December 1942

Olaf is not well at all. He has had an attack of heart palpitations. I wasted the afternoon reading the files I brought along. What nonsense! All these *acteurs* in the comedy of the DIS spend hours and hours on trivial discussions, brought about by just as trivial and unsubstantiated denunciations. Herr X is supposed to have told Herr Y about Herr Z, that the S. D. should be informed as to his activities, if . . . . This can drive you to despair. Furthermore, this childish activity gobbles up an immense amount of labor and money, only to end in nothing. Bureaucracy for the sake of bureaucracy. In the background of all these organizers is the burning desire to avoid military service. They are feverishly trying to be indispensable! An absolutely disgusting picture! In this process, of course, everyone is in the way of everyone else and everyone is suspect, for all are striving for the same goal: not to be sent to the front.

31 December 1942

The last day of the year, deep in snow, at least here in Baden-Baden! Levetzow was here at noon; he described life with Ulla H.[25] Tea in the afternoon with St. [Steffen]. He was also talking about U. H., but in less complimentary terms. Olaf still has a rather high fever and suffers from

and Ph.D. (1961) at Harvard University. Rising through the academic ranks at Case Institute of Technology in Cleveland, the University of Massachusetts at Amherst, and Kent State University in Ohio, he now serves as professor of anthropology at the latter institution.

24. Emil von Oldershausen was an employee of the Dresdner Bank.

25. "Ulla" is Ulrike Haniel von Rauch, from the family of Prüfer's former superior in the AA, Edgar Haniel von Haimhausen, who was secretary of state from 1919 until 1922. The wife of a Ruhr industrialist, Frau von Rauch was later implicated in the scandal that forced the resignation in 1969 of Eugen Gerstenmaier, the longtime president of the *Bundestag*.

severe coughing. In the evening his condition was worse. A bad beginning for the year. We are reporting a success of our naval surface forces as a sum for several months. One can argue whether that is smart. Do we want to raise the slight December quotas of our U-boat sinkings?[26] Worries, nothing but worries, this year ends with them. The greatest worry is Africa. I have the impression, hopefully false, that these matters are not taken seriously enough. In my opinion the loss of Tripoli and Tunisia would mean the defeat of Germany, may God forbid. In that event the enemy would be on the borders of those "allies" who only help us because they have to, but not because they want to. They would all turn unreliable if German control could no longer hold them at the yoke. It is our tragic fate that as soldiers we can defeat a foreign people and temporarily control them, but that we are never able to befriend these people. We are either hated and subsequently expelled, or we accommodate ourselves and are assimilated by those we conquered. Just like the old Roman Empire and North America.

---

26. Prüfer's suspicion that the number of enemy ships sunk by German submarines had declined was correct. The war waged by the Germans at sea was close to its high point in June 1942, when submarines sank 122 Allied ships totalling 600,000 tons. Because of the Allied convoy system, improved technology, and increased air protection for Anglo-American shipping in the Atlantic Ocean, only 72 Allied ships (418,000 tons) were sunk from Aug. through Oct. 1942. After sinking 105 ships (650,000 tons) in November, the submarines had increasingly less success.

three

January 1943

New Year in the rain. Olaf [Prüfer] has a sore throat, but Dr. Rossi does not think it is serious.

Abominable weather; went downtown this afternoon with A. [Anneliese]. Olaf feels much better. With a heavy heart I will depart this evening for Berlin at 8 o'clock. The train is already 29 minutes late in Baden-Oos. It is very crowded. Baron E. O. [Oldershausen] is not on the train.

Arrived in Berlin at 10:30 a.m., after a tolerable night without incident. Moved into the house on Thanner Pfad. It is snowing and storming, but without freezing. Fräulein Rohde came over in the afternoon. Grobba apparently passed himself off as my deputy. He is also making efforts on behalf of Granow, apparently in order to keep a foothold in the Arab section. The Turkish ambassador should soon be returning from Ankara.[1] I will then have to meet him in an alcoholic social setting. In the Arab vein, I composed the following verses for this occasion:

> The diplomat, a drunkard though he be,
> Is welcomed by the state to which he's sent.
> For, failing other means his tongue to free,
> Give him some booze and he will soon relent.

> A diplomat? Someone like this?
> Across from me the valiant drinker sits
> And while I probe, he babbles on in bliss[2]
> To our private mutual benefits.

> And thus depravity is turned to merit.
> Officially the lout is well-respected.
> A character so flawed one cannot bear it.
> Is, in this case, officially protected.

> Where otherwise the simple philistine
> For drunken drivel is disgraced,
> His service to the state has made him clean
> And useful—in the context he's been placed.

4 January 1943

Announcement of a *Revirement:* Moltke replaces Stohrer, Ott takes over Sthamer's [*sic*] position, and Thomsen, Wied's. Erich Kordt will be Chargé d'Affaires in Nanking.[3] The Embassy in Madrid is to be completely reorganized as far as personnel is concerned. Embassy Counselor will be

1. The ambassador was Saffet Arikan. Grobba had protested the transfer of his friend and former subordinate in the Arab section, Ulrich Granow, to the AA's Latin American desk.
2. Prüfer later added a footnote here: "Prüfer, presumably your ancestors were Küfer [cellarmen], on account of the rhymes."
3. Kordt was previously assigned from 1938 to 1941 to Ribbentrop's personal staff and during 1941–42 as minister in the German Embassy in Tokyo. Viktor Prinz zu Wied was German minister in Sweden. Hans Thomsen was former chargé d'affaires of the German Embassy in the United States. Ribbentrop recalled Stohrer because the latter had resented the encroachment on his authority by Nazi party and SD officials. These had sought to abandon Germany's official policy of reservation toward Spain, to overthrow General Franco, and to push Madrid to enter the war on the Axis side.

Henke [*sic*].[4] Perhaps Becker will become economic adviser. Grobba broke his arm and used this accident, at present, to avoid going to Paris; of course he uses this as a pretext for other purposes as well. In the meantime Gailani has once again complained to the military. Granow and Tismer[5] are writing further memoranda [in their own interest]. Real peace will only come when these guardians of the Arabs disappear.

5 January 1943

Successful shopping with Nanny [Engelhardt]. Visit from Gailani and his brother.[6] This man is a clever, somewhat lachrymose fellache. We became instant friends. My impression is intensifying that these Arab quarrels are stirred up by certain interested German parties. I have a particularly bad impression of Granow, who is stubborn, stupid, and who, moreover, has a rotten character. After many minor squabbles, Gailani finally said yes and amen to everything that I said. Had lunch with Steffen in the Hotel Adlon. He is involved in business deals in the "Caucasus," just as we were in the first World War in the "Suez," [Egypt] i.e., in tobacco.[7] There he met Niedenführ, who has also secured for himself a military-economic job. A united folk of black marketeers! My mood at the table was completely spoiled by seeing Jenner, formerly from Brazil; even St. compared him to Al Capone.[8] I am not making much progress in the "DIS" investigation. No one is talking. Vague accusations that can neither be proven nor disproven.

6 January 1943

Breakfast at Weizsäcker's, together with the Spanish Ambassador, Moltke, Bismarck, Schliep, Krummer, and their ladies.[9] The Spanish knew

---

4. Andor Hencke, the AA's representative to the German armistice commission with Vichy France in Wiesbaden in June 1940, promoted shortly thereafter to the rank of minister, and assigned to the German Embassy in Madrid in Mar. 1943. Beginning in Apr. 1943, however, he became director of the AA's Political Division with the title of undersecretary of state.

5. Ettel's subordinate in the AA.

6. This was Kamil al-Gailani, former Iraqi minister in Turkey.

7. A code word for armaments and weapons.

8. Presumably Ernst Jenner, a former German cotton buyer, engaged in sub rosa purchases in 1941 in northern Brazil. Gen. Günter Niedenführ had been military attaché and Prüfer's subordinate at the German embassy in Rio.

9. Ewald Ludwig Krummer, an official in the AA subordinate to Luther in Abt. Deutschland, had been the Nazi party leader in Poland during 1939 and active in the NSDAP's contri-

nothing of Cuesta's fate. Moltke seemed to be very content with Becker's appointment. I spent the evening with Ulla. Her marital delusions and confusions are unending.[10]

---

7 January 1943

Had lunch with the Thomsens in the [Hotel] Adlon. He hid his feeling of doom with capricious behavior. We spoke about Mary Fahrney, who maintained that she was Strempel's wife and who, in reality, is a swindler.[11] The Americans wildly call her "madcap." I spoke to A. on the telephone about her mother's visit. Both tone and tempo of her speech were disturbing. In the late afternoon I saw Schröder in Luther's office. Very elegantly decorated in the former Norwegian legation. L. was not there. We waited an hour in vain.

---

8 January 1943

Visited Gailani with Grobba in a palazzo, which was formerly the house of Schwerin-Krosigk,[12] and which was too big for him, notwithstanding his many children. Reception with sycophants, who were numerous but not decorative. The maid shook my hand after G. [Grobba] passed by. Conversations full of venom. G. is really a malicious intriguer. Spent the evening with Ulla. Herr Wehr is the new *Aziz*,[13] who is already in disgrace, *parce qu'il lui montre trop ouvertement qu'il l'aime.* Lunch with Bohny and Frau von Cossel.

---

bution to the German invasion. Martin Schliep was German consul general in Tirana. Otto Christian Prince von Bismarck served as minister in the German Embassy in Italy. The Spanish ambassador was Ginés Vidal y Saures.

10. This refers to Ulla Kracht, a sister-in-law of Prüfer. She lived somewhere between Hamburg and Berlin; Prüfer had a sexual relationship with her. All subsequent references to "Ulla" in the original diaries are to her. *Irrungen und Wirrungen* was the title of a novel by the German writer, Theodor Fontane, which dealt with Berlin society at the end of the nineteenth century. Presumably Prüfer knew the book.

11. Heribert von Strempel was first secretary at the German Embassy in Washington from 1938 to 1941 and Thomsen's subordinate.

12. Lutz Count Schwerin von Krosigk, Reich minister of finance.

13. ". . . lover. . . ."

9 January 1943

I moved into Grobba's office at No. 75. Visit from Ettel, who accuses Gr. of having made a political report to the Reich leader of the S.S., via a friend in the S.S., without notifying the A.A.[14] Ulla had dinner with me.

10 January 1943

Sunday; long, necessary sleep. I telephoned Hesler. He is a lieutenant in the Air Ministry. This afternoon I visited A.'s mother, who is going to Baden-Baden on the 18th. Later a phone conversation with A., who again is very melancholy.

11 January 1943

Lunch with Ambassador Sch. [Schulenburg] in the Adlon; he complained bitterly about the confusion in his shop,[15] caused primarily by the dilettantism of Herr E. from the J.'s [Ribbentrop] outfit.[16] In the afternoon, the Grossmufti visited me, accompanied by Ettel. Nothing was said about Gailani. I agreed with the Mufti, who emphasized the importance of propaganda in North Africa.[17] I had the general impression of a smart, attractive man, who is definitely an Arab patriot, but also, of course, a very

---

14. On 2 Nov. 1942 Grobba had sent a memorandum to members of the Ancestral Heritage Foundation (*Ahnenerbe-Stiftung*), an agency devoted to the study and spread of racial doctrine and administered by Himmler's personal staff. The memorandum was forwarded to the SS chief. Grobba discussed the differences between Gailani and the Mufti so that "the Reich leadership of the SS was carefully instructed regarding these questions."

15. Original in English.

16. "Herr E." is, presumably, Erdmannsdorff. Schulenburg headed a section for Russian affairs (Pol. XIII) established in the AA's Political Division in May 1942. Pol. XIII developed from the "Russia committee" and took over certain files of the dissolved Abt. Deutschland. The Russia committee was one of eleven interdivisional "regional committees" (*Länderkomitees*) created in the AA during the war. These groups, which dealt mainly with propaganda matters, provided a wartime haven for Nazi opportunists and otherwise idle repatriated ambassadors and ministers. See p. xiv.

17. Husayni had renewed his plea that the Axis issue a declaration recognizing the independence of the Arabs in North Africa.

ambitious man. Later I received the Italian Embassy Counselor, Count Cossato, with whom I discussed certain *Avancen* made to us from Rabat via Rieth.[18] I also informed him of my conversations with the Mufti. After dinner I visited Schr. [Schröder]. It is true that Cossel is supposed to be transferred to M. [Madrid] as B.R.;[19] however, the navy has not yet agreed. Scandal regarding Urschel.[20] The secret police are after her for removing assets—artworks, etc.—to Spain and Portugal's detriment. Apparently she is not returning to Germany. El Colombiano [Ettel] will follow Rantzaner [Hencke]. I am supposed to have greater authority in Orientalibus.

12 January 1943

Had lunch with Uncle Max [Oppenheim]. The conversation was the same as 30 years ago. But notwithstanding a certain dusty atmosphere, these visits still have a beautiful nostalgic sheen for me. Young Munzel, who handles Arab affairs in the broadcasting division, visited me in the afternoon.[21] A very nice young man, he is a former bank official from Cairo who quite successfully learned Arabic from Littmann. I discussed with Habib Edib the tasks of his ambassador. He was not very enthusiastic, but nonetheless promised his help. Cossato telephoned and confirmed the agreement of his government in Rome as to the text we want to send Tangiers. I so informed the Spaniards. Schr. [Schröder] visited me in the evening. We talked about many personal matters. I have stood up for my former Rio associates and hope I have helped many of them. May God grant that I can use what is left of my life to help as many people as possible. Only in doing good for others can one experience real joy and a sense of release from one's own worries. Glock has been promoted, Becker becomes Em-

---

18. Kurt Rieth, formerly minister in Vienna and later German consul general in Tangiers, where the Reich had a large group of Abwehr agents attached to the consulate. These passed to Berlin the information that British Prime Minister Winston Churchill would soon hold talks with "friends of the Axis." Similar reports arrived from Abwehr offices in Spain; they were untrue, however, and represented a reaction to the upcoming Allied conference at Casablanca (14–25 Jan. 1943) and increased diplomatic activity by the British in the Mediterranean.

19. *Botschaftsrat*, counselor of embassy.

20. The nickname for Marie-Ursel von Stohrer, wife of the former German ambassador to Spain.

21. Kurt Munzel, an official in the AA's radio division and formerly on Grobba's staff, of whom Prüfer was especially fond. "Orientalibus" was a colloquialism for the AA's Middle Eastern section.

bassy Counselor, Henne and Übelhör are moving into the middle ranks. The medical cases, Blaschke, Kotschi, and Winter, will be transferred to the South.[22] Now do not say any more against your father! Who is laughing here?

13 January 1943

The day has done justice to its date! Nothing but troubles. A. is unhappy, because I sent her sister a bottle of whiskey. Also nothing but frustrations in the office. The back-biting between Gr. [Grobba] and his enemy is unending. E. [Ettel] accuses Gr. of having been a seventh-degree Freemason, a high degree for a German.[23] Gr., on the other hand, spreads rumors about E. that in leaving Persia, he abandoned the German colony, particularly women and children, to the Bolsheviks at the border, while he crossed the frontier to safety. Tania, too, relates similar tales. At the very least, he [Ettel] completely panicked. His only companions were party members who had seen conditions in Persia through the party eyes. I consider both E. and Gr. unsuited for their jobs. Just today I had breakfast for the first time with Gailani, Grobba, Granow, Melchers, and a few hangerson of these important gentlemen. His [Gailani's] wife was the only woman present. The meal was well-catered and the conversation stimulating, considering the confusion of languages. There still is much animosity between our host and the Grossmufti. Both are now seeking contact with the Bey of Tunis.

14 January 1943

Gr.'s [Grobba] bomb is finally about to burst. His enemy has submitted a document that proves conclusively that he [Grobba] had sent a critical

---

22. Minor officials from the embassy in Rio whom Prüfer disliked; Viktor Blaschke, for example, was assigned to the German Consulate in remote Porto, Portugal. Prüfer mentioned Winter, apparently an Austrian, in his Rio diaries. Franz Übelhör had been an office worker in the Rio embassy from 1927 to 1942 and, while working in the Berlin headquarters of the AA in 1943, was promoted to "assistant."

23. The Nazis erroneously equated Freemasonry with "international Jewry."

report about the A.A. to the R.F.S.S.[24] He does not deny it. Further frustration from Baden. There is no reason to take note of this. Everything is completely absurd. (Herpich case—the worries of Ulla and Olaf, etc.)[25] I will not stand for this much longer. A. forgets that I am really tired. It would take but a small annoyance for me to go to my final rest. And yet, I love her so much.

---

15 January 1943

This morning I visited the Mufti in his villa in Zehlendorf; Ettel, too, was there. The Mufti handed me a comprehensive propaganda plan. In the conversation he always came back to his suggestion that the Axis powers should send the Bey of Tunis written assurances as to that country's independence. I repeatedly advised him not to do anything without the Italians, and left him in no doubt whatsoever that the Duce would scarcely be prepared to accept such a written document. This evening I visited Frau v. Heemskerk [*sic*] and her children.

---

16 January 1943

A.'s birthday. Conference and subsequent breakfast with the trustees of the O. [Oppenheim] foundation. Iraq has declared war on us. Heavy air attack in the evening from 7:35 to 9:20.[26] Esterl and I were in the cellar. Our roof was heavily damaged. An incendiary bomb crashed into my bedroom. Two carpets were burned in the attic and one in the bedroom. Many houses in the area are demolished.

---

24. *Reichsführer SS*, or Himmler; regarding the incident, see n. 14.

25. This refers to the personal and political troubles of Olaf Gulbransson, one of Prüfer's longtime friends and a painter who lived in Munich. Prüfer discusses Gulbransson in the original diary entry for 3 May 1943. Herpich was a domestic servant.

26. This was one of the first major Allied bombings of Berlin.

17 January 1943

Took a walk this morning. It looks very bad. Almost all the houses in our area were "stripped" of their roofing tiles. Many had suffered fire damage. I went to see my mother-in-law this afternoon; three houses were completely ruined on the Zähringerstrasse. The inhabitants are buried underneath. Police and rescue crews are working to dig them out. The evening paper reported approximately 31 dead and 150 wounded. The Deutschlandhalle collapsed, St. Urban hospital is badly damaged. Hardly had I returned at about 7:30 when the siren sounded another alert. Again a severe raid. Even by 10:15, the all-clear had not yet sounded. It came at 10:20. Intense glow of fires in the direction of Potsdam.

18 January 1943

The British lost 25 planes yesterday. Unfortunately, today the weather is once again very clear, tailor-made for an attack. Langmann visited me today; he is supposed to "coordinate" the foreign propaganda of the [ministry's] Information Office. A new obstacle thrown in the spokes of an already ungreased wheel. Had lunch with Hassel [*sic*].[27] He seems discontent, probably because of lack of work. Schr. [Schröder] told me yesterday that the case of Schel. [Scheliha] has finally been settled. So has the one against a consular secretary, who worked in the R.L.M.[28] The center of the city was untouched by the latest air raid, whereas we on the city's periphery were the recipients of all these blessings from on high. I received a nice letter from A., and this morning she also telephoned me, just like the old A. of former days. Thus every cloud has a silver lining.

19 January 1943

A.'s letter today was another severe disappointment. If I only knew why she considers our relationship so changed from what it used to be. As

---

27. Ulrich von Hassell, the former German ambassador in Italy, executed in Sept. 1944 for his role in the resistance movement against Hitler. Otto Langmann was Germany's former minister in Uruguay.

28. *Reichsluftfahrtministerium*, the Reich Air Ministry. The identity of the secretary is unknown. Scheliha was tried and executed on 14 Dec. 1942.

far as I can judge, I am still the same with her as in the past. All this talk about whiskey is plain stupid and, after all has been said and done, it was she who attacked me, not I her. A mystery. I can do no serious work as a result of these domestic troubles. I cannot help thinking that I have a wife who is "misunderstood," and I do not know how I can help her. Yesterday evening her mother went to see her. May that help her! This afternoon I had meetings with Erdmannsdorff and Woermann. I hope that they are now convinced that I have no ambitions. Thus far they thought I did. The confusion in the office is boundless. Everyone acts on his own authority, and the most successful are *los Xobeiros*.[29] Sometimes it is difficult for me, the optimist, to suppress the mood of *Lasciate ogni speranza. Quem deus perdere vult. . . .*[30] This evening I had dinner with Arikan. Alfieri, the Spanish Ambassador [Vidal y Saures], Richert, the Argentine Chargé d'Affaires, the Swiss Consul, Feldscher, and others and their ladies. I sat between the nice Madame Luti (Argentine) and a small blonde Italian, Frau Bolla. The Dumonts were also present. She was dressed up in a grotesque costume like an *Arara*.[31] The Turk, *légèrement soul*, declared his political love for me and referred to all other members of the A.A. as bastards (literally). I made light of these drunken babblings.

---

20 January 1943

A pleasant phone conversation with A. I believe that her mother's visit has really done her some good. In the A.A. I had meetings with Cossato and del Torso regarding North African matters. I also had a very interesting conversation with the W.H.A. Tr.z.S.,[32] who deals with Indian affairs. During the conversation he spoke of the difficulties regarding the disposition of my special mission. He maintains that something is rotten in

---

29. A bad pun on the German word, *Schieber*, which means "black marketeer."

30. ". . . abandon all hope. Whom God wishes to destroy. . . ." The first part of the passage appeared over the entrance to Dante's inferno. The second is from a Latin proverb that says "Whom God wishes to destroy, he first turns mad."

31. An *ara macao*, a parrot from Latin America. Karl Hermann Dumont was a senior counselor in the AA's Economic Policy Division. Arvid Richert was the Swedish minister in Germany.

32. Adam von Trott zu Solz, an aide to Keppler in the AA and member of the Abwehr. He was also part of the conspiracy against Hitler and executed after the attempt on 20 July 1944 to assassinate the dictator. A WHA (*Wissenschaftlicher Hilfsarbeiter*) was a professional assistant or auxiliary expert appointed in the AA for special tasks.

the state of Martin [Luther];[33] he obviously does not accuse him directly, but he does [accuse] K. [Klatten]. Since he cannot prove anything, he should better remain silent. I had lunch with the Kettenbeils. Tomorrow he is returning to Lisbon; his wife was curiously distracted. K. had a serious argument with H.[34] From this and other conversations, I have the impression that we will hand an ultimatum to the Iberians, so that others will not beat us in this game. Sizeable deliveries to the Atrak in the matter of Taijarat.[35]

---

21 January 1943

An even better conversation with A. As nice as on our first encounter. I am happy and almost thankful to the Tommies, because the damage they caused saved me from something worse. This afternoon I was in the Auerallee. Meissner, Köpke, Planck, Schwarkowsky, Brand, O.W.'s son, Kiewitz, were present. The latter told interesting stories about those interned at Laecken,[36] whom he praised enthusiastically. He was not pleased with the Flemish. They are self-serving. Our soldiers prefer the Walloons. These are judgments from a mousehole perspective. Also, as everywhere else, the opinions of this group are very bad as far as the inappropriately proliferating "bureaucracy" in our Fatherland is concerned. Everything happens *ad personem*, very little *ad rem*. Sections, divisions, offices, even entire ministries with large numbers of personnel, have been created so that all these folk can justify their existence away from the fighting front. Even people who want to go to the front, my chauffeur for instance, are being denied their wish, so that the "bureaucracy," i.e., those avoiding service, can rest in peace. This might be tolerable if all these indispensables were to remain

---

33. Prüfer's "something is rotten in the state of Martin" was originally in English.

34. Baron Oswald von Hoyningen-Huene, German minister in Portugal. Karl Kettenbeil, a military officer and longtime friend of Prüfer's from World War I, was attached to the German Legation in Lisbon.

35. This presumably refers to Germany's first large shipment of armaments to Turkey during World War II, based on a German-Turkish agreement of 31 Dec. 1942.

36. The place where Belgian King Leopold III, who had chosen to surrender to the Germans in 1940, was held during the Nazi occupation. Erwin Planck was an ex-secretary of state executed in Jan. 1945 for his activity in the resistance movement against the Nazi government. Otto Meissner, a secretary of state in Hitler's Presidential Chancellery and Reich minister, had played a significant role in 1933 in persuading the aged Weimar president, Paul von Hindenburg, to appoint Hitler chancellor.

quiet; but nothing of the sort. They disturb orderly administrative procedures by being busy and by "governing" in the most amateurish and inappropriate way wherever they can. The concept of jurisdiction, which a complex government can certainly not dispense with unless an unholy mess should occur, has disappeared. Everyone pokes his nose into everything. Dilettantism is the rule. Money is no longer important. I do not want to be petty, especially not during the war, but money today is only printed paper, the all-too small format of which scarcely permits another use; nonetheless it is somewhat irksome that this scrip is used by people in the garb of government service for purposes other than those of the common good. It is curious that, just as in World War I, the demands of war elevate to positions of power, above all, the crooks among our people. I believe the German people never had to suffer as much from these sly rascals as they do today. If only there were someone who would quite openly tell the Führer about all these loathsome things!

---

22 January 1943

Today, questioning of Herr S., the business manager of "Mundus," Inc., and the R.A. Dr. M. [Moehring], who was working for the German Information Office of Don Martinho [Luther] and anonymously and simultaneously for Alis [Frau Ribbentrop].[37] The interrogation did not produce anything substantially new. It is still a picture of general uncertainty and confusion, a totally disorganized and excessively involved undertaking, held together by profiteering, ambition, and terror. Gr. [Grobba] has played another dirty trick. He apparently learned from "midget" Gr. [Granow] that the Reeder [Woermann] was very unhappy with my policies and wanted to discuss them with the boss [Ribbentrop].[38] I cornered the Reeder, who denied everything. Gr. then called me in the evening, rather distressed, and babbled about some misunderstandings. Then I learned from Melchers that a few days ago Gr. and Gr. appeared as managers for the Mesopotamians[39] during a television production at the broadcasting studio and that "midget" Gr. gave a tea reception for 16 people in his house,

---

37. "R.A." is *Rechtsanwalt*, attorney-at-law. "Herr S." is unidentified.

38. Prüfer frequently referred to Woermann in the original diaries as the "shipping magnate." Woermann's patience with Prüfer's inability to halt the bickering between the supporters of the Mufti and Gailani in the AA was wearing thin.

39. Gailani and his entourage.

of course without mine or Ettel's knowledge. The latter is right about both of them: Gr. and Gr. are intriguers of the worst sort. I had breakfast at Bose's, who is supposed to leave shortly, with Kepler [*sic*], Woermann, the Mufti, Gailani, Ghulam Siddiq, Melchers, Cossato, del Torso, and others. The enemies, now reconciled, were repeatedly photographed with us, the mediators.[40] Interesting detail: Gh. S. [Siddiq] energetically denied that his mediation was in any way the result of Gr.'s intervention. Supposedly it originated spontaneously from him. Following a conversation with Ettel, I still feel that it is necessary to submit a note to the boss regarding our propaganda in Tunisia. Although I do not expect too much from such propaganda, I am definitely of the opinion that at a point when we and the Italians are about to lose Tripoli, we should no longer support the purely theoretical claims of our allies; instead we should go in a totally different direction, promising the Tunisians and even the Tripolitanians and Senussis recognition of their autonomy in some form. The Reeder did not quite see it that way, the St.S. seemed more sympathetic.[41] In the end, there is a difference between what can be promised under the extreme stress of war and what can be kept after achieving victory. Machiavelli, you are winking at me. Your compatriots should understand this precisely. In the afternoon I went with Alfieri to a house concert at Wannsee, where a young pianist named Michelangeli performed. I have seldom heard such a good performance. This young man should have a great future. Arikan and Sztójay, among others, were there. Irrigogen expressed regrets regarding Chile's break of diplomatic relations with us.[42]

---

40. Although their quarreling had not subsided, the Mufti and Gailani had met three weeks before, which, Prüfer claimed to Ribbentrop and Weizsäcker in a memorandum of 25 Jan. 1943, had restored superficial "unity" between the Arab leaders. Subhas Chandra Bose, the former president of the Indian National Congress and a leading Asian revolutionary, had opted during the war to favor the Axis in the hope that they would help free his country from British rule. He left Germany by submarine on 7 Feb. 1943 and arrived in Tokyo in May. The Japanese, who sought India for themselves, provided little support for Bose and the Indian national army, which failed in its mission to liberate India from Britain. Bose died in a plane crash on 18 Aug. 1945, while attempting to reach Russia.

41. The "St. S." is *Staatssekretär*, the AA's secretary of state, Weizsäcker.

42. Chile broke diplomatic relations with Germany on 20 Jan. 1943, but was the only country in the Americas not to declare war on the Reich. Prüfer's "Irrigogen" was presumably Alonzo Irigoyen, Argentine undersecretary of finance. Döme Sztójay was Hungarian minister in Germany.

23 January 1943

I can no longer obtain gasoline. That means that if I want to continue my office routine to any regular degree, then I must move back downtown, preferably into a hotel. I have already mentioned this to the St.S. and, not only for that reason, have asked for my retirement. Given these purely physical aggravations involving an hour's journey—20 min. on foot—to the A.A., I simply cannot continue in the Service, at my age of nearly 62 years. But it goes without saying that even this would be insignificant during war if I were convinced that I could still serve my Fatherland successfully and honorably. I totally lack this conviction. My sphere of influence is in no way defined; thus, I appear as an irksome and threatening intruder to all those who feel they operate in the undefined area; this the more so because no one knows for sure where his domain begins or ends. Thus, with few exceptions, I meet passive resistance everywhere and am hindered or sabotaged in dealing with those matters I consider important. Outside of our narrow, local confines, e.g., as far as the Italians are concerned, I am considered to be the director of our Oriental policy; in reality I but see a small portion of it. Weizsäcker knows all this and by his silence presumably sanctions my desire for quitting the Service. Nonetheless he advises me not to carry things too far. Perhaps he also thought that such insanities, coming from an ambassador, could be catching and might influence him in his own decisions. But his situation is different from mine. He is the Minister's deputy and can demand to be heard and, if necessary, be protected by him. I, a second-class ambassador, am comparable to a fly that is not shooed away from the cake it is crawling on because no one cares. One has forgotten that this insect is not crawling on the cake because of greed but because of exhaustion. The insect is too tired to fly away.

Gr. [Grobba] formally explained to me that he had "misunderstood" the "midget" [Granow]. The latter has not spoken about a "report" of Reeder's to the boss. The 7th rank[43] is beginning to show itself. I had another conversation with Reeder about this distasteful matter. I visited Max for lunch. Poor old man! He is, after all, a good soul.[44] The trip home on the subway took over an hour. I cannot continue this way.

---

43. A reference to Grobba's former days as a Freemason.
44. Original "Poor old man! He is, after all, a good soul" is in English.

24 January 1943

A Sunday with family. I invited myself to Engelhardt's for lunch, in order to give some cigarettes to Peter, their son, who is here on furlough. It is pathetic how they try to maintain respectability in these difficult times. Peter makes a very good impression. On the way to Engelhardt's, I spent an hour and five minutes on buses and streetcars, not to mention delays. In the long run my body will not be able to endure this much longer. But what can I do? Of course I really do not matter when one considers Stalingrad and Tripoli. Bärbel came over in the afternoon and stayed for a rather frugal dinner. *À la guerre*, etc.! Later A. called. Very sweet. I wish that I could make her happier in this world that has gone completely crazy. If only we could keep Tunisia; Russia is not nearly as important.

25 January 1943

The first trip walking and riding to the A.A. It took me 2-1/2 hours, the length of a normal train ride to Dresden. I was exhausted. My undefined position brought me into renewed conflict with the Reeder, who finally insisted correctly on the nature of his jurisdiction. Schr. [Schröder] left for *Westfalen*. Undoubtedly, on the telephone today, I lost my composure with A., just as she wanted to go to the theater with Schlemann [*sic*].[45] That is a bad sign, something that would have never happened to me in earlier days.

26 January 1943

Early this morning I once again lost my composure when A. called me about the Langenns. She had, of course, spoken to Langenn about my visit, even though this occurred after I had accepted the invitation yesterday. I sounded on the telephone like a fishwife. Directly to blame is my fatigue from the trips downtown. This phone conversation occurred in the A.A.

---

45. Presumably Josef Schleemann, an AA liaison official with the German army high command and involved in the administration of Latin American diplomats interned in Baden-Baden.

Added into the bargain was the unproductive, imitating twaddle in morning devotions, in which especially the Reeder, ever unable to recognize the tragedy of the situation, persists with his League of Nations tactics à la Bülow; his everlasting deliberations and discussions really get on my nerves.[46] And now, as we and above all the Italians have lost all occupied areas in North Africa with the exception of a small bridgehead in Tunisia, we are hesitating to play our cards that still promise success, a limited success to be sure. And all this only because Mussolini does not want to give up his claim on Tunisia. He does not really need to do that. He just needs to lie. In this "total" war, which is not exactly a conclave of applied ethics, is that something so rare and unheard of? And even if he is afraid to tell his children that he promised independence to Bourguiba, then he should give it secretly and orally. This Tunisian undoubtedly knows how he will tell his own people.[47]

There is also grim news from Russia. Stalingrad is fighting for its life, and at Voronesch, which we had evacuated, the Hungarians seem to have decamped shamefully. Undoubtedly this must also affect the Turks. This morning I had a *tête-à-tête* during breakfast with Frau H.E.T. [Frau Habib Edib], whose husband is in Turkey. Apparently the purpose of the invitation was to inform me gently of some unfavorable developments. According to her, her husband is very pessimistic as to whether or not his Fatherland, even with the best intentions, will be able to avoid joining our enemies. The Americans are getting increasingly more pushy. The [Turkish] policy of neutrality had every chance until the appearance of the U.S.A. in North Africa. Since then Turkish policy has, under American pressure, veered further and further into a direction hostile to us. She spoke very unfavorably of the Ambassador here [Arikan]. According to her, he drinks a great deal and then behaves badly. At a recent dinner reception he supposedly drank to such excess that he could not reach the "Loo" and vomited on the floor and on himself, all this in front of his guests. Recently the manners of this man also met with displeasure at the Union Club, where he playfully twisted a gentleman's moustache. The latter did not think it was funny.

Frau H.E.T. warned me urgently about the Dumonts who, supposedly,

---

46. Prüfer complained that Woermann allegedly acted like Bernhard Wilhelm von Bülow, the conservative and nationalist secretary of state of the AA, from 1930 to 1936. The morning devotions [*Morgenandacht*] were the daily meetings of the AA's divisional chiefs in the secretary of state's office.

47. The Tunisian leader mentioned here was Habib Bourguiba; he has served since 1957 as president of Tunisia. Prüfer's views in this regard were presumably influenced by similar ideas held by his longtime friend, Shekib Arslan, a Syrian nationalist exiled in Switzerland.

are not only defeatists of the worst sort, but also enemies of Germany. He poses as a Frenchman before foreigners; she, on the other hand, once said that "if the Germans are defeated, it will serve them right. The main thing is that I can buy my butter." She claimed that German news bulletins are nothing but lies. She has a fierce hatred for me and Aschmann. In front of foreigners she apparently expressed her desire for my death on our return trip from Brazil. When Aschmann's son died, she loudly expressed her joy. In the presence of foreigners she supposedly denounced Frau von der H.R.[48] and some other ladies as agents of the Gestapo. I believe that it is about time to stop this family.

The boss telephoned about 7 p.m. I have to conduct another unpleasant investigation, this time related to the "visit" of the Tommies. To do that I have to go to Berlin tonight.[49]

---

27 January 1943

I took statements until 2:45 a.m. in the Wilhelmstr. 73 and reached home at 3:30. Statements about *querelles allemandes*. At 10 a.m. today, I again visited the scene of the crime in the Lentzeallee. Just imagine disturbing an ambassador because of the possible misbehavior of a concierge, about an issue an R.M.[50] considers revolutionary in nature. God protect our Fatherland! And all that in the face of the death struggle at Stalingrad. *Saluez, c'est la mort qui passe!*

Had lunch with Gh. S. Kh. [Ghulam Siddiq]. He confirms that the tension between the Mufti and Gailani has not lessened. People in both camps are fanning the flames. Gr. [Grobba] had told him, and me as well, half-truths about his own activities in the matter of reconciliation. Hilva [Boroevich-Heemskerck] visited me in the evening in order to get some advice as to the difficulties concerning her mother's house. The poor thing will have to be operated on for the fourth time since the birth of little Olaf.

---

48. The wife of Bernd Otto Freiherr von der Heyden-Rynsch, a counselor at the German Embassy in Spain. Gottfried Aschmann was formerly head of the AA's Press Division.

49. Ribbentrop asked Prüfer to investigate Goebbels' accusations of corruption. Prüfer later described the charges in pencil along the bottom margin of his diary entry for 27 Jan. 1943: "Goebbels had complained that Ribbentrop had had his house in Dahlem, damaged by bombs, immediately repaired, instead of leaving the workers free to fix other buildings more severely damaged and more socially important first. R. had nothing to do with it. It concerned his overzealous house manager, who wanted to make himself popular."

50. *Reichsminister*. In this instance, Goebbels.

The deposition and the report about the [Ribbentrop-Goebbels] quarrel have been filed.

---

28 January 1943

I had lunch with Ettel at the Grossmufti's. Long conversation about propaganda questions. I also conveyed to him [the Mufti] our general attitude on the question of Arab policy in the same manner that I had explained it to Gailani at an earlier time. He suggested that he visit Rome, so that he could speak to the Duce. I said that we would not object.[51] Ettel spoke to me about his transfer.

An investigation that Bergmann is conducting has been initiated against Grobba. I talked to Wiehl about the family [the Dumonts].[52]

The Mufti had a conversation with Alfieri about [Axis] propaganda in Tunisia. It seems that Alfieri is beginning to understand that something must happen, since the Italians will not make any headway without compromises.

---

29 January 1943

Visit from Langmann. He is now "working on" North Africa in matters of propaganda. Luther gave him this job. That is characteristic for our "bureaucracy" in the office. The man [Langmann] does not have the slightest idea about the area assigned to him. To remedy this he appoints a committee. And then the staff can begin to argue the subject to death. *Quem deus perdere vult*! In the afternoon I was visited by Dr. Felix Baehr, a man from Abbas Hilmi. He is supposed to join him in Lisbon. He [Baehr] told

---

51. This meeting formed the basis for the Mufti's renewed plea to Ribbentrop on 28 Jan. 1943 that the Axis issue a declaration supporting Arab freedom in order to acquire their support in North Africa. Such a move was even more urgent, Husayni declared, because France had "lost its last two cards, North Africa and its fleet," and because of the recent meetings of the Allied leaders in Casablanca.

52. Prüfer told Dumont's superior in the AA, Emil Karl Josef Wiehl, head of the Economic Policy Division, about the accusations against Dumont and his wife. Prüfer's denunciation of Frau Dumont in the AA apparently led to the German police's involvement in the matter, in which Habib Edib and his wife were also implicated. Bergmann, deputy director of the AA's Personnel and Budget Division, was also involved in the investigation of Luther.

me that the Khedive was deeply disturbed about the despicable treatment he experienced here.[53] We intimate our best friends—we really do not have all too many—by abrupt, obdurate conduct à la police, or worse yet, by police measures, which are devoid of any real expertise.

30 January 1943

Departure for Bellin around one p.m. There was a preliminary air-raid alert. During the journey the train conductor called out a full alert. Nothing happened, and I arrived in Bellin safe and sound around 5 p.m. Nice evening with Langenn, a house guest, Fräulein von Leyser, a friend of Ingrid's. Phone conversation with A. in the evening. Everything is all right. Earlier in the day I had a talk with Keppler. Lasch *manwittich*.[54]

31 January 1943

Good times in a rustic environment.

53. Abbas Hilmi, the ex-Khedive of Egypt, lived in exile in Switzerland; Prüfer and the AA had cultivated close relations with him since Britain had removed the prince from the Egyptian throne in 1914. During World War II, and particularly when German troops invaded North Africa in 1941, Abbas Hilmi had intrigued anew to regain his royal office. He had received little support from the Germans, however. Instead, they had established contacts with Egyptian nationalists and King Farouk, who hoped for German aid in defeating the British. The British secretly arranged for the ex-Khedive's contact with the Germans, presumably believing that this would discredit Germany with the Egyptian nationalists and Farouk, both of whom despised Abbas Hilmi. The Germans had also refused to provide a visa for the ex-Khedive to visit Turkey. As he had always done, the former prince continued to retain secret contacts with the British, although London had no interest in his return to the throne. Baehr was an official in the German Consulate General in Geneva, Switzerland; he had close ties to the ex-Khedive.

54. "Executed." Carl Lasch, whose name Prüfer spelled here in Arabic script, was the first president of the German Academy of Law and head of the Lvov Commissariat in the Polish General Government. He had been arrested and executed without trial in 1942 by the Gestapo on charges of embezzlement and thefts of works of art. The case undoubtedly interested Prüfer because no German civil servant or officer had been executed without trial; subsequently, trials were even included in the wave of terror that followed the July 1944 plot against Hitler.

four

February 1943

1 February 1943

Returned to Berlin at noon. In the evening conversation with Luther at Schröder's. The southern sector of Stalingrad has fallen. Oh poor defenders! Gen. Paulus was promoted to field marshal shortly before the end.[1] On 30.1. several enemy raiders tried to disturb the anniversary celebration of the III. Reich's beginning by attacking Berlin. A plane was shot down in Zehlendorf.

2 February 1943

Talked to Schröder about Vomberg.[2] He was very concerned about the *Ahwal malija fil Charigiga jiftikir in ennazir magnun.*[3]

---

1. The German Sixth Army under Gen. Friedrich Paulus had surrendered on 31 Jan. 1942. Stalingrad was a major turning point in the war: nearly 100,000 German soldiers died there and 90,000 were taken prisoner.
2. Unidentified.
3. ". . . financial situation in the partnership, thinking in regard to the crazy administrator." Prüfer, presumably to protect himself, wrote this passage in Arabic; the vague references were to the AA and Ribbentrop.

3 February 1943

I saw Prof. Gudzent, who confirmed the enlargement of my heart and
an increase and slight hardening of the liver. More tests will follow the day
after tomorrow. The doctor believes that 4 weeks of vacation are absolutely
necessary. Had lunch with the Dieckhoffs, Sztójay, and the Strachwitzes[4]
at the Erdmannsdorff's; his new wife is very nice, and the Countess Strachwitz even more so. Herr and Frau Boroevich visited me in the evening.
Dieckhoff, too, is dissatisfied with his job in particular and the A.A. in
general: bureaucracy as a result of excessive organization.

4 February 1943

Moved into the Hotel Adlon. Very tired.

5 February 1943

Lunch with Frau Edib. Very pessimistic views as to Turkey's attitude.
Schröder spoke with Vomberg who, without hesitation, put his finger on
the correct source. Nothing happened to Gr. [Grobba]. He lied his way out
fantastically. That, too, is a matter of indifference to me. Prof. Gudzent
ordered 6 weeks of rest for me. I so informed the St. S. and D. Pers.[5] I had
the impression that they did not believe me. Hopefully, for A.'s [Anneliese]
and O.'s [Olaf] sake, the misconceptions of these gentlemen will not soon
have foreseeable results [i.e., Prüfer's death]. Personally I would not mind,
although it would be nice if I could live in peace with the two of them for a
few more years.

4. Rudolf Graf von Strachwitz, former counselor at the German Legation in Budapest;
beginning in Jan. 1943, liaison of the AA with Rosenberg's Ministry for the Occupied Eastern
Territories. Hans Heinrich Dieckhoff, previously the German ambassador in the United
States, had been on special assignment in the AA since 1938.
5. *Personaldirektor*, director of the Personnel and Budget Division in the AA, Schröder.
Grobba had denied responsibility for his memorandum of 2 Nov. 1942, "regarding the Arab
question," having reached Himmler. See chap. 3, n. 14.

---

6 February 1943

Lunch with Ingrid [Langenn]. The boss [Ribbentrop] called in the evening to ask about the status of the DIS investigation.

---

7 February 1943

Sunday. I went to a Croatian art exhibit full of brown gravy. These people have no sense of color.

---

8 February 1943

Nothing of significance. Ingrid's girlfriends visited in the evening. Herr and Frln. v. Saldern, v.d. Bussche, Muzi.[6]

---

9 February 1943

Witzleben visited me this evening.[7] He has become much calmer.

---

10 February 1943

Went to the theater with Ingrid and Hilva [Boroevich-Heemskerck]. A shallow piece done in the French style of 50 years ago, *The Blue Straw Hat*. Afterward Muzi and Boroevich visited me.

---

6. "Muzi" was an Italian attaché whose full name is unknown. Capt. Axel Freiherr von dem Bussche was a career officer, friend of the Schulenburgs, and member of the conspiracy to assassinate Hitler.

7. Field Marshal Erwin von Witzleben, executed on 8 Aug. 1944 for his role in the attempted assassination of Hitler three weeks before.

11 February 1943

Martin Luther has fallen. Reason, disloyalty; it is unknown in what
regard he was disloyal.[8] Ingrid has left. Scherif Scheref complained about
Gailani. Gr. [Grobba] has gone to Paris. He escaped unscathed!

12 February 1943

Together with Luther, several of his people were compromised and
have been suspended from their offices. Blind[9] visited me today and said
that Ab. H. [Abbas Hilmi] was very sick and that no one had made use of
his offer to help us in '41. He was even refused a transit visa to Turkey,
evidently so as not to annoy the king.[10] Here, too, the Reeder [Woermann]
does not seem to have behaved very heroically.

13 February 1943

In the evening I went to a dinner in honor of the Turkish Ambassador, Saffat Arikan. Richert, Sztójay, the Dieckhoffs, the Erdmannsdorffs,
the Bollas, Belkeys, Kavur, Melchers, Lebrecht, Ripken, Frau Habib Edip
[*sic*], and Hilva were there. Already at the dinner table Arikan was drunk
and made offensive comments about Goltz and others.[11] After dinner he
sidled up to Ripken and indulged in jibes against Habib Edip [*sic*], whom
he called a "bastard." Ripken behaved even worse, making vile remarks in
front of everyone about Hilva's relationship with me. Arikan is undoubtedly a pathological case. There was an act of sabotage at the Friedrichstr. S
[elevated] train station.[12]

8. Luther was arrested on 10 Feb. 1943, imprisoned in the Sachsenhausen concentration
camp, and the Abt. Deutschland dissolved. This resulted from his attempted intrigue with an
SS leader, Walter Schellenberg, to oust Ribbentrop as foreign minister.
9. An official in the German Consulate General in Geneva.
10. Farouk in Egypt; see chap. 3, n. 53.
11. Gen. Colmar von der Goltz, a German adviser to the Turkish army during 1886–95 and
1909–13. George Ripken was head of the Middle Eastern section in the AA's Economic Policy
Division.
12. Inasmuch as there was no such action reported and considering the place of this sen-

14 February 1943

Sunday. Terrible weather. I am a little depressed after yesterday's rather discordant party. Rostov and Voroshilovgrad have been lost.

15 February 1943

Address by Dr. Goebbels to the highest Reich officials in the Ambassadors' Hall of the chancellery, with the Reich ministers present. We were admonished to desist from all criticism and grumbling and, instead, to encourage our coworkers by setting a good example. That is exactly what I would have said. The Schlimperts and Franzi came to dinner in the evening. For the time being, the RAM has postponed his decision as to my request for a leave of absence.[13]

16 February 1943

Lunch with Uncle Max [Oppenheim]. Earlier in the day interrogation of *l'oie sauvage*.[14] He believes that Kl. [Klatten] is *Magnun und Ilg*.[15] The whole picture of the DIS more and more resembles an utter pigsty. I saw Gr.'s [Grobba] enemy [Ettel] this afternoon. The boss was informed of Calvin's [Luther's] activities by Heinrich Himmler, subsequent to a conversation between these two at the Italian Embassy. Heinrich then spoke with the boss, who asked Heinrich to investigate the case. Calvin was *matrud minel hizb*.[16] I am certain that he will defend himself by all means fair or foul.

---

tence in the entry, one may presume that this was an ironical reference by Prüfer to something of little consequence.

13. "RAM" is *Reichsaussenminister*, foreign minister, Ribbentrop.

14. ". . . the wild goose." This was a play on words by Prüfer that referred to an elderly official in the AA, Rudolf Wildegans, whom he had interrogated as part of his investigation of the DIS. The use of special names by the career diplomats to describe Luther was not uncommon; indeed, his enemies vied with each other for purple adjectives to describe him.

15. ". . . crazy and homosexual."

16. ". . . dismissed from the party."

---

17 February 1943

L'oie sauvage [Wildegans] informed us that Kl. [Klatten] wanted to depart for Switzerland this evening. He was ordered to wait. Once again I consulted Prof. Gudzent. My kidneys, too, are affected, and they are excreting albumen and gall. He is of the opinion that I *must* have a vacation. Tomorrow the boss is going to Rome and with him his whole swarm of followers.[17] I had a long conversation with Megerle about our propaganda in North Africa. We are in a hopeless quandary between Italian, Spanish, and Arab interests and the commitment made to Pétain. It is becoming increasingly clear that the French are lying to us all along the line. Only Abetz, Schleier, Rahn etc. fail to see this.[18] Hans and Nanny [Engelhardt] in the evening.

---

18 February 1943

The trip of our noble lords [Ribbentrop and his entourage] has been postponed until tomorrow. Visit from the Mufti, who urges activation of our propaganda in the Near East by declaring the independence of all Arab countries. He is absolutely right. Goebbels's speech in the evening about total war.[19]

---

19 February 1943

The Embassy in Budapest reports new intrigues of Gailani's people against the Mufti and the new course in the A.A. I would say that these

---

17. Ribbentrop visited the Italian capital from 25 to 29 Feb. 1943, carrying a letter from Hitler to Mussolini that declared Germany's determination to defeat the Soviet Union and not to conclude a political settlement with the U.S.S.R.

18. Rudolf Rahn was the AA's civilian administrator in Tunisia. Rudolf Schleier served as counselor in the German Embassy in Paris. Ambassador Otto Abetz was representative of the AA with the German military commander in France. Karl Megerle was a German journalist on the staff of the RAM.

19. Even before the war situation deteriorated for Germany, Goebbels, certain elements in the military, and Hitler's Armaments and Munitions minister, Albert Speer, demanded that the Reich escalate the war from a series of limited conflicts (*Blitzkrieg*) into a massive and

intrigues are directed against me. Junus Bahri[20] arrived here and was received by Kamil Gailani. New symptoms of Turkey's defection: Steinhardt met with Menemencioglu and Acikalin.[21] Rumor has it that this concerns a Russo-Turkish rapprochement. By the same token, in the event of our further retreats, the Turks supposedly intend to occupy Bulgaria up to the Danube with some 20 divisions; this as a protection against Bolshevism. The Minister's trip has been postponed once again.

---

20 February 1943

Klatten visited me and talked about matters that have been known for a long time.

---

21 February 1943

Sunday. Langenn arrived in the afternoon.

---

22 February 1943

Rahn arrived and reported about Tunisia. *Naksm fi hala battāla giddan. Kull el gēsch kull el regal lakin bidun silah kifaja wa chususan bidun*

---

brutal struggle for self-preservation and assertion. Goebbels, in a famous speech on 18 Feb. 1943 in the Berlin Sportpalast, created an atmosphere of frenzied emotion, evoking the support of his listeners for mobilization for total war.

20. An Arab (Iraqi) radio commentator in the press department of the German Legation in Bucharest and friend of Rashid Ali al-Gailani.

21. Cevat Acikalin, Turkish ambassador in Moscow and, after Mar. 1943, briefly successor to the ill Numan Menemencioglu, secretary general of the Turkish Foreign Ministry. Laurence A. Steinhardt was the United States ambassador in Turkey. Prüfer had received a report two days before that Adil Arslan, a Syrian nationalist in Turkey and brother of Shekib Arslan, had refused Prüfer's invitation to visit Germany for "a long conversation on Arab affairs." Arslan viewed the Reich's military situation as increasingly unfavorable and, believing that Turkey might soon join the Allies, did not wish to jeopardize himself and his family with the Turks.

essence. Ettalaine zaj ezzift.[22] In the evening we were at Strack's with
Abetz, Megerle, Krug, Langmann, Rahn, Auer, Erdmannsdorff, Woermann, Schumburg etc.[23] The topic was the Tunisian question. There was
no meeting of the minds. Rahn in moderate form, Auer in radical form,
held the view that only the French are worth supporting, the Arabs are a
quantité négligeable. The truth is probably somewhere in the middle.
Things are not going well for Klatten.[24]

23 February 1943

Manfred and Sigrid [Richthofen] here. Niedenführ reports from
Russia: *musiha kubra wa erraijis el masul.*[25]

25 February 1943

Helmut [Langenn] has left.

26 February 1943

Lunch with Rahn. Afternoon with Langmann and the protagonists
of Tunisia. L. succeeded in bringing back an astounding number of good
pictures from South America, as well as a few carpets that were by no
means too shabby. Only the Jews had such assets in Rio. R. described his

22. "Yes, there is a very miserable situation. All the army, all the men, but without enough
weapons and especially without a good spirit. The Italians are very bad."

23. Johannes Schumburg was an official in the AA's Political Division, previously in Abt.
Deutschland. Theodor Auer was formerly consul general in Casablanca. Roland Krug von
Nidda served as head of the Vichy branch office of the German Embassy in Paris. Hans
Heinrich Strack was head of the Western European section in the AA's Political Division.

24. Because of his activities with the DIS and his connections with Luther, Klatten was
suspended from the AA in June 1943 and sent into the military.

25. ". . . it is a disaster and the President is reponsible." "President" was presumably a
code word for Hitler.

extraordinary success as a businessman in Syria and Tunis.[26] He is quite a man, even in external appearance. But it would probably have been better if he had not followed a bureaucratic career. As a conquistador or a Cecil Rhodes, he might have become a hero of his people. I do not think there is a place among us for such creatures. Here he will probably end up as a crook. Spent the evening together with Sigrid and Manfred and the very nice C. L. Diehl and his wife.[27]

---

27 February 1943

Had dinner with the Boroevichs, together with a nice young Lieutenant, Wolfgang Erich, who told interesting stories about North Africa. Very enthusiastic about Rommel who, by the way, has returned to Tunisia.

---

28 February 1943

Sunday. Most delightful spring-like weather. Lunch with Frau Edip [sic]. She feels terrorized by the Dumont woman. This woman increasingly turns out to be a gossiper and an informer. Apparently she also insulted the Edips [sic] in front of Arikan. One must beware of her. In the evening I was at Feige's with Steffen and the radio general, Ditmar [sic].[28] On the way home the latter described vividly the total failure of a *kolordu iswin*.[29]

---

26. During the spring of 1941, Rahn had been sent as a special AA envoy to Vichy-controlled Syria to organize war matériel for assisting the pro-German Iraqi government of Rashid Ali al-Gailani in its revolt against Britain. Gailani's regime collapsed at the end of May, however, and he fled with his followers to Berlin. Six weeks later, British and Free French troops defeated the pro-Axis Vichy forces in Syria.

27. Carl Ludwig Diehl, an actor; his wife was an opera singer.

28. Kurt Dittmar, the German army's chief broadcast spokesman and propagandist. Hans Feige, a previously retired officer, had rallied behind Hitler at the beginning of the war and was restored to active duty.

29. ". . . very bad situation." This presumably referred to the difficulty Dittmar and other Nazi propagandists were experiencing in broadcasting successful propaganda in the face of mounting German military setbacks.

five

March 1943

Professor G. [Gudzent] wrote the A.A. that I am in immediate mortal peril. Will I get a vacation on the strength of this testimony? A good farmer usually does not raise his best milk cow to be slaughtered. If I am really so absolutely indispensable, the powers that be should try to help me (with a 6-weeks' vacation), rather than place me in acute mortal danger. I really feel sick, although I would like to convince myself otherwise. In any case, I have gained so much distance from this entire termite colony that I can observe it dispassionately and without ambition, indeed I can even enjoy it. At least to a certain extent. The love for my mother, Germany, nonetheless strongly prevents me from assuming the objective-historical stance of a detached spectator.

There was an air raid alarm at 9:45 that lasted for 2 hours. The attack was very intense. Unter den Linden is burning in our vicinity, four buildings ablaze, among them the Hotel Bristol, where the fire is developing, but slowly. The firemen were not yet there when I went for a short walk at 12:30. A huge glow can be seen to the north. The Fehrmann family is hail and hearty, but also very scared.[1] Roof and windows of the house on

---

1. The mother and sisters of Anneliese, Prüfer's wife. Both the number and severity of the air raids on Germany increased in Mar. and Apr. 1943, mainly because of the growing strength of the British Royal Air Force and an intensification of the Allied effort to attack the Reich's major production area along the Ruhr as well as Berlin.

Thanner Pfad have been damaged again. And all this, I fear, because of "Air Force Day."[2]

---

2 March 1943

The damage produced by the cousins is rather considerable.[3] Even this afternoon several houses are still burning. Steglitz is supposed to be the worst hit area. But it also looks bad in Dahlem, Grunewald, and on the Kurfürstendamn. Sigrid's [Richthofen] house burned down with everything in it, including Gustaf Adolf's [Glock] belongings. The Hedwig church and three hospitals are completely burned out. 19 British [planes] have been shot down: a small consolation. I had lunch with Uncle Max [Oppenheim], who was, as always, serene. In his old age he is becoming calm and cheerful, and he showed me the things he is bequeathing to Olaf: a lot of silver. When I was with Dr. Kaminski[4] this afternoon, I also saw the damage on the Spichernstrasse. The house next door to his was still burning. Traffic was disrupted in many places. There still blows a strong wind, which naturally fans the flames. Prof. G. [Gudzent] is of the opinion, as he told me this morning, that I am in "acute mortal danger." Are we not all. Why, then, should I be such an exception? Ingrid [Langenn] is coming tomorrow. I advised against it, but nonetheless, she is coming. I spent the evening with the Soehrings.[5] He is the representative of the A.A. in Aarhus. I have just spoken with A. [Anneliese]. I hope I calmed her down. The poor thing is not having a good time of it.

---

3 March 1943

The night passed quietly. Ingrid is here. Alarm in the afternoon.

---

2. Widespread in Berlin and elsewhere, however, was the rumor that the RAF raids were in response to the Nazi government's treatment of the Jews. The SS had begun the brutal (and public) roundup of the Jews who still remained in the capital for their deportation to the East.

3. The "cousins" is Prüfer's code word for the British.

4. Prüfer's dentist.

5. Otto Soehring.

4 March 1943

Spent the evening with the Turks. Interesting conversation with Sauerbruch.[6] Other prominent people were the Dieckhoffs, the Weizsäckers, as well as some Finns and Slovaks. The boss [Ribbentrop] *de retour* since yesterday.

5 March 1943

Officially I still am not on leave. Sigrid was here for lunch to "take a look at the damage." She left again in the evening.

6 March 1943

I finally was granted my leave. Ingrid left. I departed in the evening.

7 March 1943

Arrived in Baden-Baden. Went to see Stockmann this afternoon for his birthday.[7] He offered me an estate, the Au castle, located in the Upper Danube region. I will look at it.

6. Ferdinand Sauerbruch, a surgeon of international repute and at one time an ardent Nazi, who eventually enjoyed the confidence of several members of the anti-Hitler resistance. However, he was only mildly involved in the plot to kill the dictator in 1944.

7. Stockmann was a real estate agent who dabbled in politics. As the following entries show, while vacationing during Mar. and Apr. 1943 in Baden-Baden, Prüfer negotiated extensively with Stockmann on behalf of an aristocratic friend, Langenn-Steinkeller, who wished to purchase property in Southern Germany or Austria. Langenn was interested in the Au castle near Wels, Austria. He wished to move because of his fear that the Russians would eventually invade eastern Germany and seize his estate there. Prüfer had previously purchased through Stockmann some Jewish property in Baden-Baden that the Nazi authorities had confiscated.

8 March 1943

Day spent quietly. There was an alarm in the evening.

9 March 1943

Left early in the morning for Wels. There in the evening I stayed in the Hotel Greif.

10 March 1943

Trip to Roitham and the Au castle. A rather dilapidated and neglected fortress, but very nicely and romantically situated. I would buy it only if it were very cheap. Enemy planes hit Munich and did tremendous damage—Schwabing and Pasing as well as the inner city suffered extensively. Spent the night again in Wels.

11 March 1943

Returned to B.B. Alarm along the way at Pforzheim. Wild flak fire and search lights over Karlsruhe and Stuttgart, as they were being attacked. Upon my arrival at 2 a.m., I heard that quite a few incendiary bombs were dropped on B.B.

12 March 1943

The church in Lichtenthal and several houses have burned. Through Stockmann I wrote to Herr de la Vigne, the owner of the Au castle, likewise to H. v. L. [Langenn].[8] Stockmann called again in the evening and told me

---

8. Prüfer was looking at real estate for Langenn. See n. 7.

that de la Vigne had made a concrete demand (90,000 m.). I immediately told H. v. L. through Anneliese. No alarm.

---

13 March 1943

H. v. L. is coming here on Monday, the 15th, in the morning. I was examined at Dr. Müller's. I will only get the results the day after tomorrow. However, he did not seem particularly disturbed. A quiet night.

---

14 March 1943

Sunday. Beautiful weather. Our offensive in Russia has begun with the recapture of Kharkov.[9] Visit from Endriss, the representative of Daimler-Benz; he is the father-in-law of young Simon, who is employed by the firm of Theodor Wille in Santos. I walked with A. to Lichtenthal, where we saw the almost totally burned-out church, the result of the last British attack. Guida and his wife visited us in the afternoon. He is Consul General in Karlsruhe.[10] No alarm. Kharkov has been recaptured.

---

15 March 1943

H. v. L. is here. We are in agreement on the Au [castle] business. Discussions with Stockmann. H. v. L. left again this evening. The completely impossible Herr de la Vigne is making difficulties, because he is negotiating with us and another party. Quiet night.

---

9. This brief notice of the war in Russia possibly reflected the slight improvement in the general mood of Germans a month after the Stalingrad defeat. They hoped for a stabilization of the Eastern front and a return of their armies to the initiative. However, the military situation for Germany was worsening, with a basic shift in power in the East occurring in favor of the Soviet Union.

10. Guida was the Italian consul general.

16 March 1943

I received my first shot of strophantin with glucose. De la Vigne declared that he will only deal with me, and not with H. v. L. The man is unpleasantly harassing. Quiet but sleepless night.

17 March 1943

No interesting events. Afternoon at the movies. Stupid film, *The Dark Day*. Early alarm this morning.

18 March 1943

Glock's parent brought some packages. Nice old Swabians. No nighttime disturbances.

19 March 1943

Disappointing report from St. [Stockmann] about Au castle. Does he intend to buy this castle? In the evening domestic discussion about the brown products [i.e., coffee] of Brazil. A. seems to be unable to understand that, after all, I am the one who has to dispose of these belongings of ours and that she has no right to control me. An ugly scene of the usual kind followed.[11] Managed to fall asleep after 4 a.m.

20 March 1943

The mood is filled with tension, although there is no reason for this. Even though we had expressly agreed to negotiate in writing, Stockmann

---

11. Prüfer wrote the previous sentences, beginning with "the brown products," originally in English. He purchased these food packages on the black market through Glock.

dealt with de la Vigne by phone. Of course, d. l. V. has rejected all suggestions. Mild heart seizure in the evening.

---

21 March 1943

St. [Stockmann] is coming in order to apologize. He has now, after all, written to de la Vigne. Memorial Day. No alarm. I am reading a book about Winston Churchill, penned by his secretary, Phyllis Moir. It portrays W. C. rather unsympathetically. He appears as a talented busybody, with poor manners and very bad taste.[12] Moltke died during an appendix operation.

---

22 March 1943

A. had a conversation with Dr Müller about the amount of wine I consume every day. This afternoon, following a rather peaceful discussion, she suffered a nervous breakdown with paralysis-like symptoms in the extremities. Dr. M. does not think her condition to be serious.[13]

---

23 March 1943

A. is better. The British and Americans are attacking in Tunisia.[14] Hopefully we recognize that the danger is a greater threat than that menacing in the East.

---

12. "Busybody" was originally in English. Since there was no German edition of the book, *I Was Winston Churchill's Private Secretary* (New York: W. Funk, 1941), Prüfer presumably read the English version.

13. Regarding her declining health and its effect on her relationship to Prüfer, see p. xiv.

14. The battle in North Africa developed during the early months of 1943 even more adversely for the Axis than the war in Russia. On 10 Mar. Rommel flew to Hitler's headquarters with a proposal for evacuating the Tunisian bridgehead, but the dictator refused the idea, ordered his subordinate to attend to his deteriorating health in Germany, and replaced him as commander of German forces in North Africa.

24 March 1943

Physical examination by Dr. Müller. All in all, everything seems satisfactory, only my ration of wine will have to be cut back. The enemy has dropped fake [military] furlough permits, pencils, fountain pens, and toy dolls with harmful materials, and some poisoned candies. The children of Wolff, the gardener, have found such things. Fräulein Dr. Kleikamp confirmed these monstrosities. It is said that in Murgtal, children became sick after eating such dropped chocolates. I rather think that our own Communists may have been responsible.

In the evening, St. [Stockmann] explained that de la Vigne has agreed to the sale conditions proposed in St.'s letter (85,000 and the right of selling *sine die*). I immediately telegraphed Helmut. For the first time I have some liver pain, obviously as a result of the strenuous examination early this morning. Every doctor makes their patients sicker than they were before consultation. Ol. [Olaf] is now very sweet and compliant. Claus v. B.'s father was killed in the Caucasus.[15] An unlucky family.

25 March 1943

I have been suffering from liver pains since yesterday. Nothing from H. v. L. In the evening, by phone, Helmut gave his agreement, rather reluctantly.[16] This was immediately followed by queries from St. [Stockmann], which resulted from a call from de la Vigne. I cannot help but think that St. is conducting this business with unusual zeal.

26 March 1943

The former Lieutenant H. [Heiden] from Karlsruhe, now a captain, is visiting me. Previously he was in Russia, where he was the quartermaster for General F. [Felmy], Gr.'s [Grobba] cousin. In his opinion, we can bring the war to a reasonably favorable conclusion within two years only if a) our submarine war prevents further Anglo-American military escalations, and

---

15. Boroevich. Presumably the husband of Hilva von Boroevich-Heemskerck.
16. Original "rather reluctantly" in English.

b) if we succeed in surrounding and destroying the bulk of Russian armed forces. But he believes that we could do the latter only in winter, because in summer the Russians regularly evade us, lure us into the Russian void, and leave us bottled up there, only, thus, in winter, to bring their toughness and numerical superiority to crush our weakened troops. Therefore, in summer, we must hold on defensively, concentrating our strength behind the front in order to destroy them in winter, when the Russians cannot evade because of the climatic condition.[17]

All this presupposes that nothing will change to our disadvantage in the rest of the world, particularly in North Africa.

Captain H. has been extraordinarily impressed by Communism and its management. Industry and technology have been brilliantly developed, the people have more than enough to feel satisfied, and intellectual and cultural needs are also taken care of; only luxuries, which are systematically suppressed, are lacking. H. went so far as to declare verbatim that, *le case échéant*, he would not fight against Communism in Germany. My objections appeared to make no impression on him.

St. [Stockmann] has made a stupid suggestion as to a co-ownership of Au [castle] between Helmut and myself. He wants to regulate the provision of co-ownership.

27 March 1943

Rejection of the co-ownership proposal. Frau Timme visited us this afternoon. The "companion" of the Mottet woman is a Frau Bayer, wife of a local eye doctor. The German Radio Network was out for 2-1/2 hours at 10 p.m. Slept very badly.

28 March 1943

Sunday. Visited Frau Guida and Frau Pilger.[18] Yesterday the enemy attacked Berlin. A. phoned the Engelhardts; they were hardly aware of the

17. Prüfer later added in pencil, "What fantasies!"
18. The wife of Hans Pilger, a Middle Eastern expert in the AA and former German minister in Afghanistan.

raid. Yet, according to the army report, there indeed seems to have been quite a lot of damage. The attacks on the Tunisian front continue.

---

29 March 1943

I do not like the reports from Tunisia, where we are "occupying new positions as planned." The German Radio Network was out in the evening. Bad, sleepless night. Another attack on Berlin.

---

30 March 1943

Last night the enemy was over Berlin and Bochum. We acquired seven chickens. Saw a stupid Fritsch film, *Love Stories*, with A.

---

31 March 1943

Helmut has agreed to de la Vigne's suggestion.

six

April 1943

1 April 1943

Dieckhoff and Schulenburg are candidates for Madrid. Twardowski is going to Istanbul. Prof. Six is his successor.[1] Kroll is recalled. Jenke will probably be his successor.

2 April 1943

Letter from Dr. Ernst. I am going to visit him in Strassburg.[2] De la Vigne is making new difficulties about the price [for Au castle].[3] We can expect much more trouble from this man. Quiet night.

---

1. Franz Alfred Six replaced Fritz von Twardowski as director of the AA's Cultural Policy Division. Six previously led a unit of SS Einsatzgruppen B that murdered Jews and others in Russia; after the war he was sentenced to prison for war crimes.

2. Robert Ernst was a pro-German Alsatian émigré who had lived in the Reich before its defeat of France in 1940, whereupon the Nazis appointed him mayor of Strassburg. After the war Ernst published a polemical and racist memoir, *Rechenschaftsbericht eines Elsässers* (Berlin: Bernard Graefe, 1954).

3. See chap. 5, n. 7 for an explanation of Prüfer's role in this real estate transaction.

3 April 1943

The defensive war in Tunisia continues. I fear the outcome is scarcely in doubt, given the overwhelming superiority of men and matériel on the other side. But the Francophiles, Rahn and his crowd, are our greatest tragedy. Now they have succeeded in having Auer, one of the most unproductive proponents of Pétain's policies, appointed official expert for French affairs in the A.A. Do these people not understand that it is just as impossible for a respectable Frenchman to follow a policy of cooperation with Germany as it was for good Germans to follow Stresemann and the "League of Nations people" between 1918 and 1933?[4] If we had really wanted to count on France's good Europeanism, we would have had to behave like "Europeans" after France's defeat. Instead, despite our beautiful words, we behaved like conquerors, just as we did everywhere else in Europe. As usual, petty people have obliterated great ideas.

Glock arrived around noon with much luggage. The news he brought was important. Things are very bad in Rahn's country [Tunisia]. There is little hope of holding the position. R. is supposed to be on the spot. I do not believe it, after he expressed his own desire to be transferred (Tangiers). Official news bulletins today sound more reassuring.

The D. [Deutschland] Division has been broken up and those remaining attached to Cult. [Cultural Division]. No one knows anything about Martin [Luther]. *Il a disparu.*[5] [The members of] my old section seem to have become cynical. Bergmann declares he knows nothing about my *démarche* concerning the promotion of Glock! God knows I have spoken often enough about this case with him and, above all, with Schröder. Loyalty and faith are still only present in Germany, still only in the opinion the German has, or professess to have, of himself.

Moritz K.[6] seems to have been kicked out by his fine minister. Probably the ever-present females have played some role in this Niebelungen feud.

Husayni has flown to Croatia without the knowledge of the A.A. and the

---

4. This reveals Prüfer's opposition on nationalist grounds to Gustav Stresemann, German foreign minister during 1924–29. Stresemann had pursued a policy of reconciliation with the Western powers and achieved a peaceful revision of the disarmament and reparations provisions of the Versailles Treaty of 1919. The minister also hoped one day to change, through peaceful means and in Germany's favor, her eastern boundaries, particularly with Poland.

5. "He has disappeared." The Abt. Deutschland was dissolved and replaced by *Inland,* an agency charged with liaison with the SS; *Inland* helped carry forward the extermination of the Jews.

6. Unidentified.

Italians. It appears that E. [Ettel], his former caretaker, had a hand in this game. The matter is not very crucial, for the man is not so important in the general scheme.[7] But it is noteworthy that such a departure was even possible. One might interpret it as a sign of decline provided, of course, that this is what actually transpired. It is also possible that only the back-benchers, the Reeder [Woermann], for example, did not know anything about this event, and that Alfieri merely *professes* ignorance.[8]

G. [Glock] left for Heilbronn at 7 p.m. Short blackout of the German Radio Network. A. [Anneliese] has lumbago.

---

4 April 1943

Sunday. Took a long walk with Olaf; weather most beautiful. I was a little tired, but the fatigue was offset by Olaf's company. He is a good, intelligent boy. The German Radio Network went off the air at 10 minutes before 11. Even now, at 12:30, it is still not back on. Today was national Army Day. I find that on such days, if they are needed at all during the war, the armed forces should celebrate by attacking Britain rather than to draw enemy air attacks onto the German population.

---

5 April 1943

Visited Dr. Ernst in Strassburg. I found him in good spirits and pleasantly optimistic as to the outcome of the war. He is, of course, proud that

---

7. Original "not so important in the general scheme" in English. Husayni left Berlin at the end of Mar. 1943 to recruit Muslims in Bosnia and Herzegovina to assist the ethnic German *Waffen* SS (Combat SS) division, *Prinz Eugen,* in combating Tito's partisans in Yugoslavia. By 1943 the needs of war had reduced racial requirements for admission to the SS to the point where it accepted recruits from foreign ethnic groups that could not by any standard be considered "Germanic." The Waffen SS, capitalizing on the traditional Muslim hatred for the Christian Serbs who made up the bulk of the partisans, was able quickly to recruit thousands of young Muslims. Although they contributed little to the German war effort, except to skirmish with the partisans and commit numerous atrocities, the Muslims eventually comprised their own Waffen SS division.

8. According to Ettel, the Croatian and Italian governments had approved the Mufti's trip. Ettel had sent a memorandum on the issue directly to Ribbentrop, apparently bypassing Woermann, as Prüfer suspected. Original "back-benchers" in English.

he, the former outlaw, is now the dictator of his hometown. Having said this, my impression, objectively, is nonetheless favorable. The Alsatians must be treated justly and harshly.[9] Gauleiter W. is correct in these matters.[10]

Dr. E. did not receive a letter from Scherer.[11] He believes, as I do, that without losing faith and honor, the prelate could not exist in Alsace today. The trip back was delayed; there were quite a few Red Cross ladies [on the train].

---

6 April 1943

Dieckhoff is going to Madrid, Weizsäcker to the Vatican, Woermann to Nanking. Steengracht will become St. S., Hencke U. St. S. Pol., Gaus, Rintelen, Hewel, Ambassador z.b.V.[12] Spent the afternoon watching a bor-

---

9. After the conquest of France, Hitler demanded that the provinces of Alsace and Lorraine be completely "Germanized" in ten years. The Nazi party organization of Baden, which was empowered to administer Alsace, viewed it as a field for potential exploitation and advancement. The NSDAP and its affiliate agencies supervised a radical purge of Alsatian teachers, civil servants, and welfare organizations. The Nazis also deported Alsatians who opposed the party to concentration camps in Germany and conscripted those eligible in the province for military service. Most Alsatians placed in positions of authority were émigrés like Ernst, the mayor of Strassburg, who had lived in the Reich before 1940 and supported the Nazi demand for Germany's annexation of Alsace and Lorraine.

10. "Gauleiter W." is Robert Wagner, district leader of the NSDAP in Baden since 1925, Nazi governor of the state, and chief of civil administration in Alsace beginning in 1940. In the latter capacity he held extensive authority in carrying out Hitler's brutal directive that Alsace and Lorraine be made totally German in character in ten years. The French tried and executed him in 1946 for war crimes.

11. Presumably Emil Clemens Scherer, general secretary of the National Association for German Catholics Abroad (*Reichsverband für die katholischen Auslandsdeutschen*), who had originally supported the Nazi regime's stress on a powerful Germany and promised the use of Catholic missionary activity to advance such a goal. By Apr. 1943, however, a major conflict had erupted between the Alsatian church and the Nazis, resulting from the Nazis' further attempt to seize control of the church by dissolving its religious orders and deporting their members to the Reich.

12. ". . . z.b.V." is an abbreviation for *zur besonderen Verwendung*, on special assignment, and "U.St.S." stands for *Unterstaatssekretär*, undersecretary of state, in this instance for political affairs. Walther Hewel was an official of the personal staff of the RAM and his representative with Hitler; Emil von Rintelen was previously deputy director of the AA's Political Division. The changes listed by Prüfer resulted significantly from Ribbentrop's purge of the AA in the wake of the Luther affair, which had drawn the loyalty of the diplomats even further into question with ranking Nazis, including Hitler.

ing Austrian film, *Summer Love*. The Americans have killed hundreds of people in Paris and Antwerp during a daytime bombing attack. This is downright murder and can in no way be explained as justifiable acts of war.[13] How should murder be punished in peacetime, if it is allowed and glorified in war?

---

7 April 1943

First [therapeutic] bath in the hospital. News from Frau Stockm. [Stockmann]; the expedition of her husband and Helmut [Langenn] to Saalfeld was in vain. I am not surprised. Too bad about the money that H. and I spent. A. is ill again. She has an alarming disorder: migraines, exhaustion, vomiting, and symptoms of paralysis.

Things are getting worse in Tunisia. That is our *locus minoris resistentiae*. If only those in the highest places would see that! The loss of Tunisia would be disastrous for us.[14]

The attack on Antwerp has claimed more than 2000 dead, among them hundreds of children! Why do the leaders of the "neutrals," the Pope, the King of Sweden, the Swiss President and consorts, fail to pull themselves together and, finally, protest against this mass murder, appealing to the conscience of those responsible? These neutrals are more detestable than murderers because they are more cowardly.

---

8 April 1943

I went with A. to Karlsruhe today. This not particularly strenuous outing did not agree with her at all. On the way back and, later, at home she developed an intense headache and weakness, accompanied by vomiting; we considered the possibility of poison. But it is probably no more than physical exhaustion and nervous tension. Because A.'s condition has de-

---

13. On 4 Apr. 1943 the Americans carried out a major and exceedingly effective attack on the Renault motor vehicle and armament works in Paris, which supplied the German army with trucks and aircraft. The raid of 5 Apr. on Antwerp, which aimed at an aircraft and aero-engine works, resulted in inaccurate bombing and heavy civilian casualties, against which the Belgian ambassador to the United States protested.

14. Prüfer added in pencil, "On account of Italy."

cidedly worsened, and because she also looks so sick, something must be done to improve her physical condition. If I only knew what! The doctors are helpless and passive.[15]

It looked bad in Karlsruhe. Many buildings downtown were in ruins. For the most part, broken plate glass store windows were boarded up with wood, a sign that high-explosive bombs had been dropped. At the cinema we saw *Dr. Crippen on Board*, a well-scripted and suspenseful detective film, which, however, was technically not as well done as Hilva [Boroevich-Heemskerck] had described to me.

Before the trip to Karlsruhe I briefly visited St. [Stockmann], who had returned from Saalfeld rather broken in spirit. D. l. V. [Vigne] appears to be a rascal of the worst sort. The business failed to materialize because, as a condition for the sale of Au [castle], d. l. V. demanded a partnership deal between him and Helmut as to the management of the estate. That was completely new. The parties seemed to have separated in considerable anger, although negotiations have not yet completely broken down.

According to today's military bulletin, things do not seem to be going well in Tunisia. Our artillery positions in the southern sector have been withdrawn. The Russians, too, are on the offensive, but fortunately without success. The submarine war is continuing well, thank God.[16] Letter from Herbert [Richthofen], wistful, humorous. I do not like to think about our happy youth, otherwise I too become melancholy, which heaven may spare me. The German Radio Network was out for 1-1/2 hours.

---

9 April 1943

Enemy planes were over Western Germany last night. "The population sustained losses." A. finally gave the House Dragon her notice![17] Perhaps her life will now be more peaceful. De la Vigne wrote me a crazy letter, withdrawing his offer. Of course it will not end like this. At the very least he will have to pay our expenses. Stockmann impressed me as being embarrassed when I spoke to him about d. l. V. De la Vigne is either a fool or a crook.

---

15. For the causes of her difficulties, see p. xiv.

16. But presumably unknown to Prüfer, the war at sea was already turning against the Germans. The last major successes of their submarines against the Allied convoys crossing the Atlantic with provisions for England and Russia occurred during 16–20 Mar. 1943. Already by April and May the Nazis were suffering heavy losses of submarines.

17. The Prüfers' maid servant, apparently named Ludwiga; see OD, entry for 12 Apr. 1943.

Spent the afternoon with Frau Timme. Further news from Tunisia sounds bad. *Le commencement de la fin.* How can a victory on the Ukrainian plain be of use to us if the enemy is close to the Balkans and Appenines?! Hannibal, the hero of the Jews, *ante portas*! Where is the Roman who will defend the gates of Europe? Winter weather.

---

10 April 1943

This afternoon the Schlemanns [*sic*], Oster and wife, Frau Pilger, and Guida, with wife and son, visited us.[18] During the bombing raids in Berlin, Oster lost everything, also what was left of his mind. Frau P. told about the problems that R., Ziehmke's [*sic*] enemy, caused for her and her husband.[19] At one point he was so drunk that his bedcovers had to be discarded because they could not be cleaned where he had vomited all night. Opinions about Frau Oja were also rather unfavorable. Her liaison with the Indian in Peschawar is beyond doubt.

Further retreats in Tunisia. This will have to end badly for us. What is Rahn, the miniature Napoleon, doing?

There was some problem here in the Hotel Kurhof with a Vichy Vice Consul working for the Yanks.[20] The French hate us more than they do all the British and American bombs.

There was an alarm at 2:10 a.m. We all awakened and spent 1-1/2 hours in the hall shelter.

---

18. "Oster" here is presumably Maj. Gen. Hans Oster. Oster was chief of staff to Wilhelm Canaris in the Abwehr, a staunch anti-Nazi, and a key organizer of the German resistance. He had unofficially extended help to Jews through various "front organizations" under the protection of the Abwehr abroad; such activities had contributed to his dismissal from the agency at the beginning of Apr. 1943, only a few days before this visit with Prüfer. The Gestapo kept him under observation and, following the abortive plot against Hitler in July 1944, arrested and executed him. Canaris, too, was executed for his part in the conspiracy.

19. "Ziehmke" is presumably Kurt Ziemke, the former German minister in Afghanistan during 1934–36 and in 1943 the AA's representative to the Reich Protector in Bohemia and Moravia; "R." is unidentified.

20. Original "Yanks" in English. Foreign diplomats, including those from the Americas, were interned by the Nazi government at the hotel. Baden was also inundated with refugees and Nazi party notables from other, less safe regions of the Reich.

11 April 1943

The British attack in Southwestern Germany was directed at several places, mostly rural communities. Letter from a notary in Saalfeld, indicating de la Vigne's withdrawal from the contract. The Stockmanns came for a visit in the afternoon. He was in remarkably low spirits.

12 April 1943

A. at the Stockmanns. I am dictating many letters, a very long one to de la Vigne, among others. Musso was with the Führer from the 7th-10th.[21] Intense fighting in Tunisia. Battle with the House Dragon (Ludwiga). Sfax and Kairouan are lost. As far as one can judge it cannot end well for us in Tunisia. The superiority of the "others" is too great. Someday history will teach why this was so; in theory the Italian fleet and army should be superior to the "others," at least in numbers. I fear that the Atlantic Wall, spoken about extensively on today's radio broadcast, will be of little help to us on the Mediterranean shores.

13 April 1943

Severe quarrel with the House Dragon, who is becoming more venomous, causing A. ever greater concern. Rehbock and his wife appeared in the afternoon. This 79-year-old man has been called to Spain as a consulting engineer to build one of the largest irrigation dams on earth. German engineering skills must be very great indeed. Our rear guard in Tunisia is slowing down the advance of the "enemy."[22] Olaf's teacher is presenting the situation to the children the way it is!

21. Mussolini, whose position as dictator had been shaken significantly by the decline of Axis fortunes in the war, met the Nazi leader at Klessheim castle near Salzburg. Although the Duce had been urged by his advisers to press Hitler to end the war in Russia, the subject never arose and Mussolini was little more than a passive participant.

22. The reason for the emphasis on the word "enemy" was that "rear guard" referred to the Italians, whom Prüfer mistrusted and perceived to be in collusion with the Allies. He had disliked the Italians since they had joined Germany's enemies in World War I.

14 April 1943

There were two air alerts this morning. The all-clear followed each time after about a quarter hour. We have made public a Bolshevist outrage that we tracked down in a forest near Smolensk. There the Bolshevists have shot over 10,000 captured Polish officers and buried them secretly in mass graves.[23] The effect of this announcement should be monstrous if there were not the atrocities against the Jews. Ilya Ehrenburg has published a book showing the abysmal hatred of the Jews against all European Gentiles. He wants to crush, trample, and gas all of Europe, together with its 350 million human beings. How can there ever be peace if Jews are the advisers of our enemies?[24] Today I requested additional leave until 3 May.

In the evening we visited the Schlemann's [*sic*], where we met Dr. Schacht and his wife. He is the same indiscreet Bramarbas as he was in the past.[25]

15 April 1943

We had an alarm at 12 midnight, and we heard shooting over Karlsruhe and Stuttgart start about a half hour later. The British planes appeared to have been numerous, coming in continuous waves. Today the military news bulletin confirmed that Stuttgart had been the target and that at least 23 planes were shot down.

The Mamsell [i.e., the domestic servant] cleared out today. Now A. has to cook. Hopefully she can endure that.

This afternoon we visited *Pasqua* and his wife.[26] He was in a wild mood.

23. The Germans, upon discovering mass graves in the Katyn forest that contained the bodies of 4,000 Polish officers, alleged that the Soviets had liquidated them. The charge had serious implications, confusing the relations among the Russians and Anglo-Americans as well as among the Allies and the Polish government-in-exile in London. One cannot assess the guilt for Katyn here, although a solid case exists that Soviet leader Joseph Stalin, was responsible for the crime.

24. Prüfer's reaction to the Katyn massacre followed the inflammatory anti-Semitism of Nazi propaganda on the subject. Goebbels seized the opportunity to blame the Jews for the murders and use the latter to intensify the Nazi anti-Bolshevik campaign, begun after Stalingrad. Ilya Ehrenburg was a Soviet journalist.

25. Bramarbas is a braggart in the anonymous satire, *Cartell des Bramarbas an Don Quixote* (1710). Hjalmar Schacht, president of the Reichsbank until 1939, had significantly aided Hitler's financing of German re-armament and preparations for war.

26. "Pasqua" is a Latin word meaning "Easter," and in this case a reference to Oster. Al-

16 April 1943

Worked a lot in the garden. The Soviet government seems to be rather at a loss concerning the discovery of the mass executions of Polish officers near Smolensk. They declared this to be the discovery of prehistoric mass graves![27] There has probably never been a more stupid excuse.

17 April 1943

Last night, at midnight, there was an alarm that lasted until 3:30. I was very tired and slept until after noon. The night attack was intended for Mannheim and Ludwigshafen, in addition to a few smaller places. 53 enemy planes—a record number—were shot down. Our planes were over London.

18 April 1943

Air alert from 11:30-1:15. Sunday with beautiful weather. Letter from Bohny to the effect that the prosecution demanded the death penalty for him and for me in the Rio spy trial.[28] I visited Oster in the afternoon. As usual he was in a grumpy and smug mood, loaded with criticism. The man is negative to the utmost degree. Yesterday the Americans bombed Bremen in daylight. 20 were shot down.

19 April 1943

There were two air alerts at noon. I am writing Dr. Heinrich Neukirchen in Vienna about a house.

---

though considerable damage was done in the outskirts of Stuttgart by the RAF, very few bombs fell in the center of town.

27. This was a fabrication inasmuch as the Soviets blamed the murders on the Germans.

28. During Apr. and May 1943, the Brazilian government conducted a series of trials that sentenced German agents of the Abwehr, who had been arrested the previous year for espionage, to lengthy prison terms. Prüfer and Bohny received *in absentia* prison sentences of twenty-five years each.

20 April 1943

Went to Strassburg with A., where we had lunch with Dr. E. [Ernst]. In the afternoon, long walk through the city. Dr. E. has been drafted by the air force for duty as a long-distance reconnaissance pilot. The Führer's birthday. All houses are decked out with flags. The German Radio Network went out at 20 minutes after 11:00. The English and Americans are celebrating the Führer's birthday. The radio did not return to the air until after 2.

21 April 1943

A woman from Mannheim told A. about the horror of the most recent attack. The destruction exceeded all that had happened before. According to her, even liquid phosphorous was dropped. Human losses were very extensive, because of the large number of heavy high-explosive bombs. There is no protection against 2000 k.g. bombs.

Even if these stories may be somewhat exaggerated, there is still enough truth to them to make us dread the future.

22 April 1943

The Japanese have executed as murderers the American pilots who attacked Tokyo a year ago. Now, of course, the Americans will do the same. Fortunately they are at the short end of the stick. But perhaps they will view the Axis as a single entity and thus retaliate against our own and the Italian prisoners. As of yesterday there is renewed severe fighting in Tunisia. So far we seem to be successful.

In the afternoon I went to the movies with A.; we saw a boring Italian-Spanish film, *In Red Hell.*

23 April 1943

Good Friday. Bohny arrived this morning to talk to me about our Brazilian espionage trial. The prosecutor regretfully abandoned his plea for the death penalty and only asked for 20 years in prison; this, because at the time when we supposedly committed our crimes, the special espionage laws providing for the death penalty had not been enacted! I will suggest to the office that we exploit this scandalous case with propaganda, in order to show it up for what it is, namely an attempt to drive Argentina into breaking off [diplomatic] relations. Our Brazilian organization—so the thinking goes—is supposed to have had its counterpart in the Embassy in Buenos Aires.

A number of women in Rio, Frau Metzner, Frau Muth, and Frau Engels among others, have been arrested and indicted.

B. confirmed that Fränzchen [Papen], as always, still believes in the unconditional neutrality of Turkey. At noon we went to the casino. Spent the evening with him, A., and Bisse in the [Hotel] Bellevue.[29]

---

24 April 1943

A particularly melancholy April day. Hail and rain. I have some liver pain and cannot shake terrible premonitions about the future. The final act of the Tunesian drama seems to have begun. I fear that it will be a catastrophe similar to the one in Stalingrad.

---

25 April 1943

Easter Sunday. Considerable liver pains that are radiating up my back. Thus very tried and depressed. Household circumstances, too, are not exactly cheerful. From 6 a.m. to 10 p.m., poor A. is nothing but a workhorse. Then she goes to bed, dead tired. I have never been so mentally barren and exhausted as I am this spring. I cannot think coherently from one moment to the next. My mind works aphoristically, so to speak, hopping around like a bunch of fleas. In Tunisia the Americans are attacking in force from the west. Today's military news bulletin sounded very meek.

---

29. Wilhelm Bisse, a former AO leader, was an official in the AA's Economic Policy Division.

26 April 1943

Easter Monday. The Schlemanns [*sic*] visited us in the evening. The rest of the day was spent quietly. My physical condition seems improved. I concentrate too much on myself and also think too much about myself. The *Ranger* was sunk. The U.S.A. denies it. Schl. thinks that Don Martinho [Luther] is dead. Heinicke [*sic*], who was here, brought this rumor from Berlin.[30]

27 April 1943

With A. at the cinema; we saw *The Companion of My Summer*, which was fair. Received a ridiculous letter from de la Vigne with the usual old excuses. All the same, St. [Stockmann] did not act correctly either. So far the front in Tunisia holds firm. When I went to bed I discovered a tumorous growth the size of a marble in the pit of my stomach. The first thought, of course: cancer. Nevertheless, I slept quite well.

28 April 1943

The growth is there, even A. noticed it. I went to Dr. Müller and—no trace of it could be discovered. He assumed that it was intestinal gas. I am very happy that the family has been spared this potentially interesting turn. We had dinner at the Hotel Bellevue, which was as clean and well-taken care of as in earlier days, and this, despite the war and general decline.

29 April 1943

A. has a bad cold.

---

30. The "Heinicke" reference is presumably to Ludwig Heinecke, a career official in the AA's Protocol Division. The American denial was correct; the aircraft carrier *Ranger* was not sunk.

30 April 1943

Ribbentrop's birthday. He is 50 years old. The A.A., represented by the division heads and led by the St. S., visited him in Fuschl to congratulate him.[31] The birthday was mentioned quite briefly on the radio. Laval visited the Führer in the presence of Bastianini. The communiqué was very flat. Apparently we have sacrificed the Italians to the French. "The questions pending between Germany and Italy on the one hand and France on the other are being examined."[32] And meanwhile, European cart grease, meaning Italian salad, for the wheels of an axle long running hot.

Morally the Anglo-Saxons have totally collapsed. *Qui en mange, en meurt*, this in regard to the Jews. The riff-raff around Churchill cannot extricate itself from the Katyn mess and the various conflicts between Soviet Jewish atheism and the hypocrisy of Canterbury. The Americans are ethically completely lousy. There is only gangsterism there. Poor old Pinkham![33]

The army in Tunisia is wonderful. Thank God, my pessimism was unnecessary!

31. Fuschl was a castle near Salzburg, which Ribbentrop seized from one of his enemies, an Austrian nobleman, following the Anschluss. Conducting the birthday festivities was one of the final acts for Weizsäcker as secretary of state.

32. Laval's aim in his visit to Hitler at the Führer's Berchtesgaden retreat on 30 Apr. 1943 was to secure further German support for both himself and the Vichy regime. Giuseppe Bastianini, the Italian foreign minister, pressed the Germans unsuccessfully for a kind of "European charter" on which to base future peace negotiations.

33. A reference to Prüfer's first wife, Frances Pinkham, an American whom he had divorced in 1927.

seven

May 1943

---

1 May 1943

A rainy first day of May! In the afternoon we had tea at the Stockmanns. Prof. Gailer, a Heidelberg jurist, and Lucius's daughter, were there. A rather interesting conversation. Later I went with A. [Anneliese] to the theater to see a nice old comedy by Hermann Bahr, *The Concert.* A story without plot, but with good points and witty remarks about the perennially new topic of love and marraige.

2 May 1943

About 2:15 in the morning we experienced a rather intense earthquake, accompanied by rattling sounds. There was an air alarm between 5 and 5:30 p.m., despite strong winds and an overcast sky.

3 May 1943

I left for Munich early this morning, where I arrived at 2. As arranged, I met with O. G. in the Schottenhamel tavern.[1] He has aged a lot, is emaciated, and somewhat depressed. He told me about his son, the Ole-mann, who has suffered a severe shell shock from the war and particularly during the last attack on Munich, where he was working with the defense. He is an architect. Olaf [Gulbransson] is always thinking of Grete, and especially of her son. He is unhappy in his marriage with Dagny; he certainly does not love her. She has broken this powerful, yet simple, man by constant nagging. A small persistent wave will smooth a large stone. Olaf complained bitterly about Th. Th. Heine,[2] who has denounced him because he expressed himself in a letter as an opponent of the N.S.D.A.P. Olaf maintains that he, indeed, wrote the letter, but that Heine changed the date to five years later. He had actually written this epistle five years before the [Nazi] seizure of power. Heine had placed it somewhere during the period of the seizure of power. He, Olaf, says that finally he has some peace, but that these attacks which, incidentally, are coming from Norway, had caused him much worry.

In the evening I visited at the Bachmanns[3] in Ambach at the Gasthof Findmeister, a beautiful old farmhouse which, to be sure, is primitive, but nevertheless imbued with the spirits of old Bavaria before the reign of Ludwig II. B. is unchanged, sparkling with life, happy, addicted to work, and he looks better than ever; he is looked after by a touchingly caring woman. He is now 80 years old. It is too bad that he quarreled with Olaf [Gulbransson]. I believe that the women were unable to get along, and if so, I think that Dagny, who is consumed by ambition, must bear the guilt.

----

4 May 1943

Took a walk this morning, in cloudy and humid weather, in a meadow which, being wild and acidic, is overgrown with beautiful vegetation: gentian, arnica, sundew, etc. I was very happy, and we dug up many plants for A.'s rock garden. Peaceful afternoon and evening with conversations about blessed memories.

----

1. "O.G." is Olaf Gulbransson, a noted Norwegian-born German cartoonist whose drawings in *Simplicissimus* and other satirical journals before 1933, some in opposition to Hitler, had not endeared him to the Nazi regime.
2. Theodor Theodor Heine, a fellow cartoonist of Gulbransson's in Munich.
3. Alf Bachmann was a German painter and opponent of Gulbransson.

5 May 1943

Early walk to a magnificent, onion-domed church in Holtzhausen, followed by a trip to Ammerland in a carriage driven by a French prisoner of war, and finally from there to Starnberg in a motorboat filled with many small communion children. Then on to Munich and a trip back home to B.B. without incident. Grobba is in Berlin.

6 May 1943

Rest. Evening meal at the Bellevue.

7 May 1943

Went to the movies with A., *The Golden City*, a nice color film with Söderbaum.[4] The Tunisian tragedy continues. Deep penetration by the enemy. Victor Lutze was buried.[5] Very melancholy mood.

8 May 1943

A thoroughly black day! Biserta and Tunis are lost. There is still fighting, hopeless of course, in the south.[6] It is easy to guess what the future will

---

4. *Die goldene Stadt* was one of the most widely seen of all Nazi pictures. Its theme was the idea of the city as a hostile force destroying those drawn to it from the country. It featured Kristina Söderbaum, who had previously played the Aryan beauty raped by a Jew in the hate-filled anti-Semitic film, *Jud Süss*, also seen by large numbers of Germans.

5. Lutze, a victim of an automobile accident, had been chief of staff of the SA in succession to Ernst Röhm, since Hitler purged Röhm during the bloody night of 30 June 1934. At the lavish Nazi ceremony mourning Lutze, Hitler and Goebbels praised him as a "hero" for not having died in bed.

6. After bitter fighting, the British, advancing from the south, had linked up in Tunisia on 7 Apr. 1943 with the Americans, arriving from the west. During the following weeks the Allies pushed the Axis into an ever-smaller bridgehead. The Anglo-Americans hammered through Tunis on 6 May, splitting the bridgehead, and two days later the Axis lost Biserta.

bring. The enemy will force Turkey to surrender its neutrality, and we will have to be prepared for attacks from Greece and from the Black Sea through the Dardanelles, aimed at Rumania and our oil supplies. Why have we been unable to keep Africa, not just Tunisia, by which time it was already too late? Did we underestimate the importance of this front, as we did in the first [World] War, or was it no longer possible, for more than a year, to send reinforcements? Stalingrad was a serious and painful defeat, but it was not decisive. Tunisia can cost us the entire war. With all these worries, I have to return tomorrow, leaving A. and O. [Olaf] here alone. This is a difficult farewell for me.

9 May 1943

In the evening, accompanied by A. to [Bad] Oos, I departed with much on my mind. It was so nice in B.B. with A. and O. The journey was quiet. We arrived in Berlin one hour late, because somewhere along the way there was an alarm.

10 May 1943

There is not much new in the A.A. The old conflict between the Arab bigwigs [the Mufti and Gailani] continues. Grobba was here until 2 May, and this fact and other intrigues generated discord in the A.A.[7]

11 May 1943

I was with Schröder. Frosty reception. Bad conscience. Sigrid [Richthofen], on her way to Sweden, came to see me in the evening. Lunch with Bohny and Cossel. Both rather depressed.[8] Who is not?

---

7. Grobba had angered Husayni by seeking to invite Gailani and a few of his entourage to Paris.

8. "Rather" was written in English. Prüfer also rewrote several passages in this entry, but none involved substantive changes.

12 May 1943

Lunch with Witzleben. Nothing he says about his country sounds very reassuring.[9] No one is speaking against the Führer, but everybody is railing against the important and, especially, the petty bureaucrats. This afternoon I had a conversation with Cossel and Glock at Reinebeck's. The latter [Glock] had spoken with Plinio Salgado in Lisbon.[10] He is prepared to work with us in secret. Gailani prattled on for an hour.

No one is interested in my trial in Rio, although it deserves a certain amount of attention because of our relationship with Argentina. Nor does anybody talk about Tunis, oil, and the Dardanelles. On the other hand, the internal paper wars are of the greatest importance. *Quem deus perdere vult!*

Following dinner, Schulenburg stayed until after midnight.

13 May 1943

I awoke with unpleasant pains in my rib cage. Then I received bad news: Tilla M. died from tuberculosis of the larynx and the intestines.[11] She was a nice girl and had the misfortune of dying too soon.

Saw the new St. S. I am supposed to visit the Kh. [Khedive] as soon as possible [in Switzerland]. I will take A. with me.

The Mufti told me about his trip to Croatia, where a Mohammedan [SS] division is to be recruited.[12] He will travel to Rome, ostensibly to persuade

9. The meaning of Prüfer's reference to "his [Witzleben's] country" is unclear. It is uncertain whether Prüfer's claim in RD (see entry for 12 May 1943) that Witzleben had been in Rumania is true. The phrase may have referred, for example, to France (Witzleben's former wartime command), or it could have been a code word for the retired field marshal's circle of acquaintances and for Germany.

10. Salgado was the leader of the pro-Nazi Integralist movement in Brazil, living in exile since 1939 in Lisbon. Both the German Legation in Portugal and the SD courted Salgado in the event he assumed power in Brazil after the victory the Axis planned for itself in the war. Salgado wished for German recognition as the ruler of Brazil and for postwar aid from the SS in building a loyal Brazilian police. He reported to the Germans on political developments in Brazil. Otto Reinebeck had formerly been German minister in Estonia and Guatemala.

11. Tilla Münchhausen was a friend of Anneliese Prüfer from their childhood days in Berlin.

12. This meeting between the two also may have included discussion of Husayni's request that the AA halt the emigration of Jews from Bulgaria to Palestine, and instead send them to Poland "under strong and energetic guard."

the Italians to enlist Islamic volunteers in Herzegovina. I no longer quite trust the Mufti. He has been thinking about postwar developments without us. He hinted as much to Gailani. I fear that he could turn out to be one of the notorious ship rats. Perhaps this is the reason why he assiduously courts Italy.

We are now mounting an anti-Jinnah propaganda campaign in India. I have convinced our "Indian experts" that they should not extend this campaign to Indian Muslims in general. As if we had not angered sufficient numbers of religions![13]

We had an alarm at 12:30 a.m. I had just undressed for bed and barely had enough time to get to the basement. It was well occupied. There was, indeed, a lot of shooting, but I did not have the impression that the attack was very intense. The all-clear sounded about 1:45. I could not see any fires.

---

14 May 1943

About half a dozen high-explosive bombs were dropped on Steglitz and Lichtenberg by planes that probably were targeted for the Skoda works in Pilsen. On the whole there were a number of severe raids on Western Germany, which we also felt. Today at noon about 70 planes hit Kiel, causing considerable damage in the shipyards. In the evening, I was at Borchardt's with Schröder, Niebuhr, Bohny, Stiege, Cossel, and Langmann. No one knows any details about our trial, which has been over for a month. Góes, again, is chief of staff. Azevedo Amaral sponsors Jewish airplanes.[14] In a few days, Cossel will leave for Palermo. Rahn was

---

13. Muhammad Ali Jinnah had been head of the Muslim League in India since 1934. The Congress movement's mass civil disobedience beginning in Aug. 1942 to force the transfer of power in India from British to native hands inadvertently aided the British by supplying them with a pretext for neglecting to seek a political settlement during the war. Also for the Muslim League, the paralyzing of the Hindu-ruled Congress party was a welcome accident, increasing significantly the prospect of the creation of a Muslim-dominated Pakistan. Jinnah's subsequent opposition to a Hindu-Muslim agreement and his pro-British attitude were opposed by the Germans, who had supported Subhas Chandra Bose, the most radical Congress leader, who was forced at the war's beginning to flee to Germany.

14. Presumably Antonio José Azevedo Amaral, a nationalist critic of liberal democracy in Brazil, whom leaders of the authoritarian Rio government liked because of his stress on social discipline, order, and hierarchy. Pedro Aurelio de Góes Monteiro was chief of the Brazilian general staff and widely believed before 1942 to be pro-German. Capt. Dietrich Niebuhr was formerly German military attaché in Buenos Aires and a key figure until 1942 in the Abwehr network in Latin America. Prüfer's guess that the British raid was intended for the Skoda plant in Pilsen was correct.

"grandly" feted in Rome with decorations out his ears. Next week I will travel with A. to Davos. The battle of Tunisia is over. All reports from Corpoli and the Near East sound pessimistic.[15] I saw Prof. Gudzent. Superficial examination. Everything the same as before. Liver enlarged, heart ditto. *Espérons le mieux.* All things considered, he was optimistic.

15 May 1943

Spent the morning with Melchers for breakfast at the Grossmufti's. He gave me a letter from a student in Paris, protesting new intrigues by Grobba. Things cannot continue like this. Grobba is incorrigible. The Mufti intends to go to Italy next week. Reason: the Herzegovina Mohammedans. Rahn is in Rome, and "maximum" victor of Tunisia. His French policies are still unexploded, although the writing is on the wall for a secret agreement between Pétain and Giraud. The French are playing double games, nothing else, but always against us. As patriots they really cannot do otherwise.

I hope to go to *Swissera* [Switzerland] on the 19th. I believe that there I can obtain some really useful information.[16] News from Rio indicates that my trial is still pending. I have suggested a formal protest and developing a propaganda campaign against this trial.

Alarm after midnight from 2 o'clock to 2:35. I did not hear any shooting. Benzler sat next to me in the basement.[17]

15. "Corpoli" refers to Turkey. The last Axis forces surrendered in Tunisia on 13 May 1943; the Allies took 252,000 troops prisoner—half of them Germans. The Italian fleet, which the Nazis failed to protect or to supply with sufficient petroleum, evacuated only 700 soldiers. This ended the Axis war in North Africa and heralded the beginning of the Allied assault on Italy and such nearby islands as Sicily and Sardinia.

16. Prüfer added in pencil, "On Oriental affairs." He thought that he could gather news on the situation in the Middle East from pro-German Arab exiles in Switzerland, including the ex-Khedive of Egypt, Abbas Hilmi. But that was also his pretext for seeking a leave from the AA to live the rest of the war with his family in Switzerland. As shown herein, p. 84, the mission had been approved by Steengracht on 13 May 1943. Prüfer arrived in Switzerland on 20 May 1943 and returned on 16 June.

17. Felix Benzler, the AA's liaison with the German military commander in Serbia; previously deputy director of the ministry's commercial division.

16 May 1943

Sunday. Lunch with Uncle Max [Oppenheim]; earlier in the morning at the Zoo. The hyena from Djibouti is no longer there.[18] Afternoon with the Fehrmanns, and then I went to the movies with Bärbel [Engelhardt]. *Symphony of Life* with Harry Bauer [*sic*] who, as always, acted very well.[19] The film is average and dragged on too long. Later we had a bad meal at Kranzler's [restaurant].

Alarm from 1:25 until 2:15. Lively artillery fire, but probably only isolated planes.

17 May 1943

Franco's efforts to produce peace were unsuccessful. One has to wait and see what Churchill has cooked up with Roosevelt in Washington.[20] The U.S.A., with its Jews,[21] are sterile soil for the seeds of peace. Today the British have reported about 175,000 prisoners in Tunisia! According to a Turkish commentary, the treachery of the French contributed much to our defeat. But Herr Rahn gets high marks!

Had dinner with Konstantin the Younger.[22] His reports are the same as all others from North Africa: our defeat is due to Italian failures, our own arrogance, dilettantism, and an underestimation of our opponents. He is

18. Prüfer, a lover of animals, had brought the hyena with him on his return in 1930 to Berlin from Ethiopia, where he had served as German minister. He eventually gave the animal to the zoo.

19. The correct title of the movie was *Symphony of a Life (Symphonie eines Lebens)*. The film, which boasted a nonstop musical score lasting eighty-eight minutes, told the story of a composer in flashback as his symphony was performed for the first time. According to one historian, the movie was "pedantic and boring." Shortly after the film passed the censor in Nov. 1942, it was discovered that the "racial" papers of the movie's French star, Harry Baur, were not in order and that he was Jewish. He was placed in a concentration camp and, the day before the film was released in Apr. 1943, executed.

20. The two Allied leaders met during 12–25 May 1943, deciding to land troops in southern Italy, occupy the Azores as a base from which to strengthen the battle against German submarines, and invade France in May 1944.

21. Prüfer later added in pencil, ". . . who themselves are obviously the most hostile towards Germany. . . ."

22. Konstantin Alexander Freiherr von Neurath, son of Hitler's first foreign minister; he was the AA's official representative to the German military forces in North Africa during 1941–43.

the first who has described to me that the Americans have greatly improved.

I visited Heribert [Schwörbel] in the afternoon, while he had the Mufti and Gailani to tea. The Mufti is going to see the St. S. tomorrow. This audience has *not* been arranged by Pol. VII. Then who did? Perhaps Ettel? I asked the Mufti. He flatly denied it and named Schlobies as the mediator.[23] The St. S. has asked me to be present at the audience.

---

18 May 1943

The audience had, of course, been arranged by Ettel, as Bielfeld, who was sitting in the antechamber of the St. S., confirmed.[24] I was present. The Mufti merely propounded his old proposition, to the effect that the German government should publish a declaration in favor of Arab independence. Baron Steengracht refused, explaining that because of Tunisia this was the wrong time. Later, the Mufti came to me and told me about a secret Arab organization, whose leader he supposedly is, that evolved from the Young Arab movement of the World War and which had been fought in vain by Djemal Pasha.[25] He said that after the Turks had been eliminated, this secret organization originally fought only France and the Jews. But later it was recognized that Britain was the principal enemy. King Faisal[26] was its secret sponsor and, since the restoration of peace between Ibn Saud and the Imam,[27] both of these Arab princes have become members of the

---

23. Hans Schlobies was an official in the AA's Pol. VII.

24. Harald Bielfeld was a member of Steengracht's personal staff and previously head of the African section in the AA.

25. Turkish naval minister and military governor of the provinces of Syria and Palestine during World War I, notorious for his persecution of Arabs and Jews. Prüfer had been one of his principal intelligence officers in the war. Already in 1942 Husayni had used his claim to leadership of the group, the "Arab nation," to insist that the Germans acknowledge his supremacy over Gailani and the Arab countries. This had produced a protest from Grobba against Husayni in Oct. 1942.

26. The founder and first monarch (1920–33) of modern Iraq. Faisal had always been associated with Arab nationalism, and during World War I he commanded Arab forces under British leadership against Turkey, eventually becoming the supreme commander of the Arab army.

27. The ruler of Yemen who, aided by Britain, settled his country's boundary dispute with Saudi Arabia in 1934. Ibn Saud had been king of the Hejaz since 1926 and was king of Saudi Arabia from 1932 to 1953.

organization, which they have financially supported ever since. Gailani had joined somewhat later, shortly before he became Prime Minister.

The Mufti then talked about him [Gailani] and warned about his unstable and inconsistent behavior, supposedly caused by chronic migraines. He admitted that Gailani and he himself are paid by the Italians. He is leaving on 21.5. for a few weeks' stay in Rome in order to deal with the Mohammedans of Herzegovina. He greatly praised Shekib and described Fuad Hamza, who had become Ibn Saud's Ambassador in Ankara, as unreliable.

Today I repeated the Arab and Italian language exams before Erythropel.[28] It was not very exciting. In the evening I spoke with Benzler about the Dutch campaign. The British make daily radio broadcasts, announcing their heavy air attacks.[29] Many rumors about peace negotiations involving the Pope, Franco, the alleged war weariness of the Russians, etc.[30] It is high time. Tomorrow I am going to B.B. in order to pick up A. for a short journey to Davos. Unfortunately I have a sore throat.

---

19 May 1943

Left at 8 a.m. for B.B. On the train I had an interesting conversation with Herr Erich Oberländer, the owner of a large Buna factory. He is an "old fighter"[31] of unbroken courage. He gave me news of his wide circle of international contacts. Arrived around 9:30 p.m. in B. Oos, where A. picked me up. Her mother is visiting B.B. Quiet night.

---

28. Wilhelm Erythropel, formerly German minister in Cuba, retired from the AA in 1938, and reactivated during the war as a WHA.

29. This was the first indication that Prüfer may have listened to foreign radio stations, an action punishable in Nazi Germany with a lengthy prison sentence. By the spring of 1943 increasing numbers of Germans tuned to such broadcasts, and denunciations for the practice lessened.

30. Franco, during an address on 9 May 1943 in Almeria, mentioned the possibility of a quick peace and end to the war in Europe. Since January he had unsuccessfully offered his services to Britain as a mediator. Spain especially needed peace to help reconstruct its economy, severely weakened by its civil war. Franco also mentioned that Spain joined the Pope in appealing to the world's conscience to end the fighting. Three weeks later, Pius XII urged the combatants to apply the "laws of humanity" in air warfare. The British particularly were stung by the inference that their large-scale attacks against German population centers were immoral.

31. *Alte Kämpfer*, referring to persons who had joined the Nazi party during the Weimar republic (1919–33) and thus before Hitler's assumption of power in Germany. No information exists on Oberländer in the Nazi party membership files in the Berlin Document Center. The

20 May 1943

Most beautiful spring day.

21 May 1943

Left B.B. with A. early this morning. We arrived in Davos at 5:30 without incident. We are staying at the Central Hotel. The large hotels are closed. The place is empty of tourists. In the evening we went to Schneider's. The only old acquaintances still here were in the Café Canova.

22 May 1943

Went window shopping and took a walk. In the evening at the movies.

23 May 1943

In Davos-Dorf. [Walk in the] forests. Memories. Dinner at Schneiders.

24 May 1943

At the Consulate in the Villa Aruno. Diehl [*sic*] is the administrator.[32] A. has indigestion. Stalin dissolved the Comintern, thus knocking the

chemical and dye trust, I.G. Farben, had produced "Buna," a synthetic rubber for use by the German military. Farben's major factory for such production during the war was adjacent to the Auschwitz concentration camp in Poland. The Buna plant drew on the plentiful supply of slave labor from Auschwitz; the inmates who became too weak to work could easily be destroyed in the camp's extermination center at Birkenau.

32. Herbert Diel, a veteran German diplomat and nonparty member whom Prüfer had

props from beneath our anti-Communist propaganda.[33] There is no longer a Third International. Our answer should be: peace with Russia, even an alliance, for henceforth Russia is just another national entity that no longer supports international claims. Japan could be the mediator.[34] Next, we would have to develop a positive program for Europe, without trying to impose our form of government on it. But perhaps Nazism, Fascism, and Communism can be welded into a single movement, considering that Russia is again a national state. Such a European Axis would be wholly unbeatable. Indeed, one could even look beyond this to the west. There might be, after all, some hope for universal peace.

25 May 1943

It is snowing and very cold. A. feels better. Spent the evening with the Diehls [*sic*] in the Alpina.

26 May 1943

Departure at 9:30 in snow. Lunch in Zurich and then on to Geneva. Arrived there at 8:30. We are staying in the Hotel de la Paix, which looks dead, forlorn, and partly gone to seed.

27 May 1943

Walk in the city, which is full of goods. Lunch with Krauel, the Kh.

known since World War I. During his two weeks in Switzerland, Prüfer kept his diaries on tiny notes of paper and wrote little, as shown in the succeeding entries.

33. The "Comintern" refers to Communist International, founded in Moscow in 1919 by the new Soviet government to promote Communist propaganda, political parties, and revolution abroad.

34. Prüfer was presumably aware that Japan, one of the Reich's partners in the Axis, had been urging the Germans for a long time to conclude peace with Russia.

[Khedive], and Padel.[35] The Kh. praised Frangoulis[36] and confirmed that the Mufti has been in the service of the Ital. [Italians] since at least '38, at a time when the Kh. discussed him with Puaud in Syria.[37] He considers him [the Mufti] politically dead, without influence, and compromised in regard to Ibn Saud and the Hashemites.

28 May 1943

At the Consulate early. Krauel very annoyed about his transfer to Berlin. Then with the Kh., who told me the detailed story about his visa denial.[38] It apparently goes back to the Mufti, and his protector, [illegible], who played a peculiar role.[39] The latter has an expensive [illegible] wife. But wife and son are not the cause of the financial difficulties. The Kh. confirms that predated 17 May. The Kh. is protected by two of Canaris's people, "forest donkey" and "big corn."[40] In the afternoon with A. to see the Fr. [French] film, *Bengasi*, pacifist and patriotic at the same time. Not bad. In the evening accidental meeting in the Bergerie with P. [Padel] and the Kh. The latter is of the opinion that T. [Turkey] is unreliable, above all the Professor [Inönü]. He speaks badly of Numann [Menemencioglu]. He is going to Corpoli in the fall *pour rencontrer sa fille et sa soeur*. The *Nimet* is supposed to cost a million francs.[41]

---

35. Wilhelm Padel, a former official in the AA's Middle Eastern section and retired from the ministry in 1931. He worked in the ex-Khedive's entourage. Wolfgang Krauel was a German diplomat who refused to return to Berlin when recalled by the AA, apparently because of his pessimism regarding the war's eventual outcome and because two German officials in Switzerland, one a businessman and the other a diplomat, had been arrested on their return to Germany and sentenced to death.

36. Unidentified.

37. "Puaud" is presumably Edgar Puaud, a French general who had directed Vichy volunteer units in North Africa in Nov. 1942 and later (1944) commanded the French SS brigade, "Charlemagne." There is no evidence, however, that Puaud served in Syria.

38. See chap. 3, n. 53.

39. The illegible word may refer to Himmler or Ettel. The "Mufti" in this sentence was written in Arabic script.

40. *Waldesel* and *Gross Korn*. It is unclear whom these code names, possibly Prüfer's own, referred to. On Canaris, see chap. 6, n. 18.

41. Original of "million" in Arabic script. *Nimet Allah* was the name of the ex-Khedive's yacht, which he hoped to leave docked on the Riviera, despite the wish of the German navy to remove it. The yacht had been constructed in Germany in 1923.

29 May 1943

Lunch with Kessel at the Bergerie. Then a visit from Blind and Baer [*sic*], who are both in disgrace with the Khedive. Certainly Pfanne played an unpleasant role here.[42] He is often jealous and envious, also of me. That was apparent during a conversation I had with him this afternoon, when we took a walk together. He would like for me to disappear from here as soon as possible. This evening I had dinner with A. at the hotel. Then we went to the Kurhalle. We left before the end of a terrible show. Again, A. does not feel well. She tires easily after the slightest exertion.

30 May 1943

Sunday. Took a walk through the old part of the city. Went to the movies. *Albion and Bibi.* Ate alone in the restaurant at the railroad station.

31 May 1943

Met the Kh. and Padel in the evening at the Café des Dames, after I had dinner at the Amphitrion. Interesting engineer and academician.

---

42. Officials in the German Consulate General in Geneva.

eight

June 1943

1 June 1943

Visited the Kh. [Khedive], who is greatly worried about the posture of Atrak [Turkey] vis-à-vis the Imam.[1] Very pessimistic parallelism with the previous activity of Murdoch Mac. Abyssinian plan for a 20 million Pound lease cut with Eg. [Egypt] and the Sudan for the Blue Nile.[2] Evening *Plat d'argent*.[3] Afternoon with Shekib's son.

---

1. Presumably a code word used by Prüfer to describe Britain. In his report of 17 June 1943 to the AA, summarizing his meetings with Abbas Hilmi, Prüfer declared that the ex-Khedive believed Turkey would preserve its neutrality in the war until its national interest was threatened. The Turks, Abbas Hilmi maintained, would grant the Allies, particularly Britain, the use of Turkish "military facilities, but above all transit through the straits to Rumania." Both the Turks and British, Prüfer quoted the ex-Khedive as saying, feared Soviet penetration into the Mediterranean. "Turkey's policy," Prüfer concluded, "is only determined . . . by the assessment of its own interests."

2. This referred to the ex-Khedive's claim to Prüfer that as Rommel and German forces had approached Alexandria, Egypt in May 1942, the British had considered dynamiting the Aswan Dam, thereby flooding and destroying the Nile valley. Abbas Hilmi alleged to Prüfer that Murdoch McDonald, a former British official in the Irrigation Division of the Egyptian government, had informed him of an agreement among Egypt, the Sudan, and Ethiopia that would pay the latter for controlling the level of water of Lake Tana and the Nile River; such an agreement would also benefit England.

3. A restaurant.

2 June 1943

Departure for Bern at 11 o'clock after a bad feverish night. Pfanne, who is going to Paris tomorrow, was at the train station.[4] Tale about the German intentions for Geneva. Shekib[5] was at the train station in Bern. Trip to the Legation. Köcher dissatisfied with senseless [personnel] replacements. Shekib defends his new Axis.[6] Pessimistic in regard to Turkey's attitude. Arrival in Zurich at 7:30 p.m. Dinner in a nice Ticino [Italian] restaurant.

3 June 1943

Ascension day. Visit with Aziz Izzet Pasha at the [Hotel] Baur au Lac. He spoke of W.C.'s [Churchill's] immense hatred, which blinds him to the Russ. [Russian] danger. He spoke with regret about our bad, overly strident, propaganda.[7] *On ne doit pas raconter à tout le monde ce qu'on veut faire.* Lunch with Rausch and his wife at S.K. Voigt's. Everyone is appalled by the personnel changes. Schellert has gone to Lugano, Hohenthal to St. Gallen.[8] Left for Davos at 5:12 p.m. Arrived there in icy cold weather at 8:30. Postcard from Kraft in Florence.

4 June 1943

Miserable cold. Bought a suitcase. Visited Sister Rosa.[9] Coup d'etat

---

4. The trip's purpose was to arrange, presumably with Prüfer's help, a visit of the ex-Khedive to Paris, scheduled for the end of Aug. 1943.

5. Original in Arabic script.

6. According to Prüfer's report to the AA of 17 June 1943, the Syrian exile told him that, despite the Allied wartime constellation, the Anglo-Americans were "natural" enemies of Soviet Russia and Germany must decide which side it would support. Arslan recommended that Germany ally with Russia, using Japan as a mediator. Prüfer again wrote Arslan's name in Arabic script. Otto Köcher was German minister in Switzerland from 1937 to 1945.

7. In his report to the AA, Prüfer confirmed this significantly more limited account of the conversation than the one he fabricated in RD, entry for 3 June 1943. Izzet Pasha was a former Egyptian politician and longtime acquaintance of Prüfer.

8. Joachim Graf von Hohenthal, Schellert, Karl Voigt, and Rausch were German diplomatic officials in Switerland.

9. Unidentified.

in Argentina. In the evening with the Diehl's [*sic*]. Röslis[10] have had bad publicity because of alleged hostilities during a brawl.

---

6 June 1943

Sunday. There was a half hour alarm at 1:30 a.m. No trace of the planes. Morning walk with A. Lunch on the Schatzalp. Back on foot. A. feels sick. Rainy afternoon.

---

7 June 1943

In Argentina, Castillo has thrown in the towel.[11] A Jew has caused trouble at Rosita's.[12]

---

8 June 1943

With Diehl. Telephone call from Strack in Lugano. In the evening with the Tailor and the Box.[13]

---

10. Swiss owners of a restaurant and the Hotel Central in Davos. See, in this connection, n. 12.

11. Ramon S. Castillo, the president of Argentina, was overthrown on 4 June 1943 by the pro-Axis Argentine army, to halt the appointment of an Anglophile as his successor. Argentina was the only American nation that retained diplomatic relations with Germany; except for Chile, which had broken relations with Berlin on 20 Jan. 1943, the remainder of the Americas were at war with the Reich.

12. The meaning of this sentence is unclear. Rosita could have referred to one of Abbas Hilmi's mistresses of that name. Rosita was the code name for Prüfer's leave to Switzerland, beginning in Sept. 1943, to retain contact with exiled Arabs there; note p. xviii. However, the reference may also have been to Rosita Stifter, the daughter of the owners of the Hotel Central in Davos and Prüfer's mistress from the early 1920s, when he administered the local German Consulate.

13. These code names, which were written in Arabic script, refer to unidentified persons.

9 June 1943

Departure for Zurich at 9:30. Arrived at 12:45. Dienstmann at the train station.[14] Lunch with [Aziz] Izzet, wife, and daughter, Princess Hassan. *On ne parle pas trop bien du Khédive.* Afternoon with Dienstmann at Voigt's. Evening with the Dienstmanns and their daughter in the Baur au Lac.

10 June 1943

Departure for B.B. at 1:13. Arrived at 8:30 p.m. There is no lack of [domestic] tension.[15] Urschel Stohrer.

11 June 1943

Tensions are on the increase. Olaf and Erna[16] are pretty undisciplined. Conversation with Melchers: the It. [Italians] are still acting up. In the afternoon, visit by Widmann and his sister.[17] He is, or appears to be, an optimist. A. is very nervous; her mother's presence does not help.

12 June 1943

Violent attack on Pantelleria.[18] The news at noon is reporting on the island because of the water shortages. In addition, reports of air attacks on

14. Carl Dienstmann was Germany's new consul general in Zurich; he had been Prüfer's deputy during 1936–39 in the AA's Personnel and Budget Division.

15. Presumably involving Olaf, Prüfer's son, who had remained in Baden-Baden; see ensuing entry (11 June 1943).

16. A Rumanian forced laborer who worked as a domestic servant.

17. Hugo Widmann-Lämmert was formerly a physician and administrator at a hospital in Rio de Janeiro. He had been dismissed from his posts in Feb. 1942 because of unauthorized contacts with Prüfer and other employees of the German Embassy, which had been closed when the Brazilian government severed diplomatic relations with Germany.

18. Allied forces, following up their triumph in North Africa, began the assault on Italy by

Cuxhafen and Wilhelmshafen. Gauleiter Sauckel made an optimistic speech in Prague.[19]

---

13 June 1943

Severe air attack on Bochum. A. is ill. Foul temper and the usual irritability at the slightest provocation. Her mother's influence is not good.

---

14 June 1943

A. [illegible]. Glock was here for a few hours. Slight domestic difficulties in the evening, which were put right during the night. Lampedusa†.[20]

---

15 June 1943

Downtown this morning with A. Complete reconciliation between G. and D.[21] Later at the movies. Silly film with Zarah Leander. Spent the evening at the Bellevue, which has noticeably deteriorated. Miserable food and dirty service.

---

16 June 1943

Departure for Berlin in pouring rain at 8:24 a.m. Huge crowds on the train. Arrived in Berlin around 10 p.m. Schlobies and Glock at the train

---

bombing its southern ports and attacking Sicily. The Anglo-Americans occupied the island of Pantelleria in the Strait of Sicily at the beginning of June 1943.

19. Fritz Sauckel was Nazi district leader of Thuringia and, beginning in 1942, the Reich government's plenipotentiary for labor mobilization. After the war the Nuremberg tribunal convicted and executed him for war crimes.

20. Prüfer used this sign to signify the "death" or surrender of this island in the Strait of Sicily to the Allies on 12 June 1943. Like Pantelleria, Lampedusa was bombed into submission; see n. 18.

21. This presumably refers to the domestic quarrel between Prüfer's artist friend in Munich, Gulbransson, and the latter's wife, Dagny; see OD, entry for 3 May 1943.

station. Tomorrow the former is leaving for Turkey. Alarm at 2 p.m. I slept in the basement.

---

17 June 1943

Routine work. There was an air raid about 12:45 a.m. I went to the basement of the Hotel Adlon, where I met Sedlmayr, who lives in Stockholm on unknown business.[22] The attack lasted until 1:45. There was artillery fire. Kettenbeil goes to Ankara as air force attaché; he was promoted to the rank of lieutenant general; we went for dinner. Plewka phoned me after the raid.

---

18 June 1943

Discussion in the A.A. about the *Nimet Allah*.[23] The three naval representatives were quite understanding and reasonable. Levetzow, who is leaving for Seville to serve as the Honorary Consul, visited me at noon. He was very satisfied with this new job, the more so because the Duke of Alba[24] recently gave a dinner for 3,000 persons, "which is the talk of Europe"—as if there were nothing more serious in this world to talk about. In the afternoon I was invited by Sztójay to the celebration of Horthy's 75th birthday at the UFA palace.[25] Solemn and boring. The Turkish Ambassador drove me home. Renewed but confused assurances of Turkish neutrality. [After dinner visited with] Count T'Serclaes in the hotel lobby. He, too, spoke of rumors circulating in Belgium regarding a separate German-Russian peace

---

22. Joachim Sedlmayr was an engineer employed after 1940 as a WHA in the German embassies in the United States and Brazil and after 1942 as an assistant to the commercial attaché in Stockholm. Sedlmayr represented a German machine construction cartel and worked abroad under diplomatic cover.
23. See chap. 7, n. 41.
24. Spanish ambassador in London.
25. Adm. Miklos Horthy. Hungary was an ally of Germany, but following Stalingrad it attempted to establish not-so-secret contacts with the Anglo-Americans to conclude peace. Nevertheless, Hitler regarded Horthy as a valuable ally and presented the regent with a yacht for his birthday.

initiative under Japanese sponsorship.[26] I regret Bargen's recall. Mayr is going to Brussels.[27] This appointment is a pretty clumsy move.

---

19 June 1943

Around noon I went to Bellin. There I received the not entirely unexpected news that Ingrid [Langenn] became engaged to Oertzen during his recent three-day furlough, which he spent in Bellin.[28] The engagement did not come off very smoothly. Helmut claims that I. has inherited Basedow's disease [goiter] from her mother and grandmother. He believes that such an illness should not be passed on to one's descendants. He says that some years ago a doctor had diagnosed this genetic condition in the course of Ingrid's routine physical examination for work [in the Reich Labor Service]. Whatever the case may be, I believe that H. fears his own loneliness if I. were to marry. She also spoke with me. She truly seems to love Oertzen; how to understand a young girl's soul? I, for one, did not have the impression that this was love at first sight. Who knows what is going on here. I do not believe in I.'s sickness; at least I do not consider it sufficiently serious to prevent her marriage. I mentioned this to H.

---

20 June 1943

Quiet, tranquil Sunday in Bellin.

26. On 16 June 1943, a Swedish newspaper announced that Soviet and German officials had been negotiating near Stockholm, and *The New York Times* printed the report. Prüfer and many of his colleagues in the AA, as his subsequent original diaries revealed, feared that Germany could not win the war and placed great hopes on a peace agreement with Russia. Between Dec. 1942 and Sept. 1943, the Soviet Union made several contacts with the Germans through the Soviet Embassy in Sweden. Although Ribbentrop and Goebbels favored a settlement with Russia, Hitler rejected the feelers, stubbornly holding to his belief in a German triumph in the war and maintaining that such negotiations would be interpreted as a sign of German weakness. By the fall of 1943, the Soviets were utilizing rumors of the peace talks to their advantage in their alliance with the Western powers.
27. Ludwig Mayr-Falkenberg had been German consul general at Genoa and, beginning in Oct. 1941, high commissioner of the Reich for the Resettlement of the South Tirol Population. He had also worked for Prüfer in the AA's Personnel and Budget Division during 1936. Werner von Bargen served as representative of the AA with the German military commander in Belgium and Northern France.
28. See chap. 1, n. 1.

21 June 1943

Returned to Berlin. Last night there was an alarm. Nothing new in the A.A. Glock is sick, which is bad news, because it prevents him from dealing with the problem of our house in B.B., which is to be commandeered for refugees. This is an absolutely intolerable situation.[29] The night was quiet.

22 June 1943

In the A.A. Visit from L.S. Röhrig, who dealt with Arab matters in the Paris Embassy. He expressed disapproval, albeit very carefully and tentatively, of G. [Grobba], who, as usual, messes around with Gailani's Arabs.[30] In the evening with Steffen and Hermann Hatzfeld's [*sic*] daughter. They seem to be rather intimate. Alarm at 2 o'clock; it lasted 45 minutes. No more than distant artillery fire.

24 June 1943

Severe raids on Oberhausen and Mülheim. "The population suffered severe losses." Wilhelm Wagner from Addis Ababa is in town. He said that British captivity was not too unpleasant.[31] He also noted that the Italians surrendered with 270,000 men in Habesch, almost without a fight. Spent the evening with Langmann and Kettenbeil.

25 June 1943

Met Kapp, who tells terrible stories about his hometown, Barmen.[32] 18,000 dead! Yesterday "they" were in Elberfeld. Casualties "heavy." The

29. This referred to refugees from heavily bombed areas who were assigned to reside in Prüfer's home. Glock eventually prevented it, however.
30. Prüfer had opposed Grobba's request that Gailani and his entourage be permitted to visit Paris.
31. This should be compared with the enormous brutality generally accorded by the Germans to their captives. Wagner was an acquaintance of Prüfer's from Ethiopia.
32. Karl Kapp was a career diplomat and specialist in Arab and Indian affairs in the AA.

army reports have never said anything like that before. This cannot go on much longer. Bad blood between Helmut and Ingrid, because he is trying to prevent her engagement or marriage, or at least put it off.[33]

---

26 June 1943

Afternoon with Ingrid at the movies. *Romance in a Minor Key* with Marianne Hoppe. A pretty good film without a happy end.[34] Dinner with Bohny and the Langenns. Afterwards another long and fruitless discussion with Helmut about the marital engagement. He disapproves, but has no grounds for his disapproval.

---

27 June 1943

Sunday. Boring walk and bad dinner. Very melancholy mood.

---

28 June 1943

Uneventful day. Conversation in the evening with T'Serclaes, who complained about and made fun of the Cultural-Pol. Div. [of the AA], an outfit that tries, overzealously, to justify its existence. He requested the release of about 500 prisoners [of war], men with more than 3 children; this would have had a good psychological effect in Belgium. Instead only those with more than five children were released, thus achieving the opposite of what was intended. Domestic problems with Erna.

---

33. Note OD, entry for 19 June 1943. Prüfer was aware of the reasons for the father's opposition to Ingrid's marrying Oertzen: he was an army officer and could become a casualty in the war, and he was part of the opposition to Hitler. How Prüfer had learned of this is unclear.

34. Original "a happy end" in English. *Romanze in Moll* was the most elegant and artistic of all films made during the Third Reich. Its theme of an unfaithful wife who committed suicide infuriated Goebbels (whose allegedly happy family life was heavily publicized by the Nazi regime) and almost led him to destroy the work. The film was an enormous public success at the time of its release.

29 June 1943

Reuter announced today that a Rio court sentenced me to 25 years in prison for espionage. In addition, many other Germans and Brazilians were given sentences ranging from 10 to 30 years. Herr Albrecht accepted this monstrous verdict with cheerful calm.[35] He did not even seem interested in detaining, by way of retaliation, the Brazilian Ambassador to Vichy, who happens to be in Godesberg; only after I threatened to go to the Minister [Ribbentrop] did he assent. I then consulted Bielfeld (under instructions from Steengracht) and Hencke, who agreed with my suggestions to lodge protests and to detain the Brazilians until the sentence has been reversed. It should be clear that, after this verdict, I will never be able to travel abroad. No nation will ever grant a visa to a man with a previous conviction. What will happen to me if the enemy one day occupies our country?[36] Meanwhile the enemy mounted a most severe raid on Cologne and caused great losses. The cathedral is badly damaged.[37] The Mufti apparently wants to return from Rome. Signs of an impending Anglo-Americ. attack in the Eastern Mediterrranean are increasing.

30 June 1943

A day I spent totally alone, morose, and full of worries.

---

35. Erich Albrecht was an experienced career service officer from the Weimar era.

36. On 27 July 1943, a Brazilian appeals court, citing diplomatic immunity, dropped the charges and sentences against Prüfer, Becker, and Bohny. Prüfer mentions the verdict in OD, entry for 11 Aug. 1943.

37. On the night of 28–29 June 1943, 540 British planes dropped 1,614 tons of bombs on the city, killing 3,460 persons and leaving 400,000 homeless. In sixteen massive raids during May and June, the British waged what they termed "the battle of the Ruhr," dropping over 24,000 tons of bombs on German cities, most of them in the industrial zone along the Rhine and Ruhr rivers. Prüfer's immediate reaction to the attack on Cologne appeared to parallel Goebbels's ensuing propaganda campaign, which emphasized the loss of such historic cultural monuments from enemy bombings over that of the enormous loss of human life. Although the damage to the cathedral aroused many emotions, it was the deaths from Allied bombing that particularly incensed German opinion against the enemy and raised demands for revenge.

nine

July 1943

1 July 1943

Lunch with Gailani, Ghulam Siddiq, Melchers, and Glock. The conversation centered around a projected declaration of Germany and Italy favoring independence of the Arab countries. After Gailani left, Ghulam Siddiq and Melchers stayed on. The former spoke very urgently in favor of a separate peace with Russia. In the afternoon, Schröder also favored such a plan and noted that even Musso was favorably disposed in this matter. So far, however, diplomatic negotiations have failed because of the resistance from upon high. This evening I had dinner with Schulenburg. He immediately discussed the same topic, likewise in a positive sense. He also confirmed the Italian efforts.[1] Even Jo. [Ribbentrop] is inclined to send out

---

1. Schulenburg knew of the informal German-Russian contact in Stockholm firsthand from the principal German official involved, Peter Kleist, who had served under both Ribbentrop in the AA and Rosenberg in the Nazi Ministry for Occupied Eastern Territories. Kleist, however, had acted since Dec. 1942 on his own, and before he returned to Berlin on 19 June 1943 he had met twice with Edgar Clauss, a Soviet agent. Moreover, A. M. Alexandrov, formerly counselor at the Soviet Embassy in Berlin and head of the Russian foreign ministry's European Division, had arrived in Stockholm in mid-June 1943 en route to London and sought unsuccessfully to meet Kleist. However, when Kleist arrived in Berlin, he was arrested by the SD and interrogated. Hitler learned of Kleist's activity through the Abwehr, labelled the affair a "Jewish" provocation, and ordered that it be ignored. Two months later, Ribbentrop met with Kleist and then consulted Hitler, who permitted the resumption of the contacts with the Soviets, but solely for obtaining information from them.

feelers, but he has not been able to accomplish anything fruitful. Vlassov is in disgrace and can no longer be mentioned.[2]

2 July 1943

Lunch with Plank [sic], along with Köpke and Popitz.[3] Pessimistic discussion of the situation in the Rhineland. The Osters visited me in the evening. Afterward I saw Niebuhr at Bohny's. Everywhere the mood is rotten.

3 July 1943

An unpleasant event: thievery in the Hotel. I am missing a cake of soap and a knife. Another sign of the times. This afternoon, visit from Hilva [Boroevich-Heemskerck] with son, Olaf. Diehl's wife died in Salzburg.

4 July 1943

Spent thé entire day with Schröder. Exceedingly interesting conversation. He feels as I do about the negotiations in St. . . .m [Stockholm]. Something must happen. The matter has not yet been scotched. Supposedly there are ongoing secret negotiations. Two men appeared in the

---

2. Andrei Vlasov was a Soviet general captured by the German army at the Volkhov front in July 1942 and used by the Nazis to head a "Russian Army of Liberation," comprised of Soviet prisoners of war and other elements recruited inside Russia, to fight alongside the Germans. Vlasov, however, opposed Nazi forced labor, terror, and murder in the East, which alienated extremists in the SS and party. Hitler and his military leaders, moreover, soon feared that the Vlasov movement might blossom into a genuine political force that would rival the Germans. During June 1943, Hitler undermined Vlasov by limiting his activities solely to propaganda appeals across the front lines.

3. Johannes Popitz, career bureaucrat and Prussian minister of finance from 1933 until his arrest, which resulted from his role in the failed conspiracy to assassinate Hitler in July 1944.

evening, Friede, the L.G.L.[4] in Turkey, and a man from Alfred Rosenberg's office. Both are nice people. Don M.L. [Luther] is still where he was. Walter Z. has disappeared from sight.[5]

---

5 July 1943

The Mufti has returned from Rome at the request of H.H. [Himmler], who wants to discuss the Bosnian [SS] division and its religious concerns. Sikorski died in a crash off Gibraltar.[6] Our press talks about an assassination instigated by the Soviets. That does not exactly fit into the new picture [of a separate peace]; it probably means that we have abandoned this project. In Brussels Bargen has been replaced by Mayr-Falkenberg, who will be totally out of place. Count T'S. [T'Serclaes] has bitterly complained about this choice.

---

6 July 1943

The Mufti visited me. For 1-1/2 hours we discussed the proposed declaration of Arab independence to be made by Italy and us, i.e., a lot of hot air.[7] In the evening Herbert R. [Richthofen] came to see me. We talked until 3:30 a.m.

---

4. *Landesgruppenleiter.* Viktor Friede was removed to Germany after 1942 following his disagreements with Papen, the Reich ambassador in Turkey.

5. Walter Zechlin, an official in the Press Division of the German Embassy in Madrid, refused to return to the Reich when recalled and instead fled to a monastery near Burgos. Because of his socialist background, he feared that he would be imprisoned if he went back to Germany.

6. Gen. Wladislaw Sikorski was minister president of the Polish government-in-exile headquartered in London. He perished on 4 July 1943 with British and other Polish officials in an air crash near Gibraltar.

7. Husayni, by agreement with Gailani, had drafted an extensive proposal in the spring of 1943 designed to persuade the Axis to issue a public statement making greater promises of Arab autonomy than those issued previously by the Allies. Although the Italians favored the declaration, the Arab question had now become a decidedly secondary issue with the Germans, whose officials differed with the Italians over the nature of the promises to the Arabs. Berlin postponed the matter further. Only in Nov. 1944 did the Germans issue a much-too-belated statement on "the acknowledgment of the independence of all Arab countries and the demand for their unity."

7 July 1943

Lunch with Herbert at Uncle Max's [Oppenheim], whose nephew had reported terrible tales from Cologne. The downtown area is almost completely destroyed. Fatalities are pegged at 20,000, those rendered homeless at 300,000. Ingrid [Langenn] arrived towards evening and is living with Töpfer.(!) Helmut has finally agreed to her engagement.

8 July 1943

Lunch with Ingrid, who plans to leave this evening. I was alone during and after dinner. So alone that I wrote some bad poetry to A. At least it is sincerely meant.

9 July 1943

I probably had some fever last night, because this morning I had cracked lips and felt as if I had been beaten. But that is, of course, no surprise in these wonderful times. Once again the British bombed Cologne. The Reich Foreign Minister is ill and has to remain in bed. We are "governing" by means of countless inflationary committees which have usurped positions formerly held by individual experts. The sole result of this "sovietization" of the authoritarian system in the A.A. is an unbearable slowdown, a kind of paralysis of the entire organization. The worst thing about this is that the "committees" are almost entirely staffed by amateurs. In the Indian committee, for example, the three principal members, the "Indian experts," have never been to India. The head of the America committee, which has for its main task the downfall of Roosevelt, is St. S. Steengracht, who is a dilettante in this area. His deputy is Rahn, the "victor" of Syria and Tunisia, who does not know the U.S.A. and only knows South America from a short trip on economic assignment! In these *Gremien*—another new German term—the subject is simply talked to death.[8] No useful results whatsoever. At most, propaganda sheets are printed in mass quantities, but

---

8. *Gremien* is translated as "bodies" or "committees."

they usually do not reach their intended audiences—but that, at least, is no great misfortune. In Fuschl there is talk of a declaration regarding independence and eventual unification of the Arab countries. This has been discussed ever since I returned to Germany. Because of misgivings and various other considerations, this project has failed to pass beyond the "planning stage," to use the expert term from the era of the League of Nations. Meanwhile, we are no longer anywhere in the vicinity of the Arab countries. Although today our declarations of autonomy for this region are only pious platitudes, we have not even been able to bring ourselves to make such a declaration, and we still bow to the Italians in Libya (where they are no longer present), the French in Syria (where de Gaulle and the British are in charge), and to the Turks, who will ultimately side with the enemy.

In Russia, a violent struggle has developed in the region of Bielgorod and Orel; both Russia and Germany claim to be on the offensive. Probably the Bolshis were preparing a large attack that we noticed early enough to forestall. In the propaganda "sector" (another nice word) against Russia, we are continuing to harp on the Katyn forest [massacre]. There are a few new tunes in the same key: Vinnitsa, Odessa, and others.[9] Anyway, I hope that these discordant notes do not chase away the all-too-weak angel of peace in Stockholm! Sikorski's death is very mysterious. Who had him killed? Perhaps the Bolshis did it, perhaps someone from his own ranks. The death of Victor Cazalets argues against a British plot.[10] A few days ago, I heard a strange tale; it sounded so improbable to me that I will only record it: the Anglo-American attack [in North Africa] did not surprise the Abwehr, but the Führer's entourage told him about it too late, *pour ne pas le troubler.* Even after having been informed, he [Hitler] remained incredulous. I think this version is spread by the "little bird" [Canaris] in order to lessen his own culpability.

In the evening Steffen, Countess Hatzfeldt, and her sister, Barbara Baroness Brummer, dined with me. St., who stayed after the ladies left, told me about his unpleasant experiences with the "little bird." A. called me during dinner. Our conversation was unpleasant, probably because I was in a hurry.

---

9. Nazi propaganda maintained that, as the German armies had advanced into the Soviet Union during 1941, the Soviet secret police had massacred its prisoners in the two Russian cities before evacuation; Reichsminister für die besetzten Ostgebiete, ed., *Amtliches Material zum Massenmord von Winniza* (Berlin: Eher, 1944).

10. Cazalets was a British colonel, member of parliament, and liaison officer with Sikorski who also died in the crash.

10 July 1943

Last night the enemy landed on the southeastern coast of Sicily. "The battle is in progress."[11] A *façon de parler* of disastrous memory that we adopted in North Africa. The *propriétaire*[12] gave me further details on the Stockholm intermezzo. The emissary, Alexandrov, wanted to contact us through one of the "guys" from the *défense*.[13] That was enough to discredit him, although he is well-known personally to both of his bosses and was even in Berlin with no. 2 [Molotov].[14] The notion that he was a "little man," therefore, does not exactly fit the facts. In any case, nothing more seems to be said about this initiative. Only from Vatican circles are there reports that rooms are reserved in Venice for the Russian delegation. Today Schr. [Schröder] again mentioned the plan for my transfer. *Utinam!* Mainly for A.'s sake. Bochum was the target of yesterday's attack. The number of planes we shot down is not so magnificent in comparison to the number of raiders involved. During the second assault on Cologne, the ratio was about 700 to 39, thus not quite 5%.

11 July 1943

Sunday and therefore boring. I had lunch with Frau Edib. She told a noteworthy and supposedly true anecdote about Arikan, which she credits to an eyewitness, Bilbes: A. [Arikan] was drunk, as usual, and at the dinner table had kissed the hand of the lady seated next to him, a Frau von D. He then told her that she smelled bad, indeed that she even stank. B. claims to have told this tale to his boss. Henke [*sic*] is supposed to have been present. The Dumont woman is still causing trouble. She is now persecuting Frau E. in the silly second-class diplomatic circles (Mello, Brandao [*sic*], Hudacek

---

11. Anglo-American troops landed on Sicily on 10 July 1943. It took the Allies thirty-eight days to win the island; both sides suffered heavy casualties, especially the Axis.

12. A cross-linguistic reference to Werner von Grundherr, a career diplomat, longtime friend of Prüfer's, and head of the Scandanavian section in the AA's Political Division.

13. "Abwehr," Prüfer pencilled in later. On "Alexandrov," originally written in Arabic script, see n. 1.

14. Vyacheslav Molotov was the Soviet foreign minister. During 12–13 Nov. 1940, Molotov had visited Berlin for discussions with Hitler and Ribbentrop about differences between their governments, which at the time were allied, regarding Eastern Europe. The reference to the "bosses" is to Molotov and Stalin.

[*sic*], etc.),[15] claiming that the latter had "turned her in" and has set the police after her. The truth is that, based on Frau E.'s stories, not on her denunciations, I informed the Pers. Div.[16] of the Dumonts' conduct. I never involved the Gestapo in this matter. It seems that great quantities of food are smuggled in from Turkey. That is all right with us.

---

12 July 1943

A directive, signed by Bruns, arrived from the R.M.'s [Ribbentrop] office.[17] I am supposed to go every three months to Switzerland to maintain contact with the Orientals [i.e., the Arabs]. My report was submitted to the R.M. only in "excerpts." Of course Shekib's advice had been withheld from him.[18]

Meanwhile the battles in Russia and Sicily continue. The "committees" are supposed to report successes of their propaganda efforts for presentation to the Führer every 14 days. But if the successes (as in the Arab committee) fail to materialize, what then? Should we lie? Becker arrived from Madrid. He is complaining about Kroll, who "governs" in Barcelona. Becker shares my opinion that in no case should the Brazilian Ambassador from Vichy be allowed to leave Germany. He is the last trump card in our hand. Yesterday the Gauleiter of Cologne arranged for a celebration. A somewhat daring undertaking, considering the 20,000 casualties.

Since I was not shown the "edited" version, I do not know which changes or deletions in my report were made by the youngsters of the camarilla. [Incredibly] an ambassador's report addressed to the R.A.M. has been doctored and corrected by some flunky, without concern for its further disposition. The Americans lost many positions, and the British are making no

---

15. Karl Hudeczek, an Austrian, was head of the Southeast Europe section in the AA's Economic Policy Division. Hans Brandau was an interpreter in the ministry. Regarding Frau Dumont, see OD, entry for 26 Jan. 1943.

16. Personnel and Budget Division in the AA.

17. Georg Viktor Bruns had been an official since 1938 in the Büro RAM. Prüfer had initially written "Karl Megerle."

18. Prüfer's intent was to acquire a leave that would enable him to reside in Switzerland permanently. He apparently believed that portions of his lengthy report to the AA of 17 June 1943, summarizing his recent trip to Switzerland to interview Arabs exiled there and which he hoped would justify his request, had not been shown to Ribbentrop. The Büro RAM had asked him on 29 June to submit a new request "in a more precise form" to the minister, and on 9 July Prüfer's temporary leave was approved.

progress. God grant that it so continues! Met Braun-Stumm, who is leaving
for Istanbul this evening. He does not believe that peace can be made via
Stockholm. Rather via Vlasov. Had dinner with Sigrid Richthofen.

13 July 1943

Today's news from Sicily does not sound as good as yesterday evening's. The British and Americans have landed on a coastal strip, about 160
kilometers in length, between Licata and Augusta. That is a very considerable frontline. I have no confidence in the Italian defensive enthusiasm.
Had lunch with Sigrid, who was bubbling over with happiness. In the afternoon I met Hans Schr. [Schröder]. He was disgruntled because of difficulties with the boss [Ribbentrop] who, once again, is ill. Tomorrow he will
talk to Steen [Steengracht] regarding my Swiss plans. Bohle has said very
kind things about me to Steen and Schr. Schr. said: "Ernst Wilhelm [Bohle]
idolizes you." Ingrid's engagement is due to be announced, so says her
father who just telephoned me. I cannot but agree.

14 July 1943

The news from Sicily does not sound good at all. An A.A. [Anglo-
American] breakthrough would be disastrous. Our Italian friends are soft,
very soft and tired. Musso is an exception, a white crow. I had lunch with
Uncle Max, who will be 83 years old tomorrow. No word about Rosita.[19]
Tomorrow I will have lunch at Steen's with Prince Lichtenstein [*sic*]. Late
last night, a policeman came to see me because I was robbed. Actually the
theft was trifling, but the mere fact of thievery makes me feel insecure. Last
night there was an especially heavy air raid at Aachen, the first on this city.

15 July 1943

We had an hour-long alarm at 1 a.m. There was some pretty intense
anti-aircraft fire, but we did not hear any bomb explosions. The discussion

19. The code word for his proposed mission to Switzerland; see p. xviii.

about Rosita has been postponed until this afternoon. A.P. [Associated Press] reports that Juneck, Cossel, and some other Germans in Rio have been indicted. Among them Braulio Guimaraes. Lunch today at Steengracht's, given in honor of Prince Liechtenstein. Hencke, Schmidt (interpreter), Bargen, Moraht, Fröhlicher, Dörnberg, and some young people were present.[20] I spoke to St. about the situation in Brazil. He strongly favored Albrecht's ideas. In the afternoon I traveled to Boroevich's in Gross Glienicke. There I met a movie director who made a good impression. At 1:30 a.m. another alarm, which lasted 3/4 of an hour. One can no longer sleep any more.

16 July 1943

Met Ehlert from Rio. He reported that Tulio[21] did not spill the beans regarding the more important matters; on the other hand, probably under torture, he confessed to all sorts of untrue stuff: he was supposed to be with me daily, I supervised and led all of his flights, and similar nonsense. The trial against Christensen and Co. is to follow, among them Glock. João was likewise in prison, but he did not betray anything. König and Zabel are not living up to standards on the Ilha das Flores;[22] they accuse us because

20. Alexander Freiherr von Dörnberg was chief of protocol of the AA. Hans Moraht was head of the South and Central American Section in the AA's Economic Policy Division. Paul Otto Schmidt, once Hitler's interpreter, was in 1943 chief of the Büro RAM. Guimaraes was a lawyer in Santos, previously retained as a counsel by the German government. Eugen Juneck had been a low-level member of the German Embassy in Rio de Janeiro while Prüfer was ambassador; following the break of diplomatic relations between the Reich and Brazil in Jan. 1942, Juneck remained in Rio assigned to the Spanish Embassy's division for acting on behalf of the interests of belligerent powers.
21. Presumably Tulio Regis do Nascimento, a Brazilian army captain and Integralist recruited in 1942 by Prüfer to head an Abwehr spy ring comprised of Brazilians of non-German descent.
22. The main Brazilian prison in which many of the arrested German agents were held. Zabel had been an acquaintance of Prüfer's in Brazil and had informed the ambassador regarding Prüfer's counterpart from the United States, Jefferson Caffery. König was presumably the official of that name who had worked at the former Reichsbahn headquarters in Rio and was arrested by the Brazilians in the spring of 1942. João Miranda had been Prüfer's chauffeur in Brazil who, Prüfer added later to this entry, "knew much." The ambassador had used Miranda in 1942 to remove much incriminating material from the German Embassy in Rio de Janeiro. Nils C. Christensen was a phony name for an Abwehr agent in Brazil, Josef Starziczny, arrested in Mar. 1942 for espionage; he eventually provided extensive information to Brazilian and American authorities.

they—i.e., their wives—did not get enough money. Juneck needs money. Relations to Tovar are as unpleasant as ever. Oswaldo is actually supposed to have been against the trial.[23] Ehlert advised most earnestly that the Brazilian Ambassador, Sousa Dantas, should not be permitted to leave Germany because in that event the Germans in Brazil would be at the mercy of the unrestrained Brazilian and Jewish caprice. The discussion about Rosita took place yesterday. I do not know the results yet.

Glock reported that ever since 24.6., Schwörbel's entire family, including his mother-in-law and brother-in-law, are enjoying the hospitality of Gailani in Bansin, i.e., they are living and being cared for courtesy of the Reich. Frau Grobba and the Granows are also invited. If that is not corruption!

17 July 1943

Schr. [Schröder] informed me that the Rosita matter has been approved by the St.S. All I have to do is to find the proper formula for the boss. I informed Schr. of the Bansin affair. The Mufti joined me for lunch; in addition Djendeli, Melchers, Schlobies, Winkler,[24] Munzel, and Glock were present. The conversation revolved almost entirely around the issue of Arab independence; the Mufti kept insisting on "getting rid of the Jewish settlements in Palestine"[25] and listing the individual Arab states involved. Time, meanwhile, is working against us, especially in Italy.

18 July 1943

I had lunch with the "young gentleman" from the trip to China; he now serves as a grenadier at Leningrad.[26] He describes the mood of the

---

23. Oswaldo Aranha was Brazilian foreign minister. Conde de Tovar was Portuguese minister in Berlin; he had done little to aid the Germans imprisoned in Brazil.

24. Hans Winkler, an Ettel protégé and specialist for Middle Eastern affairs in the AA's Cultural Policy Division.

25. It is curious that Prüfer emphasized this. However, considering that he apparently knew of Husayni's efforts to block the emigration of Jews from Bulgaria to Palestine in 1943 and have them sent instead to the Nazi death camps in Poland, it is likely that he used "getting rid" as a euphemism for the Mufti's intention to murder the Jews in Palestine. Certain sectors of the Nazi bureaucracy often employed such expressions in referring to the Holocaust.

26. Prüfer had vacationed in China from Jan. to Mar. 1939. In the margin of this entry, he later identified the "young gentleman" as Ferring.

soldiers in terms of bleak resignation. Prepared for death, no desire for revolution, but by the same token, also no *élan*. Yesterday afternoon I saw F. St. [Frau Steffen] and heard that Hilva's father maintained an affair with Gertrude Strauss for some 17 years. He[27] even showed me pictures from this period in H.'s life. I would never have thought this possible. It makes this man, who always appeared so cold, seem a little more human. In Russia we are everywhere on the defensive. The Anglo-Americans are making slow but steady progress. Can no one see that it is high time, more than high time, to end this war, hopefully through diplomacy? There are no more weapons, and our "propaganda" has long been discredited as a sham.

---

19 July 1943

Bad news is piling up. In Sicily the Italians have surrendered Girgenti, and today Rome was severely bombed. It should be interesting to see how the Pope reacts to this. By now he is a ridiculous figure without power and courage and, no doubt, he will swallow this monstrous affront to Christian humility. The Italian air force seems completely exhausted; the fleet is inactive at La Spezia. I despair. At lunch I starved with Ferring and Achenbach.[28] The food in my hotel is getting worse and worse. Even among these young people, fear and anxiety about our declining opportunites dominate. The Führer is a great, a very great man, who made our nation—at that time facing ruin—into the most powerful country on earth; and this in an incredibly brief and victorious period of time between 1933 and 1941. Suddenly a drastic change occurred bringing us one defeat after another. What caused this? I believe that we must reserve our judgment in order to gain some distance from the events: the deterioration of human and material resources; miscalculations, especially in the area of aviation (Meyer);[29] the flagging physical strength of the population, which is exhausted and overworked. This is particularly true of undernourished women. There is also the matter of the crippling of policy by sovietization (committees!), not to

---

27. Presumably Hans Steffen.

28. Ernst Achenbach, an official in the AA's Cultural Policy Division.

29. The correct spelling was Meier. At the beginning of the war, Hermann Göring, Hitler's Reich marshal and head of the Luftwaffe, had sworn with typical Nazi arrogance that enemy planes would not reach Germany or his name was "Meier" (one of the most common surnames in Germany). In the Rhenish-Westphalian region, the population often referred to "Meier's French horn" when the air-raid sirens wailed.

speak of the replacement of policy by "propaganda," corruption, and blackmarketeering, caused by hunger and greed. Nonetheless, these factors cannot account for our rapid decline. Perhaps this is no more than the vortex around the center. We used to call it the camarilla. All this is terrible for me to see, not only because I have always been a person who is very attached to his homeland and always will be, but also because I was sincerely converted to some of the beautiful ideas of National Socialism. Even if it had not been mandatory, I was always nationalistic and social-minded. Is what we now have National Socialism? What calls itself that? All that which goes by that name.

Dumont visited me. Everything that Edip [*sic*] said about police investigations concerning D. [Frau Dumont] is incorrect. Either someone has told her a bunch of nonsense, or she is lying. In any case, Schr. [Schröder] confirms that the police are not looking into the matter.

Discussion with Albrecht and Ehlert in Henke's [*sic*] office. Results: before lodging a protest, we want to ask via Spain for the text of the indictment and the tenor of the sentences. Meanwhile Sousa Dantas stays at Godesberg.

Inquiry in Sofia about Alexandrov. *Albulgàr sa'alu bi wāstat safûhum fi russia wa biṭṭab'al-gawâb kân errâgil musch ma'arûf.*[30]

It seems that the Rosita matter is settled. I have sent it to the Dir. Pers.,[31] to be forwarded to the St.S., who is in Fuschl. I hope the decision does not come too late, as is common in such cases! In that event I would no longer be able to follow through because of my physical condition, thus leaving A. and O. in the witches' cauldron. I recall a French fable that I read in my youth, *La chèvre de Monsieur Séguin.* I no longer know who wrote it. In this fable a goat continues to defend a dilapidated barn against a wolf storming the door, trying bravely to save her offspring. The goat—in fables animals do indeed talk—says: *Oh, pourvu que je tienne jusque'à l'aube!* But she cannot hold out, and the wolf devours her and her offspring. My situation and that of A. and O. seems to be similar. *Pourvu que je tienne*

---

30. "The Bulgarians asked their ambassador in Russia to look into the affair, but after much difficulty the answer came back that the man was unknown." This confirms scholarship that has discussed reports of East European sources in 1943 on alleged discussions between German and Soviet agents in Sofia. After the war Prüfer claimed that the Germans, and specifically Hencke, the undersecretary of state in the AA, had asked the Bulgarians to verify from the Soviet Union the intentions of Alexandrov and his peace mission; the reply was negative.

31. Director of the Personnel and Budget Division in the AA, Schröder. On 19 July 1943 Prüfer submitted a memorandum to Schröder and Steengracht, requesting the leave anew and containing a lengthy rationale and plan for it.

jusqu'à l'aube! I ate off paper plates in my lodgings and then went to visit the Engelhardts.

---

20 July 1943

S. Lorenzo in Rome was badly damaged. Apart from that, no historical monuments seem to have been damaged. The raid was aimed at working class districts, Porta Tiburtina and Porta Maggiore. The British communique implies that the pilots had instructions to spare cultural monuments. But what does an American clod know about that kind of stuff? [These raids] are and remain unheard of and are completely unnecessary barbarism. Today I was visited by General N. [Niedenführ], who is here on a short furlough from the central sector of the Russia front. The bleakest of pictures: general confusion, bureaucracy, and infighting among the army, S.S., O.T., and civilian authorities.[32] In addition, bad partisan terror far behind the front. Nevertheless N. does not believe that the Russians will gain serious advantages; nor will we. The situation in Sicily is very serious. Catania [is] about to fall. The Italians are very exhausted. Had lunch with Uncle Max. I have advised him to leave this area with as many of his scientific and artistic possessions as possible and to move to Austria. Becker, whose mother died, visited me in the afternoon. Tomorrow he returns to Madrid. Dined with Niedenführ and Bohny.

---

21 July 1943

The Führer and Mussolini met the day before yesterday, somewhere in northern Italy. What they decided has not yet been revealed. Apparently it concerns military matters.[33] The Americans have taken Caltanissetta and

---

32. "O.T." is *Organisation Todt,* a semi-military unit of the Nazi government for constructing military installations and special highways suitable for armored vehicles. It was administered by Fritz Todt until his death in Feb. 1942 and then by Speer, Reich minister for armaments and war production.

33. In their meeting at Feltre on 19 July 1943, the same day of the first Allied air attack on Rome, Hitler and Mussolini discussed German aid to Italy. Mussolini had been urged by his advisers, who hoped for an Italian withdrawal from the war before it reached their country, to inform Hitler that Italy was at the end of its resources and might not be able to continue fighting. Mussolini, however, did not do so.

are thus in the middle of Sicily. Enna has also been lost. Tonight, for the first time, the newspapers contain no anti-Russian propaganda. Coincidence or new propaganda line?

22 July 1943

H.L. [Langenn] arrived. We spent a long, melancholy evening together. This afternoon with Else Stinnes.

23 July 1943

Had lunch with H. [Langenn]. He is more cheerful. The Americans have made further progress along the south and west coasts. The news has just arrived that Palermo has been taken. The collapse of Italy, in my opinion, is only a question of a few days. What will our remaining allies and supporters do then? They certainly will not perish heroically with the rest of us.

24 July 1943

Lunch with Gailani, Steengracht, Henke [*sic*], Schwörbel, Melchers, Schlobies, etc., and a few Arabs. In the evening departure for Seichau, where I arrived at the small train station around midnight, met by Sigrid [Richthofen], beaming as usual. Trip in a horse-drawn wagon under an indescribably starry and shining sky.

25 July 1943

Spent the morning in the fields, where we looked at the harvest in progress and where the forester shot a small, pitiful fox in a wheatfield. The afternoon passed with witty conversation in the park and manor house. In the evening we overindulged with a man named Rosenberg, who is a masseur, locksmith, singer, and God knows what else. A crazy odd-ball with a pretty, but unschooled, voice. Musically, he is completely untrained. He was discovered by Max v. Schillings and now serves as masseur for Manfred and Sigrid. Renaissance patronage, for he also takes care of them, if now and then incorrectly.

26 July 1943

My birthday. I was treated with touching attention. I really have good friends. Roses at every meal and culinary delicacies from an almost forgotten era of peace. Disturbing news this morning: Mussolini has abdicated. Fascism is done for. The King has taken over the high command, Badoglio is head of the government, Guariglia, the Ambassador in Ankara, became Foreign Minister. According to Badoglio's proclamation, the war will continue. But the Fasci are being removed in Rome, and the city is flying flags. Obviously the intent is to maintain public discipline, in order to conduct peace negotiations without chaos in the background. There can be no doubt that the Fascist dream is over. According to British reports, Mussolini is supposed to have been captured while attempting to cross the German border.[34] Scorza and several other *fascisti prominenti* were also arrested.[35] M.'s decision to resign, if it was done voluntarily, was a great and noble deed. Can we summon similar courage?

27 July 1943

Returned to Berlin at the break of dawn. I found Chrustschoff[36] in the hotel. Everyone is talking about the revolution in Italy. How is this going to

34. The Fascist party Grand Council voted on 24–25 July to give the Italian king, Victor Emmanuel III, command of the armed forces. Mussolini met with the monarch and was then placed under arrest iñ the palace grounds. He was eventually transferred to a hotel in the Abruzzi mountains. A new Italian government under Marshal Pietro Badoglio, a previous chief of the supreme command, proclaimed martial law throughout the country, dissolved the Fascist party, and banned political meetings.
35. Carlo Scorza had been the Fascist party secretary since Apr. 1943. Contrary to Prüfer's information here, Scorza remained free for a while, but in August the Italian police hauled him in along with a few other Fascist officials.
36. Unidentified.

affect the situation in Germany? Our military situation appears to be very serious. If Italy lays down her arms, then the Balkans will be outflanked by the enemy, and large parts of the Balkan peninsula, e.g., Albania and the portions of Croatia and Greece occupied by Italy, will automatically fall into its hands. Hungary will not defend herself, Rumania weakly at best. *Facit*: loss of the Balkans. Consequence: the rolling up of the Russian front from the south. And given this situation we have failed to build golden bridges toward the East!

---

28 July 1943

Negotiations in the A.A. with Kranzfelder,[37] Melchers, and Padel regarding the *Nimet Allah*. Alarm at 11 a.m. during these discussions. The conversation continued in the totally inadequate cellar of the A.A. Lunch with Chr. [Chrustschoff]. Evening in the Behrenstrasse.

---

29 July 1943

Ingrid arrived from Bellin. Lunch with her, Steffen, and Ch. [Chrustschoff]. Weary conversation. Helmut arrived late in the afternoon, only to continue, this evening, to B.B. Visited the Osters. There was an alarm during the night. With Ingrid until 2 a.m. in the Adlon cellar.

---

30 July 1943

Ingrid is going to Bellin this afternoon. Parting visit with Uncle Max, who was very depressed. After many efforts lasting for days, I received permission from Steen to depart for B.B. For four days, Hamburg has been

---

37. Presumably Alfred Kranzfelder, lieutenant-commander in the German navy, inasmuch as the talks Prüfer mentioned concerned the German disposition of the ex-Khedive's yacht anchored on the Riviera.

most terribly bombed for an hour and a half on each occasion. Little is supposed to be left of the city.[38]

---

31 July 1943

Departure for B.B. at 8:23 a.m. in an overcrowded train amid terrible heat. In Halle, the train was jammed with even more refugees from Hamburg; they are in pitiful condition and tell hideous tales about the horror that occurred there. The death toll is estimated at between 40- and 70,000. Arrival around 11 p.m. in B.B., very exhausted. A. and Helmut picked me up in B. Oos.

---

38. The RAF staged six massive raids on Hamburg and its immediate suburbs from 24 July through 2 Aug. 1943. The assaults, significantly worse than those on Cologne a month before, forced a large part of Hamburg's population to seek refuge outside the city. Goebbels described the raids as "a catastrophe the extent of which simply staggers the imagination."

ten

August 1943

1 August 1943

Sunday. It is very hot. I feel weak and not well. Visit in the afternoon from Schlemann [*sic*], who has been called to Berlin in order to accommodate the Chilean diplomats in B.B.

2 August 1943

Phone call from M. R. [Rohde] in Berlin. The city is supposed to be evacuated. Only people absolutely necessary will remain. Melchers wants to have my house [in Baden-Baden] for his two sisters. Unfortunately, difficulties concerning our departure have arisen, because Schr. [Schröder] does not dare to consent on his own authority. R. [Ribbentrop], who is no longer in F. [Fuschl], has to be consulted. Munich was visited by the planes. *Hinc illae lacrimae*? Helmut [Langenn] leaves for Bellin this evening.

3 August 1943

Extremely hot day. Last evening the German Radio Network went off the air about 12:30. Once again, Hamburg has been attacked. In the afternoon, there was an air alert for two hours. Afterwards we went to the movies (a weak French mystery, *And Then There Were Six*).

---

4 August 1943

Took a walk with Olaf to Gunzenbach. He was a very good boy. The A.A. will be evacuated to Wriezen.[1]

---

5 August 1943

Orel has been abandoned. The situation in the East is now critical. I have sent, via the A.A., the Swiss Legation the questionnaires for our passports. Clärenore [Söderstrom] is in Germany and has invited A. [Anneliese] and O. [Olaf] [to Sweden]. Downtown at Stockmann's in the afternoon. Many rumors and general depression. Schlemann [*sic*], just back from Berlin, talked about the confusion that permeates the A.A. It is still uncertain where this agency will be "relocated."

---

6 August 1943

Schr. [Schröder] informed me that R. [Ribbentrop] has agreed to Rosita for the next three months. Catania has capitulated.

---

7 August 1943

Sigrid [Richthofen] has gone to Finland. Ribbentrop had a discus-

---

1. For several months previously, Allied air raids on Berlin had forced AA officials to work in concrete bunkers below the ministry buildings and in special quarters beneath the nearby Hotel Adlon. With the autumn 1943 intensification of the raids, which struck the ministerial quarter, including the foreign ministry and Ribbentrop's official residence, with deadly accuracy, the evacuation of ministry records and diplomats began. The AA transported many of its files southeast to Krummhübel, a Silesian mountain resort near the old border of Czechoslovakia. Some offices were moved as far to the southwest as Lake Constance, near the Swiss border, and Bavaria and Thuringia.

sion with the Führer and Bormann at H. Qu. [Headquarters]. Why is this publicized? Are there great decisions in the offing? Göring was in Hamburg and has conferred with Speer. Again, why is this shared with the people?[2] At the same time, there was a Cabinet meeting in Rome.[3] Sweden has blocked German seaways to Norway for both people and matériel. This is bad news for our troops in Norway and Finland; it also indicates our weakness.

8 August 1943

Our Sicilian front has been retaken. The British are comparing 5.8.43 with the tragic 8.8.18, when Hindenburg told the Kaiser in Spa that the war could no longer be won militarily. But people like Sauckel in Paris are still prattling on about victory and perseverence rather than negotiations with the enemy. Apparently, we cannot bring ourselves to do that. We are mere saber rattlers; when things are going well, as when this war began with great élan, there are no limits to our goals. Full of hubris we always believe that we can conquer the world. But as our strength declines, we have neither the wisdom nor the courage to be content and begin negotiations with the enemy, which might still lead to an honorable and beneficial way out, albeit with sacrifices.

9 August 1943

O. and A. have colds. Alarm between 1:30 and 3 a.m. Manheim [*sic*] was raided.

---

2. At the end of July 1943, Hitler had decided to place all war production under Speer's ministry, thereby curtailing the role of other agencies, including Göring's Four-Year Plan, in such matters. Hitler's deputy, Martin Bormann (as well as such party leaders as Franz Hofer, Reich governor of the Tirol-Vorarlberg), played a role in the German policy of hanging on to vassal Italy in order to keep the Allies far from the Reich and to exploit Italian manpower and economic resources.

3. This presumably refers to a conference on 6 Aug. 1943 between the two Axis foreign ministers, Ribbentrop and Bastianini, and chiefs of staff, in the frontier Italian town of Tarvisio, to discuss Italo-German relations.

10 August 1943

With A., notwithstanding her poor health, at the movies; *Flea in Her Ear*, a rather nice rustic comedy. Alarm from midnight until 2:30. The target was Nuremberg.

11 August 1943

The Swiss have our passports. In Rio I was acquitted on appeal; so were the other members of our Embassy.[4]

The Lorenz church in Nuremberg has been destroyed. When will this insanity end? A British radio announcer—obviously a German Jew—explained with pleasure that 1,500,000 kg. of explosives were dropped on Nuremberg. Nuremberg is as far from England as Leipzig and Brandenburg. These cities, in turn, are only 60 kilometers from Berlin. Draw your own conclusions! The German Radio Network has been off the air since 12:15 a.m. It is now 1:15. Berlin?

12 August 1943

Berlin was not attacked; merely a nuisance overflight. On the other hand, this morning our "guests" hit Bonn and Bochum, causing considerable damage. 34 were shot down. There was an alarm from 12 o'clock midnight to 1:30.

13 August 1943

Last night, the enemy hit Western Germany and Berlin, but without doing much damage. St.S. Kepler [*sic*] is here to commandeer B.B. What a hare-brained idea! Instead of getting as far out of the path of the British as possible, we do the opposite and risk B.B., which is totally unprotected. Telegraphed I. [Ingrid von Langenn] that she should come here to help

---

4. See OD, entry for 29 June 1943; and chap. 8, n. 36.

pack our belongings; the Wendt woman refuses or is unable to assist.[5] It is high time that we come to a decision. Guida visited us this evening. He said that the coup d'état in Italy had been carefully planned. So well planned, in fact, that on 25 July, the day of Mussolini's resignation, most of the former democratic newspapers and organizations were operational, in part under their original managers. Mussolini is supposed to be in the vicinity of Rome. The conduct of the army, which felt that it merely fought for Musso, was crucial to his downfall. He, too, feels certain about a separate peace. In this connection he also mentioned rumors of a separate German-Russian peace. *Utinam*! Rome has been bombed again.

---

14 August 1943

Conversation with Melchers and Schlemann [*sic*]. The commandeering of B.B. has apparently been postponed, because the Führer, happily, did not approve. This notwithstanding, nothing has been decided as to the future of my house; Melchers seems rather pessimistic. We have given up the Aetna massif in Sicily, and thus the fate of the island has been decided. The capitulation and subsequent occupation of Italy will not be long in coming. The same will happen in vast areas of the Balkans. At Stockmann's in the evening. Dr. and Frau Heinrich Bauer and Prof. Gailer and daughter were there as well.

---

15 August 1943

Boring Sunday morning; air alert in the morning.

---

16 August 1943

Afternoon at the movies (*Late Love* with Paula Wessely and Attila Hörbiger). Rather illogically constructed, but nevertheless a touching and well-acted show. At the Schlemann's [*sic*] in the evening. Still no decision about our trip.

---

5. "Wendt woman" is a reference to the Prüfers' maid in Berlin, who was of Slavic extraction from eastern Germany.

17 August 1943

This morning air alarm for 1-1/2 hours. More of the same at night. Dinner at the Bellevue. Sicily evacuated.

18 August 1943

Glock arrived this morning and departed in the evening. He is accompanying Gailani to Reichenhall. Confusion in Berlin. It is still uncertain whether the ministries will be evacuated. We received our Swiss visas. Schröder has found a renter for our house. Short alarm during the night.

19 August 1943

Very hot weather. I do not feel well. Brief alarm during the night. Nuisance raid.

20-31 August 1943

Preparations for our departure. I. v. L. [Langenn] is here to help A. Frequent alarms. Two bad air raids on Berlin, the most recent on 30/31/1.[6] Massive Russian offensive along the entire front. We abandoned Kharkov and Taganrog. Himmler was appointed Minister of the Interior. Frick became Protector of the Reich in Bohemia.[7] Nanny [Engelhardt] arrived on the 31st and left for Berlin on 1.9 to pick up her belongings, insofar as they are still there after the recent air raids.

---

6. This date indicates that Prüfer really wrote the entry on 1 Sept. 1943. The major attacks on the capital during the nights of 23 and 31 Aug. and 3 Sept. 1943 represented the prelude to the massive and sustained "battle of Berlin," as the British termed it, in which Allied bombers especially pounded the city from Nov. 1943 until Mar. 1944.

7. Wilhelm Frick was Reich minister of the interior since 1933 and one of Hitler's closest advisers during the NSDAP's "struggle for power" (*Kampfzeit*, the years of the Weimar Republic).

eleven

September 1943

6 September 1943

After much ado, alarms, and final dispositions, we left for Oos at 9 a.m. with much luggage and escorted by Schlemann [*sic*] and Ingrid [Langenn]. Hardly had we arrived when there was an alarm, and within minutes a large formation of "Flying Fortresses" was over us. Soon we heard rolling detonations from the south, southeast, and southwest. The attack ended around 11:30, and we soon learned that the target was Bühl, where the train tracks were destroyed. Tremendous confusion prevailed at the train station in Oos. No train connections either south or north; Mannheim experienced a bad raid last night. Finally around 12:30, a local train comprised of a few cars brought us to Rastatt. Our luggage, except for 10 handbags that we had to carry ourselves, was left behind unattended on the platform in Oos. Fortunately it was forwarded to Davos. The personnel was just as helpless in Rastatt as in Oos. We simply awaited whatever came next. The station was full of people. Finally, a local train arrived and, after many transfers, brought us to Strassburg, which had been bombed only a few hours ago. We changed trains, lugging our suitcases and helped by a few young girls from B.B. After a slow trip, we reached Basel aboard an "express train" that came from Hamburg, via Colmar and Freiburg, finally arriving around 10 p.m. We were treated very kindly by customs and then spent a long night in the Hotel Euler, only to be disturbed by an air alert which, in Switzerland, is meaningless; rolling thunder from across Germany. As we learned later, the enemy attacked Munich.

Davos, 7 September 1943

In the afternoon, we traveled on to Davos without incident and checked into the Hotel Central. The news from the Eastern front and Italy sounds very bad.

part two

The Revised Diaries, October 1942 to September 1943

twelve

October 1942

Baden-Baden, 16 October 1942[1]

After almost a three-year absence to the day, we, that is, my wife, my twelve-year-old son Olaf, and myself, stepped onto German soil. Accompanying us was the group of Germans returning home from Brazil, mostly women and children, and the last members of the German Embassy and consulates still remaining in Brazil, who were greeted ceremoniously by the civilian and military authorities in the "Römer" [town hall] in Frankfurt am Main which, until now, has not suffered any air attacks. Our transport dispersed in Frankfurt. I traveled with my family to Baden-Baden, where I am a resident.

Our trip back to Europe on the *Cuyabà*, the steamer of the Brazilian Lloyd, was not especially comfortable, but under the prevailing circumstances we had no reason whatever to complain. The ship was old and tired, so tired that once it just stopped in the middle of the ocean because the life

---

1. There are no original diaries from Oct. 1942 in the private papers of Prüfer held either by his son Olaf or by the *Politisches Archiv des Auswärtiges Amt* in Bonn. O. Prufer informed the editor in an interview on 20 Feb. 1987 that original diaries never existed for Oct. 1942 and that the following entries were a complete fabrication for the time his father claimed to have written them. They are printed here because the elder Prüfer included them in his revised version and because they allege views on German politics, diplomacy, and the persecution of the Jews that are frequently contradicted by the original diary version and by other sources.

had gone out of it. The behavior of the officers and crew was irreproachable in every regard. We all had reason to be thankful for these well-behaved seamen, even though our countries were at war. During the month-long crossing, we noticed nothing about the actions of the war.

In Lisbon we had a few days' wait, which we passed visiting and replenishing our travel provisions.

The trip from Lisbon by way of Portugal and Spain and on through Hendaye and Paris went off trouble-free. A brief stay in Biarritz, which almost reminded us of peacetime and where we had a surely expensive, but by no means scanty, wartime meal, did not exactly seem to confirm the news spread in Brazil about France being in want.

On the other hand, after our long absence, the first conversations we had during the trip with Germans from the Homeland seriously unsettled the optimistic views we held on the basis of German radio news reports picked up in Brazil, concerning the situation in Germany. On the trip through Spain, I heard for the first time about the mass deportation of Jews spoken of casually from the mouth of a German, an S.S. man to be sure. In fact, rumors about these deportations had reached us from Germany as well as from enemy sources; however, they seemed to us to be so dreadful that we held them to be "atrocity stories," or at the very least exaggerated, like so many other reports of enemy propaganda that had proved to be incorrect.[2]

The unfavorable impression increased during the rest of the trip. The gentlemen sent to meet us from the Foreign Ministry and the NSDAP spoke among themselves with such total abandon about things that sounded so incredible, that we would not have believed them had some traveler told them to us. In these conversations, "organizing," the illegal procurement of every kind of imaginable, essential commodity of everyday life, and shady deals played a paramount role. It seems that any kind of moral scruples are hardly any longer a matter of concern in Germany. Everybody procures for himself whatever is offered, how is no longer an important question.

In France, on the other hand, as was evident from the information of our fellow travelers, we paid cash—and not too badly—for whatever there was to be had, on the black market of course. I was offered wine *en passant* in Paris. It was certainly not cheap.

We also learned on this journey that the food and general supply situation at home was by far not as favorable as we had thought. But the most unsettling thing for us from the stories of the passengers was the mood of

---

2. For the reasons to suspect that Prüfer knew more in Brazil than he indicated here, see pp. xvii–xviii.

the German people, which left much to be desired. The unwavering confidence in victory, still prevailing among the Germans in Brazil, can scarcely be felt among the passengers on our train. They are not exactly pessimistic; on the contrary, they stress almost too loudly the absolute faith in the Führer and the army, only then to whisper about all sorts of misgivings, rumors, and doubts behind a hand held in front of their mouths. They seem to speak two languages, an official one intended for the public and perhaps the Gestapo, and another whispered behind closed doors and directed to a trusted circle.

So before we came to Frankfurt, we had already heard more about smuggling, profiteering, whitewashing and, unfortunately, also about persecutions and denunciations than we would ever have dreamed of in Brazil. Still, perhaps these are only exaggerated instances and the unavoidable concomitant symptoms of a war which has now lasted already three years.

In the evening I arrived in Baden-Baden with my family, happy and fortunate to be home again despite everything. We found our house still without billeting and maintained passably well.

---

17 October 1942

I have been disappointed in my hope to find at least some rest and recuperation after the strenuous journey from Rio. Today I received a telegram from the Minister [Ribbentrop], stating that I should report to him immediately on my activities. I left for Berlin the same evening, in pouring rain and in an appropriate mood.

Berlin, 18 October 1942

Already early this morning, on my arrival at the train station, I learned that Ribbentrop expected me without delay at "Feldmark," the name of his headquarters, which is located somewhere in Russia.

I had several short conferences in the Foreign Ministry with Secretary of State von Weizsäcker, the Personnel Director Schröder, and Ambassador Ritter, my predecessor in Rio, now filling the post of military adviser principally in charge of economic matters within the ministry. I lunched with him [Ritter] in the Hotel Adlon and took this opportunity to ask him about the events—totally incomprehensible to me because of my express warning—that led to the torpedoing of a number of Brazilian coastal ships in Brazilian territorial waters, and thus to war with Brazil.

For an understanding of this incident, the events that prompted my warning are described below.

On 3 August, six months after relations between Brazil and Germany were severed on 29 January, I had almost a two-hour conversation with Oswaldo Aranha, the Brazilian Foreign Minister. In this conversation, conducted by both parties in the most open and loyal manner, we discussed the developments that had led to the breaking of diplomatic relations between our countries, notwithstanding all our efforts during the last two years. Despite all the malicious and insulting diatribes directed at him from Germany, which greatly hampered my work in Brazil, I have always had the best impression of Aranha; he now held the opinion that the previous developments had for the present come to an end, but need not necessarily lead to war.[3]

When I expressed my opposing skeptical arguments, he replied that Brazil did not desire war because it considered a later resumption of our economic relations very important.[4] Perhaps he was thinking, although he had always emphasized to me that he was not anti-German, that as a democrat he probably could not give much trust to our regime, but that in the event of a change of government in Germany, Brazil wanted to keep a free hand for the future.

The Brazilian government—this is also the opinion of the president[5]— had never intended to enter the war against Germany, and would rather let the matter rest with the rupture [of diplomatic relations] as long as no acts of aggression against Brazil were to be undertaken by Germany. Especially attacks on Brazilian shipping in the coastal waters of the country, i.e., within the three-mile zone, would be perceived as such. To be sure, Brazilians found the repeated sinking of their cargo ships on the open sea, in the North American coastal areas or in the Caribbean, to be extremely painful, but they would be willing to disregard this, as they had other such losses up to now, since actually such trade, according to the laws of war, warranted German countermeasures. But it is different with Brazil's coastal shipping. Such internal trade offers Germany's enemy no immediate advantages but, on the other hand, it is of vital importance for a country which does not

---

3. Prüfer omitted here, however, his role in the Reich's propaganda attack on Aranha.

4. This account of their meeting ignores how Prüfer denied to Aranha Germany's responsibility (especially its deadly submarine attacks on Brazilian ships) for the imminent declaration of war between the two countries.

5. Getulio Vargas was president and virtual dictator of Brazil from 1932 to 1945.

have sufficient railways or roads across its tremendous expanse to deal with domestic trade and traffic. The torpedoing of such ships within the internationally recognized zone of sovereignty will, of course, be seen as an attack on Brazil itself, and would thus inevitably lead to war.

He emphasized this statement to me earnestly and emphatically, even though it was delivered orally and unofficially because a written démarche was no longer possible after the rupture of relations. For that reason I did not hesitate to telegraph Berlin immediately, which was still possible at the time. I received confirmation that my message had reached its goal and, at the time, I believed that, at least from the German point of view, the immediate cause for the outbreak of hostilities between the two countries would be avoided.[6]

Instead, on 16 and 17 August, fourteen days after the dispatch of my warning, five small Brazilian steamers were torpedoed in sight of the coast. This was the first action of its kind since the beginning of the war and had to have been viewed by me and those in the know, and above all by the Brazilian statesmen, as the answer to my efforts: a deliberate provocation designed to produce war.

The sinking of these ships claimed a considerable toll in human lives. Five days later Brazil found itself at war with Germany.

As a result, the situation of the Germans and their interests worsened disastrously, and the [Brazilian] people's feelings of hostility, heretofore unknown, erupted against everything that was German. What that meant can easily be surmised, because there lived in Brazil about 80 to 100,000 Reich citizens and approximately a million Brazilians of German descent, against whom the full hatred of the population now exploded. This hatred had been unleashed by the conduct of the German navy.[7]

How was it possible that such a provocative attack occurred. [*sic*] It seemed simply inconceivable that in the late summer of 1942, when matters in North Africa and Russia were no longer optimal, we should have thoughtlessly and eagerly sought a new enemy. Considering our generally poor evaluation of power factors abroad, it was easily imaginable, although foolish, that we did not assess the Brazilian war potential very highly. All the same, one has to admit that in this situation every law spoke against us, that we had large traditional interests in Brazil to protect, and that its entrance into the war, being the strongest power in South America,

---

6. Serious questions, however, exist about whether he sent the telegram.

7. This pro-Brazilian and anti-German account should be contrasted with Prüfer's complete absence of concern in Aug. 1942 for Germany's action against Brazil and with his belief then in an Axis triumph in the war.

would not be without effect on the rest of the countries of the Western hemisphere.

This attack, hitting five ships at almost the same time, becomes an even greater riddle when one considers that during the entire six months following the rupture of relations, German submarines had cruised off the Brazilian coast and even left unmolested the huge troop transports, the *Queen Mary*, *Queen Elizabeth*, and the *Pasteur*, ships that repeatedly docked in Rio.

The German press and likewise the radio were quiet about this daring exploit of a young submarine commander, for that is how this aggression with its serious consequence appeared to us at the time. Neither an official German explanation nor an apology was forthcoming. The damage was done and could not be repaired.

Ritter, apparently in good faith, did not have any information for me concerning this mysterious incident. He explained that he had known nothing about my warning telegram. The incident became even more incomprehensible because my dispatch fell under his jurisdiction and must have been handled in his department.

I did not have more time to concern myself with the matter during my short stay in Berlin, because I had to spend the rest of it obtaining a [diplomatic] uniform without which, typically, I would not be permitted to appear at headquarters. I had not needed such theater props in Brazil.

"Feldmark," 21 October 1942

On the evening of 19 October, I left with two younger men from the Foreign Ministry for "Feldmark," without having a precise idea where this geographical point was located. We only learned that it was someplace in the Ukraine.

Because of the danger of partisans we traveled in a military furlough train, heavily guarded from the Polish border onward. Since mine attacks occurred repeatedly, the locomotive was preceded by two carloads of sand. After a short stay in Warsaw we arrived on the 21st, at about three o'clock in the morning, at Berdichev in the Ukraine. It was cold and very dark. After some highly uncomfortable delay in the empty and inhospitable station, the convoy, made up of trucks and passenger cars, was ready to depart, supposedly taking us to headquarters. We traveled under a heavy military escort. The trip was forbidden for single vehicles, because attacks were hardly rare.

The journey, lasting about two hours, took us slowly past deserted villages, over endless country roads, through the forests, and across open land until, after passing several barbed wire barriers, we finally stopped in the early dawn in front of a long one-story building, the guest house of "Feldmark."

During the day I had the opportunity to look around "Feldmark," the living quarters of the Reich [Foreign] Minister and his staff. "Feldmark," a part of general headquarters, was spread over a wide area, protected by the military. Every department that belonged here, and that, of course, included Ribbentrop's, was quartered several kilometers from the other departments. Each consisted of new barracks and buildings that were still there from an earlier time. The staff of the Foreign Minister had settled in a former Russian military training camp, whose various living quarters had been supplemented by wooden barracks. The Minister himself lived in the most stately of these houses, together with his closest aides. A wide parklike area stretched out from these buildings with groups of trees lining an open meadow, suggesting that this was formerly the estate of a noble family during the czarist period. Further away, but still within the restricted barbed wire compound, a few pathetic villages were located near a small stream. The closest larger city was [word missing].

All of the houses, even that of the Minister, were makeshift and furnished without luxuries. Interestingly enough, we newcomers were warned that it was not advisable to go unarmed alone on extended walks because the area was in no way secure from partisans. The front was hundreds of kilometers away, thus making this warning appear even more striking. This did not exactly suggest that we had been successful in pacifying the country whose liberators we claimed to be.

What I saw this morning of the Ukrainian peasantry on a tour in the immediate vicinity of "Feldmark" did not convey a warlike impression, although it was not particularly friendly, either. This impression notwithstanding, the partisans, who are dropped by plane and parachute, find willing support from the Ukrainian population.

"Feldmark," 22 October 1942

The Minister did not feel well and could not see me. Thus I spent the day talking with members of the staff and the doctor who is treating Ribbentrop. Spirits here, too, are low, and the atmosphere does not suggest victory. All are overworked, tired, and worried. Work is totally irregular, that is, not bound by any time frame, and it consists mostly of waiting. Nonetheless it is exhausting, perhaps precisely because of the idleness. Most of the time the men on the staff and the great number of secretaries sit and stand around, gossip and intrigue, or they are suddenly engaged in the most hectic activity, brought about by some sort of sudden unforeseen "higher directive." There does not seem to be a regular work schedule.

"Feldmark," 23 October 1942

Today I finally had a *tête-à-tête* with Ribbentrop at lunch, i.e., I ate and he looked on. He is still not well, looks very tired, and has aged considerably in the three years that I have not seen him. He had little to say about my report concerning the situation and my activities in Brazil. It did not particularly seem to interest him. In contrast to his behavior in the past, he was generally rather quiet, did not pontificate as before, and appeared to be absent-minded.

I naturally brought the conversation around to the causes of the outbreak of war and my telegram, which seems to have disappeared in such a puzzling manner. Ribbentrop listened patiently to my story and finally explained, just like Ritter, that he did not know anything about this telegram. I did not have the impression that he was lying. He even advised me to make further inquiries, which seemed to prove his good faith. Apparently the matter did not seem to interest him further, since the damage could not be undone. He was probably used to such slip-ups within the operation of his staff. In leaving, my request for a several-week furlough was granted. My wish to retire was flatly rejected because of the necessity of retaining all personnel in these times.

It goes without saying that I could not leave the question about the outbreak of the war between Brazil and Germany unanswered. Therefore, in the afternoon I visited the Minister's cabinet chief, Baron von Steengracht, and learned to my astonishment that he indeed remembered the telegram in question. Searching together in a folder of old files, we quickly located the telegram, which, unbelievably, had not been acted upon. [As the initials on the original revealed] it had passed all the appropriate offices of the Foreign Ministry, including those of the Minister and Ritter, only then to disappear into the aforementioned folder. Since the telegram contained other insignificant messages in addition to the warning about torpedoing Brazilian ships, the only important item it contained was apparently overlooked. Whether this was actually an oversight or perhaps the malicious intent of

some saboteur will probably never be known. In any event, careful handling in the central office [responsible] for German foreign policy[8] of an
ambassador's telegram could have avoided a declaration of war against the
German people, if not in the long run, then at least for the time being.

Berlin, 25 October 1942

I arrived back in Berlin this morning. The only interesting experience
on the return from "Feldmark" was meeting General von Niedermeyer
[*sic*], a well-known geographer, geopolitician, and Russian expert since his
campaigns in Afghanistan in the first World War.[9] Niedermeyer [*sic*],
whom I have known for years, boarded the train with two young officers
somewhere in the Ukraine and joined me for lunch. As he explained, he is
entrusted with raising and leading a Caucasian anti-Bolshevist troop of
division strength, which will be trained in the region of Poltava. He spoke
very favorably of these people. Particularly the Mohammedans among
them he considered to be extraordinary men, patriots, and soldiers. On the
other hand, he talked disparagingly—rightfully so—of our Russian policies in general,[10] and especially about Alfred Rosenberg's confused Eastern
Ministry, and above all of the measures taken by the Gauleiters [Nazi party
district leaders] working in the East, who have thoroughly muddled
things.[11] Instead of trying to make friends with the population of occupied
regions, especially in the Ukraine, they carry out an unworkable settlement
policy, entailing cruel and embittering expulsions of the indigenous popu-

---

8. The AA's headquarters in the Wilhelmstrasse in Berlin.

9. Oskar von Niedermayer had led a German expedition to Persia and Afghanistan in 1915
and 1916, but failed to persuade them to join the Reich and its allies. He had also served in
Russia from 1922 to 1931 as an adviser to the German government for military and armaments questions. Having taught at the University of Berlin after 1933, he entered the German
army during World War II and became commander of the 162d infantry division in Russia,
which consisted of foreign and especially Turkic legionnaires.

10. It is unclear whether Niedermayer voiced such criticism to Prüfer, although the general
was widely considered pro-Soviet. Prüfer, by the time he wrote this in 1945–46, probably
possessed knowledge of Niedermayer's removal from his post in May 1944 and subsequent
trial for remarks opposing German policy in Russia. As Prüfer wrote this, Niedermayer was in
a Russian prison, where he died in 1948.

11. Hitler had appointed Rosenberg minister for the occupied eastern territories in July
1941, as the German armies overran vast chunks of Soviet land. The *Ostministerium*, a civilian administration, differed little from the SS in its draconian policy towards the Jews—
ghettoization and then extermination. Similarly, Rosenberg supported the brutal Germaniza-

lation in exchange for a senseless colonization of small groups of unsuitable and helpless German peasants in its place. According to Niedermeyer [*sic*], the result of such policies is a general disappointment and hostility of the Ukrainians, who were originally favorably disposed toward us. In addition there is disharmony and rivalry between the individual German dictators, who behave in their district like petty tyrants and who are feuding with each other to the detriment of the resident population. The idiotic experiments carried out by the civilian government, devoid of any knowledge as to the local situation, have destroyed all hopes among the anti-Bolshevist national elements, hopes that had arisen following the penetration of the [German] army with its generally correct behavior. Only on account of these factors can the increasingly more dangerous activities of ubiquitous partisans behind the German front be understood. In the Ukraine, people have lost faith in our claim that we are bringing them independence and liberation from Bolshevist methods of oppression. If one has to be ruled by such methods, so say the Ukrainians and the Russians, then better to be tyrannized by one's own commissars than by foreign ones.

I fear that Niedermeyer [*sic*] is right, for even in "Feldmark" I heard very similar views expressed among Ribbentrop's staff members. We condemn the Bolshevist regime and know nothing better to replace it with.[12]

Here in Berlin I again had discussions with Weizsäcker and, more importantly, with Ritter. It goes without saying that I told the latter about the discovery of my telegram from Rio concerning the conversation with Oswaldo Aranha. He now dimly remembered this document, and laid the blame for the tragic "oversight" onto the fact mentioned above: that the telegram had also contained other information in addition to the only really important one; thus the latter had been "overlooked" among these communications. This does not sound very plausible. In any event, it was a case of gross negligence which has cost us dearly.

---

tion of the subject peoples of Russia, especially in the Baltic lands. His opposition to such subordinates as Erich Koch, the Nazi gauleiter of East Prussia and Reich commissioner for the Ukraine, against establishing bloody slave-states remained ineffective because it disagreed with the ultimate objectives of Nazi rule in the East: the enslavement and murder of the allegedly "inferior" Slavs.

12. But in his original diaries, Prüfer defended German policy against the Soviet Union and Communism; see entry for 26 Mar. 1943.

Berlin, 27 October 1942

Today my former colleague, Legation Counselor M. [Melchers], had lunch with me. He was in a most depressed and pessimistic mood. For the most part, work in the Foreign Ministry is devoid of substance. No one knows for sure what is actually going on. The information from the Minister's staff and from headquarters is totally insufficient. Apparently from time to time something like foreign policy is discussed between the Führer and the Minister, but the Foreign Ministry is informed only according to the needs and whims of the lords. The [Reich minister's personal] "staff" shares with the Ministry, still nominally responsible for the conduct of foreign affairs, only what it considers important, but in Berlin one learns of important matters rarely and belatedly, if at all.

In the capital, on the other hand, there is an ongoing and unpleasant paper war between the ministries, to the extent to which they are still located there; a similar situation also pertains between the various divisions of the Foreign Ministry, where people battle over questions of jurisdiction and prerogative, or whose offices work in isolation, each on its own, as if they were behind the watertight bulkheads on a sinking ship.

It is particularly bad at his [Melcher's] desk, Middle Eastern affairs, where in addition to and independent of him, two Ministers [Grobba and Ettel, who held this rank, *Gesandter,* in the AA] directly responsible to the [Reich Foreign] Minister are "working," each for himself, and in bitter enmity toward each other. In addition to this, there is a division, created by the Foreign Minister out of the clear blue sky, which acts like a dilettante debating club and, to prove its justification for existence, involves itself in anything and everything; thus it does nothing other than be obstructive.[13] The [division] members prattle on in endless meetings, leading only to paper results that waste precious time.

Instead of exploiting the political situation in the Middle East, still reasonably favorable for us, and instead of strengthening elements friendly to Germany by giving clear explanations as to our policies toward these countries, these people shy away from making their own intentions clear because of consideration for some kind of promises Hitler made to Mussolini, promises which ought to be rejected or revised since they are no longer in accord with current events.[14] All urging for action at headquarters leads to

---

13. A reference presumably to the AA's Abt. Deutschland; see p. xiv.

14. The "promises" refers to Hitler's notorious wartime disinterest in the Middle East and Mediterranean regions, a result of his obsession with conquering Europe and Russia and his wish not to alienate Germany's Axis ally, Italy, which held imperialist ambitions in the area.

nothing. All suggestions are protracted and watered down. Above all, noth-ing is done to put a stop once and for all to the mutual petty jealousies of the Orientals [Husayni and Gailani] currently in Berlin. The intrigues of these Orientals have been passed on to their German caretakers [Ettel and Grobba], and thus any common political policy has been completely lost.

   The picture that my colleague drew for me was truly terrible. I left in the evening for Baden-Baden with a heavy heart.

thirteen

November 1942

Berlin, 11 November 1942

I returned to Berlin today. The long-awaited vacation went by all too quickly. Unfortunately it was nowhere near as enjoyable as I had imagined.

Getting our house, unoccupied for four years, somewhat refurbished required unusual efforts on the part of my wife. All of us had underestimated the technical difficulties which make the smallest structural or manual changes difficult in these times. All building materials are lacking, and above all [there are no] workers; the few remaining specialists are old and in such a bad mood because of overwork and never-ending frustrations, that working with them is not always a pleasure. All the same, it is astonishing that despite these difficulties, houses can still be made livable.

During my stay in Baden-Baden I was visited by Professor L. [Littmann], an old friend from Tübingen. Although this "great period" has also brought him much worry and concern, he is still full of cheerful stories and anecdotes that he tells very well in a loud voice, unconcerned about who is listening, even when these anecdotes cannot always be judged as politically in line with today's Germany. In Southern Germany one is essentially more free and courageous in voicing opinions than in Berlin. Even if people do not often dare to complain openly, they make no secret of their feelings in trusted company. Most people do not seem to have friendly feelings towards the ruling system. There is absolutely no talk of enthusiasm [for the government], but also no open revolt either, which would indeed be completely hopeless. The general view is that we have unfortunately said A and now must also say B. We cannot go back, because on the home front all resistance would shatter in the face of terror and because the external enemy relentlessly seems to desire the destruction not only of Hitler, but of everything German. If England and America would give the German people a chance to extricate themselves from this dilemma with acceptable losses, it would all be over for the Nazi regime. But unfortunately from the other side we only hear threats and pronouncements about the terrible future in store for us. How could we set up a domestic front against Nazism under such conditions? People tell themselves that it is better to stick it out with Hitler, as long as there may still be a prospect for a reasonably favorable end to the war, rather than lose the war by rebelling against him and capitulate, only then to be handed over defenselessly to merciless destruction by the spiteful Allies. Thus enemy propaganda works right in tandem with that of Goebbels, who preaches resistance to the last man.[1]

The last two days of my vacation in Baden-Baden were particularly ruined by the news from the new front in French North Africa. It seems that reconnaissance and the intelligence service of the Axis powers have totally collapsed, otherwise the surprise attack of the English and Americans in Morocco and Algeria would not have been possible in so many places at one time. In any case, the result is a bad situation for the already hard-pressed Rommel, and a further weakening of Italian strategic and moral positions.

Today we invaded previously unoccupied Southern France, in order to take over the protection of the coasts. It is also planned to occupy Corsica before the Allies do. They have achieved their first great victory, and our French policy has collapsed decisively.

The mood here in Berlin seems to be a shade more pessimistic than in Baden-Baden, although this is not meant to imply that it was reasonably good there, either. Particularly noticeable here is the edginess of the people and the impoliteness, even rudeness, in the way they behave towards one another. A lack of patience and friendliness is especially noticeable among the personnel in restaurants and public facilities. The tone in the hotel where I was [*sic*] temporarily lodged defies description, it was so vulgar and odious. Although the prices are very high, the guests are treated by the waiters as if they were beggars. Only the black marketeer is well-served, the one who comes to the table with countless boxes, cans, and packages full of

---

1. For an explanation regarding Prüfer's deception here, see p. xii, n. 15.

rare foodstuffs. The waiter hopes to receive a few crumbs from this illicit booty, or at least he counts on considerable hush money.

Again we are on the surest road to disaster because of internal decay, brought on by hoarders, black marketeers, and swindlers.[2]

This evening I was visited by an acquaintance from the Rhineland, who described the same gloomy conditions and popular attitudes that I have observed here. The background there is more Catholic. The population is justifiably offended by the persecution of the Church, which does not play such a large role here. National Socialist excesses against the clergy only upset a small minority in this predominantly Protestant part of Germany, which is not so much a church-going area anyway. This is especially so because many pastors have lost all standing in matters of faith resulting from their deals with the Nazis or their opportunism. People are not so ready to grant to those called to preach the gospel permission to compromise, a matter that is excusable in the case of laymen.

Berlin, 13 November 1942

Today, for reasons unknown to me, I was invited to a meeting with Undersecretary Woermann, where one of the many superfluous discussions took place. These meetings have as little influence on the course of events as I have on their results.

The theme of the conversation was the so-called "Arab training division," whose existence I did not even know about until then. These troops, consisting of only three companies and made up of deserters from the Maghreb, Iraq, and other Arab countries, have mysteriously been sent to the foothills of the Caucasus, from where they apparently are supposed to reach Mesopotamia via Persia. Just how one expects to execute this adventurous plan, even the instigators do not seem to know, because for the present the Russians are still in the Caucasus and Persia, and the English in Mesopotamia.

One can scarcely drive the enemy out of there with three companies of Arab deserters. For the time being these people are hanging around idly and, of course, are unhappy in this country alien and hostile to them; they have—I am tempted to say wishfully—no hope of ever reaching their destination. What are these few hundred soldiers, barely trained, reluctant, and

---

2. See chap. 1, n. 7.

half-coerced, supposed to do in Iraq? A German General [Felmy], who fell into disgrace on another occasion, probably without [it being] his fault, now commands this unit.[3] A Minister [Grobba] in the Foreign Ministry has to deal with this questionable affair officially; the Minister is related to the General; both find this to be an unpromising sphere of activity.

Of course the Minister has an adversary and competitor [Ettel] in the Foreign Ministry who does everything possible to make this already unproductive activity completely ineffective. And so there emerges a pretty picture of wartime collegiate and patriotic cooperation.

The discussion naturally came to naught in the midst of jealous quarreling and mutual accusations.

Berlin, 14 November 1942

The news from the Mediterranean region sounds more and more threatening. Following the disaster of El Alamein, we are in full retreat in North Africa. Tobruk has been evacuated. Derna is to be the next assembling point—for how long? There are only very weak forces in Tunisia.

The Allies took Morocco and Algeria almost without effort. How was that possible? A member of our Lisbon Legation [Weber] told me that a warning about American intentions in North Africa was sent from there. The Consulate in Casablanca is also supposed to have sent a warning. No one seems to know why these alerts were not acted upon so that countermeasures could be taken in good time. What did the apparently so reliable and omniscient counter-intelligence of Herr Canaris do? Was it sleeping or. . . ?[4]

The Italian fleet was scarcely deployed because it allegedly has no fuel. I can only ask, why does it not have fuel in the face of this enormous threat? That is indeed a planning error of the worst sort. If we no longer have the most important raw materials for the most important operations, then this is an especially catastrophic symptom of our weakness, and there is nothing left for us other than to liquidate the entire war, regardless of the cost

---

3. This presumably refers to the participation of a special German military mission (*Sonderstabes F*), led by Felmy, in the failed German attempt of 1941 to seize Iraq, headed by its pro-German Prime Minister Gailani, from the British.

4. Here Prüfer betrayed the lack of authenticity of his revised diaries by claiming knowledge of Canaris's traitorous activity at a time when it was unkown even to the German police.

involved. Or are we perhaps, again, underestimating the significance of the Mediterranean as we did in the first World War?

Berlin, 17 November 1942

Today I received a small package of apples from friends in the country. This was a wonderful gift in this city where there are no fruits. Why the supply of fruits is so bad is another of the many difficult things to understand. Fruits are spoiling in Southern Germany because they cannot be shipped. The transportation difficulties cannot possibly be the only reason for the poor fruit supply. Just as in the case of alcoholic beverages, particularly wine, people have the impression that much is being diverted to the black market, despite threatened punishments.

In the Foreign Ministry today the "important" question about medals was a topic for long discussion. Even I was asked to make suggestions. Because the worth and moral justification for decorations seems to me to be rather doubtful, especially since after three years of war medals have lost nearly all meaning, it is not a question of who receives a medal, but rather who is refused one. As far as I am concerned, whoever is made happy by these metal trinkets should receive one. There was a lot of disgusting haggling about this business.

I had lunch at Weizsäcker's with the Italian Ambassador Alfieri, Woermann, and some gentlemen from the German and Italian Foreign Services. The talk was mainly about the situation in North Africa and Italian interests there. We are at the mercy of Mussolini, to whom Hitler seems to have granted the decisions about everything that touches the Near East. The Italians are very stubborn and make no concessions whatever to the Arabs, although they have, to all intents and purposes, lost North Africa. We do not dare to act energetically against them, and consequently we are losing face with our Arab friends in the process.

During this affair I also had a conversation with a functionary of the broadcasting division in the Foreign Ministry, a new man from Ribbentrop's camp. My impression of conditions even in this area were quite unfavorable. Here, too, disputes concerning jurisdiction, favoritism, and jealousy reign rampantly. In discussions regarding the personal merits or demerits of a broadcaster, whatever of substance he has to say receives little attention. A dangerous dilettantism results. This man, who should be giving instructions to the radio division, does not have any more understanding than an ordinary newspaper reader of the area of competency we touched on in our discussion.

Berlin, 18 November 1942

Today, for the first time since my return, I was in a famous Berlin restaurant. *Quae mutatio rerum*! One sees almost only black marketeers, who know how to use all sorts of tricks and bartering in order to gain small advantages with the manager and staff. The normal, inexperienced guest, not knowing all these maneuvers, and not understanding how to make himself popular, is relegated to the sparse food and drink accorded him by food ration cards, that is, if he is seated at all, rather than being turned away at the door because of the apparent or real overcrowding in the restaurant. I had the dubious fortune of being invited by a habitué of the establishment, and the meal was accordingly almost like in peacetime.

Berlin, 19 November 1942

I had a long conversation with Gauleiter Bohle, the head of the Foreign Organization [AO].[5] He spoke in great detail about the case of Rudolf Hess and the role he [Bohle] had played in this affair. It almost brought him to the end of his career, if not the end of his life. He said—and I believe truthfully—that Hess, when he fled to England, had acted completely on his own initiative without the knowledge of Hitler and the ruling circle of the N.S.D.A.P. He probably honestly believed that he was going to be able to initiate a separate peace with England because of his relationship to the British, or rather Scottish, nobility.[6] Hess was always opposed to the war with Great Britain and had been an advocate for a general political compromise with this country. For this reason, he had always opposed Ribbentrop. He did not tell the Führer anything about his move in order to be secure against any meddling by the Foreign Minister. Hess hoped that he could bring back an offer of peace to Hitler, who basically had always tried to achieve an understanding with England.[7]

5. On Bohle and the AO, see chap. 1, n. 29.

6. A reference to the intention of Hess, Hitler's deputy leader, to contact the Duke of Hamilton as his intermediary with the British government; contrary to the implication in Prüfer's account, Hess had no "relationship" of substance with the Duke (nor with other Scottish nobility), but had only met him briefly at the 1936 Berlin Olympics. Bohle told Allied interrogators after the war essentially what he had said to Prüfer; he also said he believed Hitler had known of Hess's plan.

7. A view that is no longer accepted by scholars, several of whom have shown that Hitler's armaments program was aimed at conquering England even before the Anglo-German naval agreement of 1935.

Bohle's own role was that of a handyman, who had not known what purpose the work demanded of him would serve. Hess, his immediate superior, had requested him to translate a completed memorandum into perfect English. This memorandum contained the political situation Hess wanted to suggest to his Scottish friends, as Bohle only learned later. He, Bohle, did not hesitate to carry out the directive of his boss, because he, of course, did not know how the memorandum would be used, especially since it contained Rudolph Hess's thoughts and views regarding German [*sic*] relations with the Third Reich, views that were already known to him [Bohle]. Apart from all that, Hess was the deputy of the Führer, without whose knowledge and consent, he [Bohle] had to assume, that the document could not have been written.

When he then had to convince himself of the opposite, he was not spared some unpleasant hours. He was questioned personally by the Führer, and only after lengthy interrogation had Hitler understood that Bohle acted in good faith.

I have known that Hess maintained close relations with the Scottish nobility since 1938. A South German doctor, who ran a sanitorium in the Allgäu and who was Hess's friend, had already told me at that time that Hess took great pains to improve Germany's relationship with England, and that he himself had undertaken many trips to England under instructions [from Hess] to act as a mediator. This doctor is supposed to have been arrested temporarily after Hess's landing in Scotland. I do not know his fate.

Berlin, 21 November 1942

The squabble in the Oriental section of the Foreign Ministry between the two Ministers [Grobba and Ettel], commissioned by Ribbentrop to handle the troops in exile [Gailani and the Mufti], is taking on grotesque proportions. They are accusing each other of sabotage, even treason in *optima forma*. And all that only because of the personal, petty jealousies and vanities of the Arab leaders which have rubbed off onto the ones administering them. A doctor visiting me today [Schrumpf], an adventurous figure himself who typically works for the Abwehr in Oriental matters in the Balkans, maintains that one of the Ministers [Grobba] is suffering from *dementia paralytica progressiva*. One can tell that from his pupil reflexes. In addition, he shows clear symptoms of megalomania and paranoia. If this diagnosis, which seems to me to be a little daring, were correct, it would not be particularly comforting to know that such people are occupying politically important posts with us.

Every layman can see and feel that the other Minister [Ettel] is a manic-depressive psychopath. In such circumstances it is not astonishing that we are losing one position after the other in the Orient.

I had lunch at Baron O.'s [Oppenheim]. Despite his eighty-two years and, although formerly a famous gourmet, who is now terribly emaciated, he is extremely interested in political questions, particularly those having to do with the Orient, his old sphere of activity. Amazingly, the Nazis have left him, half-Jewish as he is, unscathed. He is probably too old for them and therefore seems safe. This remarkable man has a bad heart condition, yet smokes and drinks, and even with all that keeps intensively busy with his Oriental work. In addition, he has continual money worries and, of course, suffers psychologically under the oppression of the regime without talking much about it.[8]

I also saw again an old acquaintance from Tiflis, a half-Russian [Tania], whose father came from the Baltic. She is here on her way to Norway, where she will be a nurse. She experienced the expulsion of the Germans from Persia and told me how bad it was for all of them there, and how feebly the Embassy, beforehand so "staunchly" National Socialist, defended the Germans when the situation became serious. The Minister [Ettel] left the country without concerning himself for the Germans, mostly women, who were badly mistreated and plundered by the Bolshevists and who were fleeing into Turkey. For the most part, the German men were sent from Persian to Indian concentration camps. The "neutral" Persian government capitulated miserably under the pressure of the Allies. Perhaps we will finally learn from this example what such political friendships are worth, particularly in the Orient. Unfortunately in the East, more than in any other place, only power counts in political matters.

I spent the evening with an officer's family in the circle of old acquaintances from the first World War.[9] The conversation turned almost completely on food and other essentials and how one can "organize"—that is the catchword—eggs, butter, meat, and other hard-to-get items, legally or illegally. All feeling for the general suffering pales in the face of personal worries. The Nazi slogan, "The general welfare comes before the private welfare," no longer has any value, certainly not for the well-off. Everyone only thinks about and looks after himself.

---

8. There is no evidence that Oppenheim endured "oppression" from the Nazis because of his background. He had converted from Judaism to Christianity long before World War I. Prüfer presumably wished in this passage to leave the impression for the reader that he was sympathetic to Jews.

9. Langenn and Tiller.

In these conversations there erupted repeatedly the hatred toward the regime which had promised so much and has delivered so little.

The discussion also came around to the Jewish question. It appears that it has finally come hereabouts to grave Jewish persecutions, to the veritable extermination of the Jews. They are all said to have been rounded up and carried off to the East, where they are supposed to have been exterminated—men, women, and children—by gas or machine guns. If these stories really correspond to the facts, only hatred can result from this, which will never die and will cause us unspeakable harm.

My sources confirm that all this is true. The fact is that one seldom sees Jews on the streets.[10] They are identified by a star on a yellow armband. They all look careworn and are badly clothed.

The Jews, who traditionally were not seen in aristocratic officers' circles, are actually popular today in these groups because of a certain chivalrous reaction resulting from the injustice that has been perpetrated against them. Everyone speaks of them with the greatest sympathy. Even here Hitler has achieved the opposite of what he intended.

Berlin, 23 November 1942

A reunion with an old Turkish friend [Habib Edib] brought me further disappointments. On the basis of reports from our Embassy in Ankara, the atmosphere regarding the current and future position of Turkey is very optimistic in the Foreign Ministry. The conversation with my friend, who has always been a politician well-disposed toward us, has completely destroyed this optimism, which had almost infected me as well. Ismet Inönü, so he asserted, is very careful and does not want a war. But he is completely convinced of the inevitability of our eventual defeat. Therefore no one can know how Turkey will react to the increasing pressure of the Allies. If the Allies make further progress in North Africa and should hold up to the Turks the nightmare of losing the straits, it would be very uncertain how Ismet and his cabinet would react. The country is terribly poor, and very bad inflation reigns. The upkeep of the army, already mobilized for a long time, exceeds the entire military budget, a situation which cannot last long

---

10. Contrast this entry, with its equivocal passage sympathetic to the Jews and written by Prüfer in 1945–46, with his original diary entry for 22 Nov. 1942, in which he admitted to knowing and believing the information about the mass murders and worried only about their effect on foreign opinion against Germany. See also pp. xvi–xviii.

if political advantages do not appear on the horizon, advantages that could only be attained by the deployment of the army.

In many cases German policies are very undiplomatic, particularly in the economic sphere, where well-intentioned, but politically inexperienced, people are dabbling around. The embassy counselor [Jenke] was perhaps a good businessman, but has hardly any idea as to general political conditions and interrelationships, and above all, he knows nothing of diplomatic methods and customs, just like his brother-in-law, Ribbentrop. But in Turkey, despite all modernization and democratization of the state, one is basically still very conservative and bound to tradition.

The ambassador [Papen] enjoys only limited confidence, because he makes promises too lightly and liberally. His degree of influence in Berlin, and therefore the success of his optimistic promises, are not entirely in accord. Papen talks far too much anyway. Since Ribbentrop does not like Papen at all, as is commonly known, it is clear that he can accomplish little in Berlin.

For the first time since my return from Brazil, I went to a movie during the afternoon, where the Bismarck film, *The Resignation*, with Emil Jannings as the imperial chancellor, was playing. Although it was a workday afternoon, the theater was overflowing with movie-goers or customers, just as in peacetime. The same holds true for all theaters, concerts, and amusement centers. As often as possible, everyone wishes to escape from the grim reality of the war atmosphere into the beautiful illusion of the former peaceful life.

Berlin, 24 November 1942

A hopelessly dreary meeting of approximately thirty people, unknown to me for the most part, about the type and goal of our foreign propaganda. I do not know why I was invited to this drivel, which rightfully took place in the infamous Information Division of the Foreign Ministry, one of the most recent divisions Ribbentrop created helter-skelter during the war. The chairman was Undersecretary L. [Luther], a man who perhaps comprehended his former sphere of work, municipal construction and real estate; but he does not understand anything about foreign countries and propaganda methods used there.

The result of the meeting, lasting several hours, was exactly zero. I would be embarrassed if I were supposed to say what these people were actually talking about. It was a *soviet* of the worst sort, but without a Stalin. Every one of the participants, mostly still young, felt duty-bound to say something, thus believing to have proven that he was completely justified in being freed from service at the front. Words, words, words!

The Bismarck film was technically very well made and shows a clear bias against William II and the camarilla surrounding him, without emphasizing a clear anti-monarchist view. The emperor is only incidentally and personally an inadequate and unsympathetic figure. In appearance this enactment of William II was not similar to Ribbentrop, but surely in character and speech there was a powerful resemblance.

After the movie I had dinner in a restaurant on the Kurfürstendamm, where I was often a guest in peacetime. This formerly very elegant restaurant is terribly run-down. The waiters still look the best. The poor guests unpack sandwiches and apples from paper bags, because the food served is entirely insufficient. When I wanted to leave the restaurant, the manager recognized me, and immediately began to sing a pathetic lament about the situation in general and his in particular. I tried, not with much success I believe, to give him courage and told him that the crew of a ship in danger cannot complain to each other, but as long as there is a little hope, must work together to deflect the danger. Complaining would only hasten the sinking. If the man told such things to all of his guests—he only knows me by appearance—then our propaganda and its successes are in a bad way. I fear that tenacity and optimism and, let us be candid, moral courage in adversity, are not the virtues of our bourgeois middle class. We are also more materialistic than we ourselves and others want to believe. The unceasing talk about food is simply unpleasant and completely undignified, particularly in the mouths of the affluent and well-educated. Precisely these classes should take pains to endure their deprivations, which are still bearable, with more propriety.

The women exhibit heroism and greatness to a much greater degree than the men. Life today for them is without question exceedingly difficult because, apart from deprivations, they still have to bear the daily trials and humiliations of shopping and the difficult housework, mostly without help. A woman who today remains calm and confident is in truth a silent heroine. And it seems to me that there are a lot of them. That was different in the last war.

Berlin, 25 November 1942

Frightening news from the Eastern front. The Russians are attacking everywhere and have done us severe damage southwest of Stalingrad. Everywhere there are rumors, as people are whispering to each other that more than 100,000 men in and around Stalingrad are supposed to be surrounded. The situation is nearly hopeless. In addition, one says that a rescue of these troops would have been possible if the Führer had not insisted on keeping Stalingrad at any price for purely prestigious reasons.[11]

In Turkey the influence of Tewfik Rüshdi, always an enemy of ours, is becoming noticeable.

Berlin, 27 November 1942

There is no longer an unoccupied zone in France. We have taken Toulon, but Dakar is lost. Thus the shortest route from the United States to Africa is open.

All these Job-like news stories are barely noticed by the broad masses. There is nothing unfamiliar about such news, and people avoid open discussion of any kind, because such could be interpreted as defeatism. "The enemy is listening," the internal enemy, the Gestapo. Moreover, no one knows exactly what the general situation is like, even in the highest positions of the Foreign Ministry. One always hears something only in pieces, and even then never anything coherent or complete on which one could build a fairly accurate judgment. Everything is rumor, gossip, suggestion, and tittle-tattle in the halls. And that in the highest circles of authority, where foreign policy for the great German Reich is supposed to be made!

Berlin, 30 November 1942

Scandal in the Foreign Ministry. Legation Counselor Sch. [Scheliha], the nephew of my old boss, the late Minister M. [H. v. Miquel], has been found guilty of espionage favoring an Eastern power. Whatever one

---

11. Here Prüfer intended after the war to foster the view of Germans as being anti-Hitler and victims of Nazism. His original entry for 25 Nov. 1942 did not mention Hitler. Nothing in Prüfer's original diaries after the battle indicated that the defeat at Stalingrad lessened his positive attitude towards Hitler. Contrary to his claim that Germans were already critical of Hitler in Nov. 1942, secret police and SS reports on public opinion in the Reich barely mentioned Stalingrad or Hitler. One report even stressed that in contrast to the battles in Africa, "the events on the Eastern front have stepped significantly into the background of general interest."

wants to think about the regime, what Sch. did is treason and a grave disgrace for all members of the Foreign Ministry. Naturally this is grist for the mills of the Minister [Ribbentrop], who mistrusts us anyway. In Japan probably the whole caste of diplomats would commit hara-kari if one of them had done something similar.

The only comforting thing in the case of Sch. is that the man, according to his ancestry, is not a pure German. He has much more Slavic blood. Therefore perhaps he became a traitor not solely for the money.

In the highest places one is supposed to have nearly written off North Africa. Then Hannibal would be standing *ante portas*. Nevertheless, in the Orient we continue making every concession to the Italians, and we are squabbling with them and among ourselves about Arab policies.

fourteen

December 1942

Berlin, 5 December 1942

I found a house in Dahlem. It was occupied until now by a division head of the Gestapo, Dr. Best, who has gone to Copenhagen as our Reich commissioner. I knew Best, one of the most influential men in Himmler's Gestapo, because of a highly unpleasant affair in the Foreign Ministry that took place in the fall of 1937. The final details are still obscure.

Ribbentrop had become Foreign Minister at the beginning of the same year,[1] [and] Papen, who had not liked Ribbentrop from an earlier time, was minister in Vienna. The mutual animosity between these two men, although not openly acknowledged, is likely to date back to an old personal conflict, in which Ribbentrop's membership in an exclusive club was rejected when Papen was its president. Ribbentrop never forgives such small insults that may injure his excessive personal vanity. In any event—notorious among those in the know—Papen and Ribbentrop did not like each other at all.[2] In passing it should be noted that, in my opinion, Ribbentrop is incapable of love or friendship. Either people are immaterial to him,

---

1. This was incorrect; Hitler appointed Ribbentrop as minister on 4 Feb. 1938.
2. Prüfer's information was faulty regarding the cause of the enmity. Papen and Ribbentrop disliked each other for a much more sinister reason: their competition for Hitler's favor. Antagonism between them dated from their mutual jealousies as Hitler relied after 1933 for advice in foreign policy on Ribbentrop and ignored Papen and other conservatives.

living entities outside the sphere of his ever egocentric character, or they are hated enemies, whom he tries to destroy because they actually stand, or could stand, in his way.

If Ribbentroop nonetheless overly hid his resentments from Papen, it probably was because he knew that Papen was always certain of the Führer's backing. Notwithstanding Papen's compromising behavior during the events of 30 June 1934, this [Hitler's] support of him continued.[3] Hitler must have known that Papen—the Catholic feudalist, the wealthy snob from Union and aristocrat clubs, the cavalry officer, horse racer, and the man of the reactionary military and industrial clique—distrusted him from the bottom of his heart and regarded him, at best, as a trailblazer for the restoration of the good old days of the monarchy.[4]

In 1936, during the regime of Neurath, I became chief of personnel in the Foreign Ministry; as such I was also entrusted with the management of technical operations and the financial administration of the Ministry.

In late summer of the following year, when Ribbentrop was already Minister,[5] I received a report which claimed that a secret device had been installed in the building of the Foreign Ministry, making it possible to eavesdrop on all telephone conversations of the higher officials. Beyond that, this device also permitted the surveillance of all conversations these officials had with office visitors.

An immediate investigation confirmed the accuracy of this strange report. In fact it was revealed that from a windowless room in the basement of the Ministry, all conversations, whether direct or by telephone, conducted in the Ministry's senior sections, were under the control of a subordinate employee. This operation included the offices of ministers, state secretaries, and section directors. This individual used his knowledge, gained in such a devious manner along with similar data he presumably obtained from other ministries, to complile a sort of secret news bulletin. Copies of this document occasionally turned up in the Foreign Ministry; its actual origin was unknown. These anonymous sheets carried information about

---

3. This, too, was inaccurate. Papen, outmaneuvered by Hitler for power in 1933 and 1934, epitomized the bankruptcy of the conservative upper classes (to which Prüfer belonged) in their sympathy for and opportunism in collaborating with Nazism. After Papen had belatedly voiced fears regarding the Nazi regime and narrowly escaped being shot during Hitler's purge of the SA on 30 June 1934, he privately pledged his loyalty to the dictator and Hitler sent him as German minister to Austria, primarily to get rid of him.

4. Although Hitler disliked and mistrusted Papen, the latter supported the dictator's policies while acting as Germany's diplomatic representative during the Nazi regime in Austria (until the Anschluss in 1938) and Turkey.

5. This was incorrect; see n. 1.

confidential transactions, opinions, and gossip from the highest circles of the Reich government and National Socialist party. Such information generally tended to be detrimental to the person involved in the surveillance.

At Ribbentrop's instigation, an inquiry was conducted by Dr. Best who, at the time, was working in a high-level position with the Gestapo. This investigation revealed that the aforementioned Foreign Ministry employee was acting under the instructions of Minister von Papen, and that his news sheets were forwarded to Papen in Vienna by a special courier, paid for by Papen.[6] Supposedly—I have not been able to prove this—the sheets are said to have found their way from Vienna into other countries. Additionally, transmitting these bulletins to the individual offices of the Foreign Ministry probably served the purpose of lending this enterprise the face of legality in case of discovery.

The employee, as well as the courier, were arrested and interrogated by the Gestapo, which was conducting the investigation on its own, without involving the Foreign Ministry.

After several months I heard that the employee had been released from custody, that indeed he is supposed to be working again in the domain of another ministry. When I had occasion to ask Dr. Best about the results of the investigation, he answered evasively and hid behind "higher" instructions. To my knowledge, Papen's position vis-à-vis Hitler has not been shaken by this peculiar incident, although Ribbentrop was very angry about the discovery of the listening devices.

Incidentally, the employee maintained that the [bugging] apparatus in the Foreign Ministry had been placed there many years before under the direction of a ministerial director who is no longer living. His explanation, therefore, could not be disproven.

At the time this mysterious affair, which throws a peculiar light on Hitler's relationship to Papen, brought to my mind a conversation I had several years before the war with a German ambassador. He claimed to have proof that Papen, while he brought Hitler and President von Hindenburg together, had at the same time intrigued in France against Hitler and

---

6. It is dubious whether Papen masterminded such an operation. Although an arch intriguer, even the little courage necessary for such petty spying seemed out of character for him, and he surely would have gloated about the action in his postwar memoirs, in which he sought to relieve himself of complicity in the Nazi debacle by falsifying his role in it. Furthermore, none of the major scholarly studies of the AA mention his bugging of the ministry. Finally, one must consider that even as Prüfer was writing such a defense of Papen in 1945 and 1946, the latter was on trial at Nuremberg.

the National Socialists.[7] Since one may presume that Hitler knows Papen's true feelings towards him, perhaps the unusual patience of this relentlessly hateful leader with Papen can be explained, on the assumption that Papen has some incriminating material kept in a safe place. The publication of such material might well be uncomfortable for Hitler. Such deviousness would be entirely in Papen's character, passionately suited to conspiracy and intrigue.

Berlin, 8 December 1942

Today I was invited for lunch at a former colleague's [Köpke], along with some of his friends from heavy industry. The individual is now employed by one of the largest German firms. A conversation full of discontent dominated the whole table which, incidentally, was quite well provided for, as though we were living in peacetime. People are well informed, and unfortunately all too precisely, as to the present situation. My former colleague, although regarded as one of the most capable people of the old Foreign Ministry, was obliged to leave the Service because of a "weaving defect" in his ancestry and was bitterly disposed toward Ribbentrop. Despite the caution he acquired in his former position—he was once a secretary of state—he judged him to be a dynamically ambitious idiot who views everything egocentrically and directed at himself, and who is utterly devoid of objective judgment. He is nothing but a lackey of his lord and master, without whom he would be an absolute zero.

The gentlemen from industry enthusiastically applauded this view. Embarrassed, I had to listen to this outburst of anger. I would have found it difficult to contradict.

Berlin, 9 December 1942

Once more the Arabs are trying hard to obtain a declaration from the government, unequivocally establishing as our policy in North Africa the

---

7. Quite to the contrary, Papen did everything possible to help Hitler into the chancellorship in 1933 in order to destroy Papen's rival, German Chancellor Kurt von Schleicher, and place himself back in power as vice chancellor; Papen expected that he would then control Hitler.

political independence of all Arab countries. We do not dare give such a declaration, first because we do not want to prejudice Italian aspirations, although they have become virtually ridiculous, and second because we seem to have committed ourselves to Pétain. We entirely ignore that Pétain, a good Frenchman, is undoubtedly playing a double game with us, and would have already gone over to de Gaulle's side, if we did not appear to be so strong. We are showing the cold shoulder to the Destour party in Tunisia because of him, and are also messing around with Esteva on Rahn's recommendation.[8] It is a true miracle that we are still in Tunisia.

Legation Counselor B. [Becker], too, a specialist for economic questions and my old coworker from Rio, has found something to quibble about in the economic division where he now works. Everywhere there is over-bureaucratization and overcrowding, a condition that is the more grotesque when one considers that dangerous shortages are beginning to show up in all areas of economic life. In place of action, nothing but words and empty formalities.

This became particularly and ridiculously apparent during a conference of the section chiefs in the Political Division, which I attended as a guest. No fewer than thirty people were present and reported on events in their domains that have been known for a long time. No new suggestions or plans as to the situations were produced, no resolutions were passed, and no directives given. The whole thing was only a political debating club whose members were buttering each other up.

Berlin, 14 December 1945 [sic]

I have received a rather unedifying job. I am supposed to examine the economic status of the Mundus Corporation, which deals with literary propaganda abroad and which was set up by Undersecretary of State L. [Luther]. The investigation has been ordered by Ribbentrop himself, because of recent doubts about the business practices of this company.

This organization is quite typical of everything we have achieved in the propaganda sphere. Some task that allegedly must be dealt with immediately and which has been brought up by someone out of the clear blue sky, will be entrusted to an individual who has an "in" and who at that

---

8. Adm. Jean Pierre Esteva was the Vichy resident-general inTunisia; Rahn and the AA had sought his support for the German military effort there.

moment happens to be a favorite of the Minister; in the present case, this is a publisher who wants to escape the draft and who has the good fortune of being a protégé of Ribbentrop's brother-in-law. The "immediately" matters more than the "how."

The "Mundus" is a publishing organization that was designed to market German publications in countries accessible to us; this on the assumption that such literary output is of propaganda value to the German cause. To achieve this purpose, bookstores were set up at great cost in the Balkan countries, the occupied Northern and Western territories, and neutral countries, either through outright purchase or by other means. Perhaps this idea would not have been so bad if two important prerequisites had been taken into consideration: the right materials and the right people.

Unfortunately, what has passed for literature in wartime Germany is so wretched and devoid of any standards, that it can only cause the opposite reactions of those that were intended. All this propaganda and all these resounding clichés cannot hide the fact that in this war we have no political concepts, or more accurately stated, those that had barely been born, are already dying. To foreign nations this war must appear as pure piracy on the part of National Socialist Germany. No one in Europe any longer believes in the "New Order,"[9] which we talk about and have talked about so much without ever defining its meaning. On the other hand, the whole world sees only our inability to befriend people, people on whom we want to bestow this "New Order." Indeed, it does not exist, except as a meaningless cliché.

What we have served up in fiction and poetry, in descriptions of the war, and in popular National Socialist "scholarship" is crass, arrogant, kitchy, or boring, to say nothing of the writing that attempts to proselytize, but convinces no one, because our terrible deeds are not in accord with our beautiful phrases.

The personnel at the Mundus organization is even worse than its finances. The employees were brought together in great haste from one day to the next, without serious regard for their qualifications. Consquently, friction and disagreements ensued everywhere, leading to quick firings and

---

9. The belief of Hitler and his subordinates in a brutal rearrangement of German and European life to conform with the Nazi *Weltanschauung,* or worldview. It included the conquest, enslavement, and even murder of the populations the Nazis considered racially "inferior," including the Jews and Slavs. Contrary to Prüfer's claim here, the Nazis had possessed a horrifying blueprint for Europe, had begun implementing it during the war, and continued almost to the end of the conflict, long after Germany's defeat was assured, to harbor fantasies about its completion.

subsequent hirings of new employees, who turned out to be worse and even less adequate than their predecessors.

The picture of the central office looks almost more unpleasant than that in the Mundus offices abroad. With the exception of few creatures entirely dependent on him, the director of this publishing enterprise is unanimously hated. Denunciations are the order of the day. There is no confidence whatever, and this includes the financial integrity of the management. It is high time this strange enterprise be investigated.

There is a rumor that right now Ribbentrop's position with Hitler is insecure. The Führer does not want Ribbentrop to be present during Mussolini's pending visit. Most likely this is no more than one of those customary minor storms, given the unrelenting tension prevalent within the intrigue-laden atmosphere of the party. As the saying goes among the lesser breeds: birds of a feather flock together, but there is no honor among thieves. Incidentally, Ribbentrop is in an unusually good mood. Perhaps this has something to do with the fact that he is currently out of favor. Today he expressed entirely reasonable views as to the export of party wares. He urged greater caution and more restraint in party propaganda abroad. He claimed that we had no desire to convert anybody.[10] That is also supposed to be the opinion of the Führer, which he claims to have heard often enough.

Berlin, 20 December 1942

The investigation of the "Mundus" affair—I have passed the technical busines aspects on to the Reich Trust Company—is making slow progress. There is no proof, and yet there is certainly much that is "rotten in the state of Denmark." No one dares to testify, everyone is afraid of the boss and his high connections. As everywhere else, there is terror here, too.

"Mundus" not only controls a large number of foreign operations selling books and propaganda materials, but it also conducts businesses that are supposed to camouflage its real activities. However, the general impression, which so far could not be proven accurate, is that most of these side

---

10. Contrary to this claim, what especially concerned Ribbentrop was his battle throughout the war with Bohle and Nazi Propaganda Minister Goebbels to secure control for the AA over the NSDAP's propaganda abroad. Ribbentrop, in fact, appeared to win the struggle when Bormann, Hitler's powerful deputy, directed in June 1942 that the party's foreign propaganda should be subordinated to the AA.

businesses not only serve political purposes, but also the personal enrichment of their founders.

Berlin, 21 December 1942

In addition to Stohrer, Ott is supposed to be recalled. That means Moltke or Dieckhoff will go to Madrid. The present ambassador in Nanking, Stahmer, a former businessman from Hamburg and Ribbentrop's man, will take Ott's place. Even before he joined the Foreign Ministry he was active in the so-called *Dienststelle Ribbentrop*, where he was supposed to have been decisively involved in concluding the Anti-Comintern pact.[11] I do not envy any of them their new posts, for under today's conditions, one can easily lose one's honor and reputation in the service of the state, almost without being aware of it.

Berlin, 22 December 1942

Today I am traveling to Baden-Baden for Christmas, fortunate to escape the Berlin atmosphere.

Baden-Baden, 26 December 1942

A sad, but beautiful, Christmas has come and gone in the peaceful quiet, only occasionally interrupted by rather harmless air-raid alerts. To be sure, life here, too, is full of deprivations and material difficulties. The women must work hard without appreciable household help, and all personal comforts, formerly so abundant in this peaceful and elegant spa, have disappeared. But even so, Baden-Baden is a paradise compared with Berlin.

Nothing here suggests the Nazi party goings-on, the denunciations and

---

11. The pact was signed between Germany and Japan on 25 Nov. 1936 and joined a year later by Fascist Italy. *Dienststelle Ribbentrop* was the office of Ribbentrop in his capacity before 1938 as foreign affairs adviser to Hitler; it held decreasing importance after his appointment as foreign minister.

terror. People are like a large, but discreet, family, conscious of its shared misfortune. Of course, the people give the Hitler salute in public, whenever strangers are watching, but for the most part, party customs are ignored when possible. In trusted circles, complaints are voiced openly and nobody withholds criticism. Here the party has but a very slight following. People are much too humane, too cosmopolitan, to be as rabidly National Socialist or as fanatical as National Socialism demands. The country is too lush, the climate too mild for such dark excesses of the soul. People here are more balanced than in the north. Thus there also are not as many crooks and profiteers.

The last group of American diplomats and consular officials, brought here from Vichy, have been interned in the Hotel Kurhof, one of the many first-class hotels in a town rich in such establishments. It appears that these people are not badly treated, even if they do not enjoy the same freedoms that had been granted to their South American predecessors. A counselor of legation from the Foreign Ministry takes care of them, as well as is possible under prevailing conditions. The Americans' freedom of movement is only restricted insofar as they are not permitted to stray beyond the extensive hotel grounds unless accompanied by a policeman in civilian dress. Together with their keeper, the counselor of legation, they may also take excursions in the beautiful environs of Baden-Baden. They can indulge in sports, tennis, swimming, and golf. According to the counselor of legation, their meals are much better than those of an ordinary German family.

Baden-Baden, 30 December 1942

Today I wasted the entire afternoon reading the Mundus files, which I brought along. What dangerous nonsense! All these *acteurs* in the comedy of this company, as well as their superior in the German Information Office, a division of the Foreign Ministry, spend days in meaningless and unsuccessful discussion of unsubstantiated denunciations. Herr X is supposed to have said to Herr Y that Herr Z must be turned over to the S.D., if . . . this highly important case will then be discussed at length and finally ends up at the insurmountable wall [of silence] in the S.D., where on principle no information is released about any reports. One can only despair, especially because such affairs always leave a taint on the informers as well as on those denounced, so that in the end everybody is compromised among all those concerned. Thus this childish activity consumes much time, money, and many man-hours, only finally to result in nothing. Bureaucracy for the sake of bureaucracy. In the background of all these bureaucrats is the burning desire to dodge military service. They work feverishly, even against each other, in order to look indispensable. At the same time they try to obtain, by hook or by crook, whatever may be obtainable. An absolutely disgusting picture! In the process, of course, everyone is in the way of everyone else and everyone is suspect, because all are striving for the same goal that not all can reach: not to go to the front.

Baden-Baden, 31 December 1942

On this last day of the year, the land is deep in snow, something rare in these almost southern climes.

For the past several months we have now reported the success of our surface forces as a total sum of our sinking of enemy shipping. I am not certain that this line of argument is smart. Perhaps this serves the purpose of concealing the small number of sinkings by U-boats in December. It is common knowledge that the enemy has found defensive means against the submarine danger, means which have almost crippled the activities of our submarines. This year is ending with worries. Most pressing is the concern about Africa. There I have the impression, hopefully false, that we are not taking the situation seriously enough. In my opinion the loss of Tripoli and Tunisia would be the final defeat of Germany. In that event the enemy would be geographically in the immediate vicinity of our "allies," who help us only because they must, but not because they want to. These folk, including the Italians, would be unreliable if Germany were no longer able to control them, in which case they could switch allegiance to our enemies.

It is our tragic fate that as soldiers we can conquer foreign peoples and subjugate them momentarily, but that we are incapable of converting those conquered into friends. We are either hated and expelled [over and over] again, or we accommodate ourselves and are assimilated by those we conquered. German hstory is proof of this unfortunate trait in the character of the German people.

fifteen

January 1943

Baden-Baden, 2 January 1943

It has been raining since yesterday. This is symbolic of my mood, which is as gloomy as it can possibly be, because tonight I have to go back to Berlin, into the hateful environment of the Foreign Ministry I once loved.

Berlin, 4 January 1943

After a tolerable night in a sleeping car, without air-raid alerts, I arrived and moved into my new house in Dahlem. Located on a quiet square, it is a small villa surrounded by a garden. I am staying here quite alone with my old servant.

Meanwhile a *Revirement* in the Foreign Ministry has taken place. Moltke is going to Madrid replacing Stohrer. Ott is being replaced in Tokyo by Stahmer, Wied in Stockholm by Thomsen. My former subordinate, the excellent Becker, is supposed to go to Madrid as the Embassy's economic adviser. Apparently Stohrer has made himself very unpopular with Ribbentrop, because contrary to his usual custom, the Foreign Minister has approved Stohrer's requested retirement. Why Wied is finally disappearing no one really knows, even though he has always been regarded as one of the least reliable supporters of the regime.[1]

Berlin, 6 January 1943

Farewell breakfast at Weizsäcker's for Moltke with the Spanish Ambassador [Vidal y Saures], Bismarck, and other gentlemen from the office and the Spanish Embassy. Moltke does not appear to be going to his new post with great hopes. A heavy, oppressive mood is affecting everyone, resignation in the face of something inescapably bad that can easily be foreseen.

Probably even Moltke anticipates a thankless task awaiting him in Spain. By the same token, if the political events, the instruments which the conductor gives to his virtuosos, the diplomats, are so completely out of tune, as in our case, how can something other than cacophony come from them?

Berlin, 7 January 1943

The same picture today at lunch with Thomsen. He, too, does not appear to delude himself, even though he tries, as his wife does, to display some confidence. He is no more a National Socialist than Moltke,[2] but believes in serving his country in this extremely difficult and dangerous hour, even if the present government can in no way merit his approval. Like

---

1. A view probably traced back to the AO's accusation in 1936 that Wied was pro-Jewish and friendly to Freemasonry. However, he was one of the first German diplomats to join the NSDAP after 1933, and his denunciation of the former undersecretary of state in the AA, Köpke, to Hitler for Köpke's criticism of Ribbentrop, contributed to the undersecretary's removal from the ministry.

2. This was an example of Prüfer's effort to absolve his colleagues and, by implication, himself, of complicity in the Nazi regime. Both Thomsen and Moltke were career diplomats who had served Hitler and his policies with the utmost loyalty. Thomsen entered the NSDAP in Sept. 1938. Moltke, while German ambassador in Warsaw in 1939, supported fully the Nazi attack on Poland, which touched off World War II. Spain, which had opposed the destruction of Catholic Poland and closed its Polish mission in 1942, learned of Moltke's appointment to Madrid with mixed feelings.

many Germans, he feels that if the brakeman jumps off the train car, it would run more swiftly into the pit which the enemy has so carefully mined. Unfortunately, I feel that no one can any longer stop this course of events. Perhaps only Hitler himself, if he were to resign, could prevent this ultimate plunge. But he will certainly not resign.

Berlin, 9 January 1943

Today I heard an astonishing story from one of the two ministers in the Orientalibus which, if it is true, throws a characteristic light on the conditions in the Foreign Ministry and which also illustrates the degree of disciplinary disintegration in this government agency. According to this man's [Ettel] statements, which I have no reason to doubt, his opponent, the other minister [Grobba], made a detailed report behind Ribbentrop's back via an acquaintance to the Reich leader of the S.S., Himmler. In this report he [Grobba] severely criticized the Ministry's Middle Eastern policies! But in doing so, he did not count on the fact that his enemy and opponent holds a rather high rank in the S.S. himself, and naturally—S.S. blood being thicker than the water of the Foreign Ministry—he was informed of this report immediately. And to top it all off, Ribbentrop himself is a member of the S.S., and thus he is always well-informed about the intrigues of his staff.

These are the consequences of a system that has spread mistrust everywhere and which has created a state that has developed within the state.

Berlin, 11 January 1943

Today, to my delight, I accidentally ran into Schulenburg in the hotel, and we had lunch together. He complained bitterly of the confusion that dominates our Eastern policies and of the atrocious dilettantism resulting from the interference of Rosenberg's Eastern ministry in combination with that of the Gauleiters in all matters concerning Russian affairs.[3]

---

3. Although Prüfer intended this as a defense of Schulenburg, who had opposed the German invasion of Russia, it was also a support of Ribbentrop, who complained bitterly about having no part in the civilian administration of the conquered Soviet territories and Baltic states. Hitler had given this to the foreign minister's longtime rival, Rosenberg, and his *Ostministerium*.

Special interest groups are also supposed to have a most disastrous influence.

Yet, at the highest level, one does not appear to understand that the Russian war was a disastrous mistake; indeed, seen militarily, this is the mistake of the entire conflict. Even given our losses, we must somehow try to liquidate this part of the war if we wish to escape reasonably unscathed. To utter such thoughts, however, would be presumptuous in the face of the life-threatening hubris which permeates headquarters. Yet, no one can find a solution. The motto is: rigid military resistance, regardless of any kind of political solution.

Schulenburg spoke of his own position with a certain ironic anger. He is being detained in Berlin without consultation on important matters; nor does anybody listen to his advice. He seizes every opportunity to go on vacation so that he can leave Berlin, at least for a short while. Things are the same for him as they are for me.

Informed circles report that Henke [*sic*] will be appointed as undersecretary of state to head the Political Division instead of Woermann, who will go to China. Henke's [*sic*] successor will be Minister Ettel, holder of a position for which there is probably no counterpart in any other Foreign Ministry. Incidentally, it was unknown to me until now that there existed a position in the Foreign Ministry that was entrusted with the secret surveillance of the entire bureaucracy and which is responsible only to the [Foreign] Minister personally. Thus Ribbentrop has created his own *Cheka* in the Foreign Ministry—or at least he imagines that he has. In truth he has only given Himmler supervision over the Foreign Ministry, because Ettel belongs to the S.D. and therefore is more responsible to Himmler than to Ribbentrop.[4]

It is unknown to me what authority this secret police unit, supposedly unknown to one and all, possesses in this Ministry. Its presence alone is proof of the Foreign Minister's distrust of his staff and is, for that reason, a terrible danger. Trust and confidence are hopelessly gone, and without these qualities collegiality cannot endure. Thus, with his appalling and ultimately stupid methods of snooping, Ribbentrop has completely subverted the once absolutely trustworthy and honorable German Foreign Service.

---

4. Although Ettel was a member of the SS, there is no evidence that he was an SD agent.

Berlin, 15 January 1943

An extensive propaganda plan has been submitted by the Arabs. The Axis powers—such is the high point of this plan—must give the Bey of Tunis written assurances that they will recognize the independence of his country. Like many similar previous plans, this project has no chance of being approved by Hitler and thus also Ribbentrop, because of Italian intransigence and our concerns for France. No one in the Foreign Ministry dares to oppose such negativism for fear of becoming unpopular. Anyhow such opposition is doomed to be unsuccessful.

Berlin, 16 January 1943

Iraq has declared war on us; while in a material sense this will harm us but minimally, it will nonetheless have an impact on the Arab world. Meanwhile, the legitimate prime minister of Iraq, legitimate at least by our definition, lives here in Germany, from where he speaks in the name of his country, which is *de facto* at war with us.

Berlin, 17 January 1943

Yesterday between 7:30 and 9:30, Berlin experienced its first severe air attack. In the western suburbs, and particularly in Dahlem, where I was at home with my servant, it was quite uncomfortable. Almost all of the houses in our neighborhood were hit by incendiary bombs, and soon fires were raging throughout the area. Phosphorous flames bounced around like will-o'-the-wisps on the snow, which covers the yard in front of my house. We received two direct hits in the attic, but succeeded in putting out the fire before it could spread. One of the bombs crashed through two floors and finally lodged itself in my bedroom carpet.

In the morning the area looked bad. Our roof and those of other houses were ripped apart by detonations of several heavy bombs that had landed nearby. Everywhere windows and doors were blown in, and many houses are burned out.

The damage was still worse in other quarters, especially in West Berlin, Wilmersdorf, Schöneberg and, on the Kurfürstendamm, a row of big houses was totally destroyed; its inhabitants were buried beneath the rubble. The streets are full of bricks and broken glass. The population, which must have suffered considerable losses, nevertheless remains quite calm. There is no trace of panic.

A few public buildings were also hit. The Deutschlandhalle caved in, and as though by a great miracle, only a few of the thousands of people attending an animal show were injured. St. Urban's hospital and a private clinic were heavily hit. Unfortunately, many people died in these institutions.

At 7:30 p.m. the sirens sounded again. As I write these lines, it is 10:15, and the all-clear has been given. One can see the intense glow of fires in the direction of Potsdam.

Berlin, 18 January 1943

The British lost 25 airplanes in yesterday's raid. That is not much of a figure, considering that the attack was mounted by at least two hundred planes.

I met the finance minister, Count Schwerin-Krosigk, who does not live far from me in Dahlem. Like me, he was walking around in the area to take a look at the disaster caused by the British. His house was also damaged. He himself barely escaped injury when a door, forced out of its frame by the air pressure, hit him in the back.

Downtown there was not much damage. This time, we who live on the city's periphery were the recipients of these blessings from on high. Living in a house without windows and a partly demolished roof, and which, moreover, stinks of smoke and phosphorous, is no great pleasure in midwinter. I had to move out of my bedroom because the melting snow drips through a hole caused by the bomb.

Today I saw Hassel [*sic*]. Since his dismissal he is disgruntled, much more now than even before, grumbles about everything, and about Ribbentrop in particular. He, too, views the general situation as thoroughly hopeless.

With his execution during the Christmas holidays, the treasonous affair of Legation Counselor Sch. [Scheliha] came to its tragic end. He was the grandson of Miquel,[5] the finance minister from Bismarck's era.

I note with regret that in the Political Division of the Foreign Ministry, I am nearly everywhere treated with some reservations which I can only ex-

---

5. Johannes von Miquel.

plain as being due to jealousy and some peoples' belief that I myself still harbor some ambitions. Basically, Ribbentrop's system of breaking up and subverting all jurisdictions is to blame for the behavior of my colleagues. No one knows exactly what he is supposed to do and, therefore, all others, but especially newcomers, are seen as unwanted intruders into one's own heretofore jealously guarded sphere of competence. When I met today with Woermann and Erdmannsdorff, I took the opportunity to make it clear to them that I am entirely harmless and do not yearn for anything other than repeatedly requested retirement.

In the evening I was the guest of the Turkish Ambassador, Arikan. Countless members of the diplomatic corps and Foreign Ministry were present, including the Italian Ambassdor, Dino Alfieri, his Spanish colleague [Vidal y Saures], and the Swiss Minister, Feldscher, who looks after foreign interests represented by Switzerland in Germany.[6]

We had to take a detour in order to reach the Ambassador's house, because a large unexploded bomb was stuck in the middle of the road, which caused the police to close the street. Obviously the main topic of conversation at the dinner table was the most recent air raid. Just in case an alert suddenly should sound, the Ambassador had planned for the celebration to continue in the air-raid cellar.

After dinner there was a rather embarrassing scene when the host, his stiff drinks perhaps having loosened his tongue, unburdened himself about our Foreign Ministry officials. He addressed the remarks to me in a rather noisy manner and, in the process, used some German expressions not exactly common in polite society. I tried to make light of this scene, which could not remain unnoticed, but failed to succeed in the face of the Ambassador's obstinancy. The incident shows what one thinks in foreign diplomatic circles of the goings-on in our Foreign Ministry.

Berlin, 20 January 1943

Today I was visited by Secretary of State Kepler's [*sic*] *adlatus* [Trott zu Solz], who is in charge of Indian affairs. He is a young man who makes a good impression, even though he does not understand anything about India, where he has never been, just like his boss. He complained bitterly

---

6. Feldscher did not hold the rank of minister. The Swiss minister in Germany since 1938 was Hans Fröhlicher, notorious for his views sympathetic to Germany. In OD, entry for 19 Jan. 1943, Prüfer identified Feldscher as a consul.

about the prevailing crookedness and corruption in another division which, in his opinion, pokes its fingers into everything. Unfortunately he cannot prove anything, but I am convinced that he is absolutely right. Since one cat does not scratch out the eyes of another, we will probably never get to the bottom of these things. For the same reason, the results of the Mundus investigation, which also involves the division mentioned by Trott, have until now remained completely negative.

I was invited for lunch by my old friend, former Ministerial Director K. [Köpke], who now works for the Otto Wolf [*sic*] concern. There I also met Meissner, Planck, the son of the great physicist and former secretary of state in Schleicher's cabinet,[7] and Kiewitz, who is assigned in Brussels to the king of Belgium [Leopold III]. The latter told interesting stories about the prisoner of Laecken, whom he praised enthusiastically because of his dignified and correct conduct. He was less delighted with our Flemish friends; their behavior toward us is self-serving and, thus, unreliable. Basically we enjoy no more sympathy with them than we do with the Walloons.

Here too, as everywhere else, the unhampered proliferation of "bureaucracy" in Germany is disastrous. Everything happens *ad personam*, very little *ad rem*. Sections, divisions, offices, even entire ministries with large personnel expenditures are created out of nowhere for no known purpose. It seems that we take a kind of childish delight in such bureaucratic games. I actually witnessed how people who volunteered for military service because of their impression that manpower was needed at the front were rejected so that the "bureaucracy," i.e., those avoiding service, can remain indispensable. This might perhaps be tolerable if the "indispensables" were more discreet. But they are not. They disturb the orderly process of administration by being busy and by "governing" wherever they can, in the most amateurish and incompetent manner. The concept of jurisdiction, a *must* in complex government, can certainly not be dispensed with if an unholy mess is to be avoided; this basic concept of government has disappeared in Germany and is regarded by the powers that be as reactionary. Everyone pokes his nose into everything. Dilettantism is becoming the rule; restraint no longer plays a role. One certainly cannot be petty in matters of life and death, especially not in times of war; money today is only printed paper, the small format of which scarcely permits its use for other purposes. Nevertheless, it is still somewhat irksome that these lists of paper, guaranteed by the state, no less, are used by people in the garb of government officials for

---

7. Schleicher was the last chancellor of the Weimar republic, dismissed on 28 Jan. 1933 after a complicated intrigue that led to Hitler's appointment, in which Schleicher's old rival, Papen, played a leading part.

purposes that are more harmful to the state than useful to the [long-suffering] public at large.

It is curious that, just as in the first World War, the desperate requirements of war attract, in the main, the most dishonest elements among our people.

These things must be just as well-known to Ribbentrop as to the rest of us; nevertheless, he not only tolerates, but also encourages them, by retaining his creatures in office. Financial shenanigans are also part of the "Mundus" affair, inasmuch as Frau von Ribbentrop has an attorney [Moehrung] who was, at the same time, working for Mundus and for her in an inheritance case. Although, strictly speaking, the examination of this attorney did not actually reveal anything incriminating as far as the "Mundus" administration is concerned, there still remains the picture of general confusion and unprofessional behavior in a futile enterprise, haphazardly assembled, and held together only by corruption, ambition, and intimidation.

Berlin, 22 January 1943

Today, Subhas Chandra Bose, the Indian nationalist leader who took refuge in Germany, gave a farewell party before his return to the Indian border regions. There was much talk and photographing. I had dire memories of the first World War period when, in a similarly fantastic and ridiculous manner, we sheltered a few Indian hotheads and distributed pamphlets suggesting that British rule in India should be ousted. The result of our efforts was evident on the French and Oriental battlefields, where hundreds of thousands of Indians fought against us for Britain.

Bose, whom I have known from the time of the Indian unrest after the Amritsar affair,[8] is doubtless an honest patriot, fighting for the independence of his country. However, his alliance with us, the champions of racist doctrine, is pretty paradoxical, because the National Socialists, above all Rosenberg, as well as Hitler, have never made a secret of their racist perception that British rule in India is justified.[9] Only now in India have the same enemies adopted the same goals.

---

8. In Apr. 1919 the city of Amritsar in Northern India became a center of unrest during which a large gathering was dispersed by the British authorities with gunfire, resulting in the deaths of nearly 400 Indians.

9. Prüfer neglected to mention here, however, how he had defended Hitler's racial views to Bose in 1933.

To incorporate Rosenberg's anti-religious principle is disastrous for Bose and his movement; he fails to see that he cannot bring national principles into opposition to the various religious beliefs of the Indian population, which is still completely dominated by religious and mystical ideas, unless he wants to turn everyone against him and all the various factions against each other. Least of all should Bose fight Islam, which is inclined toward the British leadership because of its opposition to [dominant] Hinduism. Bose, to support his anti-religious bias, has found a fanatical assistant in the Foreign Ministry in the person of Secretary of State Kepler [*sic*], who is entrusted with Indian affairs.

Everywhere in the world we enjoy a reputation, perhaps not entirely unjustified, of being thorough and precise in scientific and, above all, organizational matters. We possess none of these qualities in our foreign policy. On the contrary, in this area we are easily taken in by every charlatan and amateur. How would it otherwise be possible that in the Foreign Ministry we do not have a single responsible person for India, someone who knows this exceedingly complicated country and its problems? It is difficult even for an expert to understand, let alone someone who has only made a cursory visit there.

Herr Kepler [*sic*], originally an engineer, is an old party member and served the party for years as a consultant on technical and economic questions. Perhaps he performed well. Undoubtedly he has read much about India and has the best intentions of applying his knowledge. But his views are not the result of firsthand experience; everything he knows and thinks about the Indian problem is pure theory; unfortunately it does not remain theory, because he tries to put his "knowledge" into practice, with the typical rigidity and obstinacy of all party members.

The rigid principles of the party are thus stupidly applied to this foreign and unusually heterogeneous region. Party doctrine is anti-religious and purely nationalistic. Consequently we appear in India to be opposed to Islam as well as Hinduism, and as advocates of purely nationalistic principles, while being entirely unconcerned about angering Mohammedans and pious Hindus.

In the case of India, National Socialist theoreticians have been blatantly stupid from the beginning. Apart from our economic interests, Germany should never have involved itself in Indian politics, unless we desired to antagonize Britain. Furthermore, especially because of our trade interests in India, there was no reason to discriminate against the Indians because of their dark skin, and thus to draw them into the circle of our absurd racial theories.

Notwithstanding all this, very soon after the [Nazi] seizure of power, Alfred Rosenberg did just that. When the Indians, and especially the [Indian] nationalist leader Pillai, then living in Germany, remonstrated with us, Hitler backed his trusty paladin, declaring that India should consider itself lucky to have such excellent mentors as the British.[10]

Given the exigencies of war, we have suddenly found our Indian heart. In the face of this surprisingly rapid racial reversal, one can hardly be surprised that the Indians do not entirely believe us, and are more inclined to see in Hitler no more than a man who wants to establish his rule in place of the British. Racial obscurantism does not really accord well with a people who want to conduct international politics.

Berlin, 23 January 1943

The scarcity of gasoline has become so great that even my little car has been deprived of this commodity. In order to go downtown, e.g., to the Foreign Ministry, I now need at least an hour each way, given the inadequate public transportation system. The mere trek from my house to the nearest subway station requires a walk of some twenty minutes through an undeveloped area which, in the evening, during an air-raid alert, is not particularly pleasant. Being 62 years old, a poor walker, and not in the best of physical condition, all this is a terrible burden.

But even these adverse personal circumstances would not be of major significance in wartime if I were convinced that I could serve my Fatherland usefully, successfully, and honorably. But I totally lack this conviction. My sphere of influence, if one even can call it such, is in no sense clearly defined. On whim, and depending on the circumstances, I am only rarely asked for my opinion and dragged into the factional battles of the Foreign Ministry. Consequently, I appear to all who are fishing in these troubled waters as an irksome and threatening intruder; this, the more so, because none of these folk even know where the borders of their activity lie.

I have discussed all this with the Secretary of State and have requested of him, too, my retirement. Weizsäcker is completely aware of the situation in the Foreign Ministry and in private presumably approves my motives for leaving the service. Nonetheless he encourages me not to carry things to extremes. Perhaps he also believes that such desires of an ambassador can be infectious and might influence him in his own decisions. But his case is

10. Again Prüfer failed to note a significant fact: he had supported Hitler's view in 1931 against the protest of Chempakaraman Pillai, an Indian leader.

somewhat different. He is the deputy of the Minister and can, if necessary, demand to be heard and to have himself protected. I, a second-class ambassador-at-large, am compared to a fly that is allowed to crawl all over the cake, because there is no particular reason to shoo it away. One has forgotten, however, that this insect is not crawling out of greed, but only from sheer exhaustion. The fly is simply too tired to buzz away.

Thus, once again, the discussions were fruitless.

Berlin, 26 January 1943

The daily trip downtown and back to my house—I spent about 2-1/2 hours, which is equal to a trip from Berlin to Dresden—tires me beyond measure. Added to this are the fruitless and annoying palavers at the daily directors' meetings, the so-called morning devotions, which get on my nerves with their League of Nations-type tactics from a bygone era. These kinds of tactics still dominate around here and, given the fact that this awful kind of claptrap in various committees and subcommittees prevents recognition of our tragic situation, makes any and all decisions impossible.

We have recently been confronted with a striking case of our political helplessness. At the very moment when we and the Italians have completely lost possession of North Africa and are barely holding on to a bridgehead in Tunisia, we are hesitating to play our last trump card which, to be sure, does not promise much, but still has some success: the matter of the Arabs. But Mussolini does not want to give up his claim on Tunisia. He does not even need to do that. All he has to do is lie. After all, he is used to it. Indeed, is that something so rare and unheard of in this "total war" which, truly, is not exactly a conclave of applied ethics. And even if he is afraid to tell his children that he promised independence to the leader of the Destour party, Bourguiba, then why not give such an assurance secretly and orally; the latter will be satisfied. This Tunisian undoubtedly knows how to convey the news to his people. This may sound and, indeed, be cynical, but in this disastrous war worse has been perpetrated by both sides.

The news from Russia is increasingly threatening: Stalingrad is fighting for its life. All attempts at relieving the beleaguered garrison have failed, and our troops, the alleged liberators, have fallen into their own trap. At Voronesch, which we had to evacuate, the Hungarians seem to have run away ignominiously. Since this is not their usual behavior, it is probably a sign of general war fatigue.

Of course, all these setbacks also damage the few political relationships which we still maintain with some neutral countries. Thus here, too, among the neutrals, one slowly begins to be more pessimistic as to whether Turkey, whatever her intention may be, will not ultimately be forced to side with our enemies. The Americans are already applying more and more pressure. The policy of neutrality had excellent chances until the appearance of the U.S.A. in North Africa. But now, Turkish policy, under American pressure, will gradually favor the enemy camp.

Ribbentrop phoned me at precisely 7 p.m. He has a new investigation for me, which is even more unpleasant than the Mundus affair. Consequently, I immediately had to proceed downtown this evening. I do not know why all the distasteful tasks are given to me: in any event, they do nothing to improve my mood and my willingness to work.

This time the matter concerns the fact that Goebbels has threatened to denounce Ribbentrop to the Führer in writing, because immediately after the air raid on 16 January, Ribbentrop is supposed to have seen to it that his damaged house in Dahlem was repaired without delay, using scarce labor and building materials. The owners of other houses in the same area, houses which were equally or even more seriously hit, requested in vain for repairs of the most serious damage. Above all, a Catholic home for unwed mothers located across from Ribbentrop's villa remained without window panes, while in the empty house of the Foreign Minister, the windows had already been replaced. In actual fact, Ribbentrop, as usual, was in the main quarter of the city; his wife and family, too, do not live in Dahlem. Neither the Minister nor his wife had taken any steps whatever to repair the house.

It is supposed to be my task to establish who gave the orders for these repairs and how such directives could be sent from the Foreign Ministry. Presumably it was Goebbels' wish to discredit with Hitler simultaneously the Foreign Ministry and Ribbentrop, whom he especially hated at the time of these events.

As usual, Ribbentrop demanded the utmost speed in executing his orders. The investigation is supposed to be finished within 24 hours, so that those responsible can immediately and mercilessly be brought to account. Above all, this is supposed to provide him with an opportunity to respond as fast and emphatically as possible to the insidious attacks of his rival, Goebbels.

Berlin, 25 [sic] January 1943

Today I questioned all the participants, however remotely involved, in the affair of the [Foreign Minister's] house. This lasted until 3 a.m. in the old Presidential palace. The results were, as foreseen, that the domestic staff, always in fear and terror of the angry outbursts of Ribbentrop, arranged for the swift repair in order to please the master. The Foreign Ministry was in no way involved. Much ado about nothing. The Minister could not make his own officials, whom he hates so much, into scapegoats. Just think: an ambassador was summoned to resolve a quarrel between two Reich ministers, and in this conflict the only matter of concern turned out to be the excessive zeal of a concierge, who should now be reprimanded! And all that in the face of the death struggle in Stalingrad.

This silly story proves in startling fashion how deep and how subjective the disagreements between our highest authorities really are.

I never heard how the quarrel between Ribbentrop and Goebbels ended. The first blow, an annoying exchange of letters, lies before me. I believe that in the last 24 hours I was close to being incarcerated in a concentration camp. Goebbels must not have much influence with Himmler at the moment, or else I would now probably be in one of those educational institutions of the German people.

Berlin, 30 Janaury 1943

Kepler [*sic*] told me today in an offhand manner that the leader of the *Rechtswahrerbund*,[11] an official of the higher judiciary, had been executed, because he was guilty of huge, financially shady, deals. Another sign of the times.

We again had British visitors by air, but without much effect.

---

11. Nazi lawyer's league. Lasch was the leader referred to by Prüfer.

sixteen

February 1943

Berlin, 1 February 1943

The man responsible for the financial management of the Foreign Ministry [Schröder] today unburdened his heart to me regarding the hopeless conditions which prevail in his domain. The Minister [Ribbentrop], whom he seriously considers to be insane, has lost all sense of moderation and purpose. There are no longer any budgetary procedures. Ribbentrop gives financial orders, regardless of whether the necessary monies are available. He is subject to no controls.

When I was reponsible for the financial management of the Foreign Ministry, I learned to my chagrin that Ribbentrop is very generous financially and is not greatly bothered by the rules of budgetary procedures. At the same time, I believe Ribbentrop would be done an injustice if he were accused of enriching himself. He has hardly any personal material desires, but, indeed, he has some for the upkeep of his prestige and official position. In such matters he knows no limits and continuously needs money, money, and more money. He does not care where it comes from. *L'état c'est moi!*

Stalingrad has fallen. Paulus was promoted to the rank of field marshal on the day before this event, by way of gratitude for the appalling and senseless sacrifices he ordered to satisfy Hitler's megalomania.[1] In my opin-

---

1. This entry, which should be compared carefully with the original, is a dramatic illustration of Prüfer's effort to appear anti-Hitler.

ion he [Paulus] is not without guilt. Had he not obeyed an idiot, he might have saved his army from senseless destruction.

Berlin, 4 February 1943

Because I am no longer equal to the strain of negotiating long daily journeys from Dahlem into the inner city, especially in the cold of winter, I have moved into the Hotel Adlon. Professor G. [Gudzent] has confirmed a serious worsening of my heart and liver ailments, and he urgently advised at least a temporary, complete rest. I immediately asked the Secretary of State for an extended vacation, especially since my official "activities" are superfluous and fruitless in the first place. He did not seem to believe that I am really sick.

Berlin, 11 February 1943

I have avoided the Foreign Ministry for a week. The investigation into the Mundus affair has meanwhile resolved itself, because both the managing director (the publisher)[2] and Undersecretary of State L. [Luther], his superior in the Ministry, have suddenly and secretly been arrested and suspended from their offices. Their principal employees have also gone down with them. The Division is supposed to have been abolished.

The end to such a stormy career as that of Undersecretary of State L. was foreseeable. Even so, the alleged mismanagement and corruption in his domain did not lead to his downfall. Instead, it was the "disloyalty" of this Undersecretary of State, originally Ribbentrop's man, that caused his dismissal and removal to a concentration camp. News of this is being disseminated only "very secretly" in the Foreign Ministry. According to rumors, L. is said to have conducted highly disparaging conversations with Himmler about Ribbentrop and his management of the Ministry. Allegedly, Himmler then mentioned this to his S.S. comrade, Ribbentrop. After one of his customary angry outbursts, the Foreign Minister reported this mat-

---

2. Unidentified.

ter to Hitler, who placed him [Ribbentrop] under his protection and ordered the immediate removal of the disloyal servant.

Even though L. did not have many friends in the Foreign Ministry, there reigns, nevertheless, general consternation about his dismissal. The incident is considered, and correctly so, to be an alarming symptom of the general disintegration of the German state. Our country has been reduced to matters of personal interests, fighting, and grabbing for power among the robber barons surrounding the Führer. The German state is merely an empty shell.

Berlin, 15 February 1943

A satyr play followed the tragedy of [Under] Secretary of State L. On the Minister's instructions, the Secretary of State assembled all the officials of the Foreign Ministry in small groups one after another, and read them a document most likely written at a higher level, in which L.'s case, without going into details, was described as a reprehensible example of serious disloyalty. The heavy penalty that L. received is supposed to have a deterring and cleansing effect. This somewhat didactic and childish declaration, which did not touch on the core of the matter, the relationships between the "bigwigs of the Reich," caused partly indignation and partly amusement among the higher officials.

Today's address in the Ambassadors' Hall of the Reich chancellery by Propaganda Minister Goebbels to the leading members of the Reich government, proves that a note of malaise and pessimism dominates the upper levels of our officialdom. Goebbels gravely admonished us to refrain from criticizing and "belly-aching"; instead, we must do our duty for the Führer and the Fatherland, and we must be models of courage to our compatriots.

All this would be well and beautiful if our superiors were good exemplars and if we did not have to be faced daily with the symptoms of disintegration for which the leading men of the party and the ministers themselves are responsible. How is one supposed to retain respect, faith, and composure if one continually sees one's own superiors disregard all rules of public and private propriety? The more so if braggadocio, sycophancy, and filth are virtually cultivated in every shape and form as counterparts to capriciousness, terrorism, and brutal oppression? This system is beyond help.

In the East we are retreating with giant steps. Rostov and Voroshilovgrad have been lost.

Once again the Minister has rejected my application for a leave.

Berlin, 17 February 1943

Professor G. [Gudzent], who wanted to see me today, believes that I most certainly must renew my request for a leave; he says that I am no longer equal, physically or mentally, to the tensions of the kind of "services" [I have to render]. I truly am seriously ill, even if I may not be aware of it. My kidneys and gall bladder, too, are malfunctioning.

Tomorrow Ribbentrop is going to Rome, accompanied by his entire swarm of satellites. Once again, this visit will only lead to further makeshift repairs of the long-standing fissures and cracks in the Axis. We are in a hopeless dilemma between Italian, Spanish, and Arab interests, and the commitments made to Pétain. It is becoming increasingly clear that the French are leading us by the nose all along the line. They are just waiting for the time when they can finally jump ship. One can hardly blame them. We have consistently talked about "collaboration," by which we have merely meant French support [for our cause]. One cannot, in all decency, expect the French to support German supremacy in Europe. It is obvious that the talk about a "New Order" which, moreover, has never been carefully defined, no longer attracts anyone in France. Furthermore, the foul behavior of the S.S. forever vitiates against good will among the French, good will that may have been created by the impeccable conduct of the [regular German] army.

Berlin, 18 February 1943

The Minister did not leave; he has postponed his trip until tomorrow. I have not been able to ascertain the reason for this delay, but it seems to be a matter of quite serious difficulties.

Today Goebbels delivered a speech about total war which, as of now, is supposed to be fought on a total basis. We are getting ever close to the edge of the abyss, instead of trying to extricate ourselves, albeit with sacrifices.

Berlin, 22 February 1943

Rahn arrived here from Tunis for a report. He painted a gloomy picture of the situation. The problem is not a matter of manpower, but of supplies, weapons, ammunition and, above all, fuel. The Italians are fighting only reluctantly. For that reason alone we can almost certainly count on the loss of Tunisia in the near future. During a dinner at Strack's, with Abetz, Woermann, Erdmannsdorff, Rahn, and others, a rather heated but unfruitful argument erupted about the Tunisian question; Rahn and the majority again propounded the old theory that the defense of our position in Tunisia is only possible with the help of the French. This would have been correct if we had taken a different, sincerely conciliatory, position toward the French after 1940, after the collapse of France. Today it is too late.

Incidentally, Rahn's description of the events that occurred at the time of our initially feebly supported occupation of Tunisia, was not uninteresting. Rahn and the military succeeded in persuading Admiral Esteva (no friend of ours) to collaborate with our forces only by means of bluff and gentle force. If the Admiral had suspected how weak the armed forces he surrendered to really were, the entire Tunisian undertaking would probably have failed on the spot.

The Bey likes neither the French nor the Italians; therefore, he does not like us either.

Berlin, 23 February 1943

General N. [Niedenführ], who has been entrusted with some kind of military-economic task in Southern Russia, visited me today. The picture he sketches of the situation in his sphere of activity is just as hopelessly dismal as everything else one hears from the various fronts. In his opinion, the root of all evil lies in the fact that Hitler has taken over the supreme command of the army and now dabbles in an area in which he obviously is an amateur; he improvises and gives orders based on intuitions, without being able to work out a clear strategic plan for the entire front, a plan that can be communicated to all army leaders. Thus, the connections between the various [army] groups are often completely lost. This behavior of the Führer has a crippling effect on the generals, who are aware of only one thing: they will be held responsible for every setback, when in reality, after all has been said and done, not they, but invariably Hitler is at fault.

Thus, the catastrophe at Stalingrad can be blamed entirely on Hitler's rigid directive to hold out, notwithstanding the advice of General Paulus and his officers. Without doubt, we could have escaped the pincer movement of the Russians by a timely retreat from a position that was too much exposed. But for reasons of prestige Hitler did not want to give up Stalingrad, perhaps precisely because of the city's name. Consequently, he sacrificed one of his best army units and, on top of everything else, he had to swallow the loss of his prestige resulting from this serious defeat.

General N. is very skeptical as to a new spring offensive in the East, a subject currently much under discussion here. Russian superiority in men and matériel is constantly on the increase, whereas our capacity to replace losses is ever diminishing. On the other hand, American superiority in the Mediterranean area is increasingly apparent and affects the Russian theater of war most disadvantageously; by opening up new approaches, greater and greater amounts of American war matériel can be shipped to Russia.

Therefore, in General N.'s opinion, on the Eastern front we must limit ourselves to defensive action. But even this would be successful only if our supreme command were returned to expert hands. This is the general assessment in the army.

Berlin, 26 February 1943

Long conversation with Rahn at the [Hotel] Kaiserhof about his Syrian adventure. According to him, we have gambled away there, too, our chances because of our ambivalent and indecisive French policies. One can only agree with his denunciations, given our uncertain conduct. On the other hand, Rahn forgets that our campaign in Syria, just like the Iraqi rebellion, was a totally senseless exploit, doomed to failure from the beginning. It only served to bring its protagonists, Rahn and Grobba, some dubious fame. This adventure was bound to end in failure militarily and politically, because it was inadequately prepared and because it was carried out with insufficient means.

Last evening I was invited to dinner by Count and Countess R. [Richthofen], together with a very nice actor [C. L. Diehl] and his wife. Even in this cultural milieu—the Countess was once a very well-known opera singer—there prevails an atmosphere hostile to the regime. People everywhere have recognized the "face of the ruling classes."[3] It bears the same features everywhere: terror and corruption.

---

3. Presumably from the title of a collection of famous political cartoons by George Grosz, *Das Gesicht der herrschenden Klasse. 55 politische Zeichnungen* (Berlin: Malik-Verlag, 1921).

Berlin, 28 February 1943

A Sunday with delightful spring-like weather. I took a walk on Unter den Linden and through the Tiergarten. Considering the huge crowds of reasonably well-dressed people, the many sightseers, the crowded restaurants and coffee houses, one can easily forget that we are living in the midst of war and that we have only recently suffered a serious air raid. Only the barely repaired, devastated and burned-out buildings and the many strange figures walking about catch one's attention. This is particularly true of the confusion of languages one hears everywhere. Today being Sunday, many foreign workers have time off and use it to travel into the city. They are mostly people from the East: Russians, Poles, and Ukrainians, but there are also many French and Italians among them. Berlin without Italians is barely imaginable. In the Hotel Adlon, e.g., the majority of the waiters is Italian.[4] There are also many people in S.S. uniforms who clearly are not of German origin. They belong to one of the many formations Himmler has recruited from among the Dutch, Flemish, Walloon, Danish, Norwegian, and all sorts of other populations. It remains to be seen whether these troops possess real value in battle. I doubt that they have come here because of their enthusiasm for the European "New Order."

I spent the evening with General F. [Feige], where I met Major St. [Steffen] and the military broadcaster, General D. [Dittmar]. F. has been cashiered because he was held responsible for the breakdown of one of his S.S. divisions. He spoke about his experiences with great bitterness, and suggested that the differences between the regular army and the S.S. are now so extreme that they may, one of these days, lead to dangerous conflict. In that event the S.S. would be supported in every respect by Hitler, who is completely under Himmler's influence.

As we returned home, General D. voiced his concerns [about the general situation]. As a broadcaster he tries to tell the truth in as restrained a manner as possible, without exaggeration; this is exceedingly difficult, because there is hardly any good news to report and because he, in his role as a radio official, also has the propaganda task of preventing public morale from sinking too low.

---

4. Such an idyllic picture of the treatment of foreign workers hardly corresponded to reality. The increase in the German labor force in 1943 resulted to a significant degree from the expanded use of foreign laborers. Originating primarily from Eastern Europe and Russia, the laborers were recruited in brutal fashion. While there were a few attempts to ameliorate the working and living conditions of the foreigners in the Reich, and while their treatment varied, it was never good. Hence, for most of the eastern workers and some of the western workers, life in the Reich was a continual nightmare of hard work, insufficient food, inadequate quarters, personal discrimination, and cruelty.

seventeen

March 1943

Berlin, 1 March 1943

Professor G. [Gudzent] wrote the Ministry that I would be in imminent and mortal peril, unless I were to take a complete rest immediately.
Although physically I have little energy, and perhaps precisely because of
that, I am in an almost cheerful, euphoric mood. I have slowly distanced
myself from this whole busy termite colony to such an extent that I can
observe it as a spectator, almost dispassionately, impersonally, and without interest; indeed, I can even enjoy it to a certain degree, but *only* to a
certain degree. Being an involved German because of my allegiance to my
Fatherland, I cannot take an objective-historical view of the adventurous
goings-on around me. [Metaphorically speaking] any son who is not a total
degenerate will be inclined to excuse even the most repulsive mistakes of his
mother.

Berlin, 2 March 1943

Yesterday ended badly. There was an air-raid alarm at 9:30. I had just
finished dinner and gone to my room when the sirens began to "sing"! Like
most hotel guests, I first believed that, as happened frequently in the recent
past, it was a question of a nuisance raid and the enemy would not get
beyond the periphery of the city. But when the anti-aircraft fire became

audible in the vicinity, I went to the hotel cellar. This shallow basement was overflowing with people; there were also many utility pipes, which would have been very dangerous if a bomb hit. I had scarcely arrived in the basement when it became clear that this time it was not just a question of a mere nuisance raid. Loud detonations followed one another at short intervals, causing the entire massive building to shake. The anti-aircraft batteries continued to fire without ceasing. Now and then the air-raid warden appeared and said that everything in the vicinity of the hotel was burning. Surprisingly, however, our building was not hit.

The all-clear followed two hours later. I went out into the street. On Unter den Linden several buildings were in flames, among them the Passage and the upper floors of the Hotel Bristol. The glow of conflagrations could be seen everywhere. A bank building was burning on neighboring Friedrichstrasse. The cupola of the Catholic cathedral of St. Hedwig near the castle seemed to be a glowing mountain. Incendiary bombs were smoldering and blazing everywhere on the street. In addition, a strong wind was blowing, fanning the flames and spreading the fires.

We have probably received an intimation of the shape of things to come.

This afternoon I took a walk through the city, mainly in the West. Many houses were still burning, particularly in the region around the Kurfürstendamm. The so-called Old West was heavily damaged. The house where I had dinner with the R.'s [Richthofen] a few days ago is totally destroyed. All the houses on Pragerplatz are burned out or have caved in. The Hedwig church is still enveloped in thick smoke.

Curiously enough, the government buildings on the Wilhelmstrasse have remained nearly undamaged, although the attack was probably aimed at them.

In many places traffic is disrupted. Nevertheless, people seem to go quietly about their business. Everywhere one sees them diligently clearing debris and removing the ruins. I would never have thought that the Berliners, usually so nervous, are capable of taking these blows so stoically.

Berlin, 3 March 1943

There was yet another alarm this afternoon. But we did not notice or see any enemy planes. They probably only wanted to look at the damage they had done.

Ribbentrop returned yesterday from his Italian trip. No report yet as to the results.

Baden-Baden, 7 March 1943

After having received permission yesterday to go to Baden-Baden, I left immediately and arrived here at noon, exhausted, but after an undisturbed night.

Baden-Baden, 12 March 1943

Here, too, the war is becoming ever more noticeable. Yesterday there was a severe raid on Munich, and tonight Stuttgart and Karlsruhe were hit. From our house one could plainly see the glow of conflagrations. On their return flight the British mistakenly dropped incendiary bombs on Baden-Baden. Luckily not much happened. Only the Catholic church in Lichtenthal was hit and completely burned out.

My doctor here ordered me to take a cure, consisting of daily injections. But, he says, I need rest above all. Of course neither he nor I know how I am supposed to accomplish this in these times.

Baden-Baden, 21 March 1943

One day passes just like another, with medical treatment, short walks (longer ones tire me out), and household worries, which today concern property owners to a much greater extent than in earlier days.[1] These concerns, however, are nothing compared with those the women have. My poor wife, who is ill, is overworked in caring for the house and has only one wholly inadequate servant. Domestic help is virtually unobtainable, and small families like ours are forbidden to hire servants. The physical size of the household is of no consideration; [this is frustrating] because one cannot scale it down easily. That is another of the aggravating side effects of these wonderful times.

Moltke died in Madrid from peritonitis, following a belated appendix operation. Probably Dieckhoff will be his successor.

---

1. Presumably to encourage the view he sought to portray of his lagging health, Prüfer omitted here reference to his intensive efforts and travels in purchasing a castle estate in Austria; see his original diary entries for Mar. 1943, pp. 56–65.

Baden-Baden, 26 March 1943

One of my comrades from the first War, the former Lieutenant H. [Heiden] from Karlsruhe, now a captain, visited me on his way to Tunisia, where he has been posted. Until now he has served in Russia.

He, too, believes that our offensive on the Eastern front has exhausted itself. At the most, we can only try to consolidate our present position.

Captain H. has been extraordinarily impressed with Russian Communism and its management. Industry and technology are developed to the utmost. The people have more than enough to eat. Even intellectual and cultural needs are taken care of, as long as they are not outside the framework of Communism. Only luxury goods are lacking and are systematically suppressed. H. went so far as to state verbatim that, in an emergency, he would not fight against Communism in Germany. My objections appeared to make no impression on him: Seidlitz [*sic*] and his cohorts have their followers.[2]

The transformation of Captain H. is all the more astonishing because, in civilian life, he is a prosperous manufacturer. The leveling influence of the war, and probably also the National Socialist emphasis on the "people's solidarity," may have severely affected him; thus he can no longer perceive that Russian Communist happiness is nothing more than an equalization towards the bottom, the deliberate creation of a community of poverty, barely able to sustain life.

Baden-Baden, 28 March 1943

British air raids on Berlin have resumed. Also the general attack in Tunisia seems to have begun. We are occupying new positions "according

---

2. Prüfer misspells the name of Gen. Walter von Seydlitz-Kurzbach, who was chief of staff to Paulus at Stalingrad, where he was taken prisoner by the Red army and later made president of the German Officers' League (*Bund Deutscher Offiziere*) in Moscow. The league's activities were identical to those of the Free Germany National Committee (*Nationalkomitee Freies Deutschland*), formed in Soviet Russia a few months before. They sought to persuade the German army and people to overthrow Hitler, end the war, and establish a "free" democratic government. Many captured German officers and rank-and-file soldiers joined the movement. The failure of the July 1944 plot against Hitler convinced the Soviets that the committee had no further use. The reference to Seydlitz's "cohorts" is interesting; the National Committee was not formed until 12–13 July 1943 and the Officers' League until August. Prüfer presumably knew nothing about Seydlitz's activity when he claimed to have written this entry.

to schedule." Everybody knows what this means. Here, too, we have alarms almost daily. Attacks are mostly aimed at the large south German cities. They [the enemy planes] are merely flying over Baden-Baden. Therefore, life here is still quite peaceful. The populace is quietly going about its business, theaters and movies are still operating in the evening, and the few hotels that are still open—most have become military hospitals or have not yet been readied for the summer season—are full of guests.

In these parts one can see many foreign workers, mostly Frenchmen, who are not particularly noticeable, because given the patriarchal ways of this small frontier town, people are more accustomed to their ways and language than in distant Northern Germany. The driver delivering our alcoholic supplies is a former prisoner of war; now a "free" worker, he is happy every time he comes to our house because he has an opportunity to converse in French and because he can gossip a little in the kitchen. He yearns for home, where he owns an *Estaminet*, and complains about too much work, probably justifiably. He does not talk about being mistreated.[3]

---

3. There may be some truth in this account. While Nazi authorities in Baden considered the foreign workers from Eastern Europe to be the best laborers, on occasion even surpassing the Germans, they were treated significantly worse than French, Dutch, and Indian prisoners of war.

eighteen

April 1943

There are now attacks on Berlin every night. But they do not appear to be very serious. It is strange how little one hears about them. The newspapers are only allowed to publish official reports, and private citizens shy away from giving detailed descriptions in their letters. Everyone is afraid to express opinions in writing, for fear of being branded a defeatist. At the same time, there supposedly is no internal censorship.

Schulenburg, among others, is also being considered for Ambassador in Madrid. In my opinion he does not have a chance. As Ambassador in Moscow he saw matters correctly, and that does not recommend him to Hitler, who saw them incorrectly.[1]

Our defensive war in Tunisia continues. I fear that the outcome can hardly be in doubt, considering the overwhelming superior strength of the opposition. But our greatest misfortune is the emergence of quasi-Francophiles in the French section of the Foreign Ministry.

These people side with the French with their hearts rather than with their heads. They still cling to the idea of collaboration and cannot understand that all that happened is our fault and that it is no longer possible for any respectable Frenchman to consider a sincere policy of cooperation with

---

1. Before the German invasion of the Soviet Union began in June 1941, Schulenburg had expressed grave doubts about the operation.

Germany. If we had really counted on France's good Europeanism, then we, ourselves, should have acted more "European" after their defeat. Instead, we were nothing but conquerors, just as elsewhere in Europe, our beautiful phrases notwithstanding. Great ideas do not come to petty people. No matter what such people say, they only talk of themselves and the satisfaction of their own miserable vanity.

Baden-Baden, 5 April 1943

I went to Strassburg. This "beautiful city" has barely suffered from the war. Only a few historical street names have been changed. It remains to be seen if this also means that the minds of the inhabitants have been changed [in our favor]. It will depend essentially on the conduct of the administration. The fact that we are appointing only Alsatians and Badenese as local officials—no "Prussians"—suggests that these people will treat the feelings of the local population with more understanding and more tact than in 1871. Only German is spoken on the streets and in restaurants. But these are superficial matters.[2] Unfortunately the S.S. is much in evidence here, too.

Baden-Baden, 6 April 1943

Dieckhoff has been posted to Madrid, Weizsäcker to the Vatican, Woermann to Nanking, Secretary of State in the Ministry will be Steengracht, head of the Political Division will be Henke [sic]. Gaus, Rintelen, and Hewel, all on Ribbentrop's staff for a long time, having done the labors of Sisyphus there, have now been rewarded for their difficult work with the title of Ambassador—Hewel will be the liaison with the Reich chancellery.

This reshuffle is not without interest, because it means a further removal of the professional diplomats from central to peripheral posts, and the consequent reallocation of their positions to Ribbentrop's people. In the minister's eyes diplomatic posts are irrelevant. Ambassadors and ministers, in his opinion, are nothing more than mailmen or, at best, executors of the

---

2. Prüfer's original entry for 5 Apr. 1943 suggests that he knew the Nazi treatment of the Alsatians was much harsher than he alleged here.

Minister's instructions. They do not need to have opinions of their own and, even less, do they need to state their views. He believes that those in the Ministry [offices in Berlin] who are in daily contact and communication with other government offices are dangerous obstacles. He sees them either as unwelcome alarmists or as people who meddle in matters which really only concern him, the one and only chosen adviser to the Führer. Perhaps shame also partially plays a role, the secret knowledge of his own inadequacy, which he wants to hide from the experts. He may feel like an amateur hunter who does not want to go hunting with the professional forester.

Consequently, Ribbentrop has always shown a tendency to remove all career diplomats, particularly the ones from the pre-Hitler period, or he hopes to place them in distant posts and remove them from influence. A few well-qualified specialists, such as Gaus and Ritter, who were indispensable to him, he neutralized by flooding them with meaningless routine work; thus he transformed them into mere technical machines who could not seriously influence the shaping of policy.

Likewise, he places liaison people such as Rintelen in his immediate, thus controlled, environment. Apparently he finds Hewel, who is not a career diplomat, particularly useful, because he is one of Hitler's former cronies and fellow prisoners from the N.S.D.A.P.'s period of struggle; as such, he always has easy access to the Führer.

Baden-Baden, 7 April 1943

Things are heating up in Tunisia. Our *locus minoris resistentiae* lies there. The loss of this last bridgehead in Africa could be disastrous, because of its likely repercussions in Italy, both in political and military terms.

Even now the atmosphere there seems more than depressed. An Italian Consul General [Guida] in a South German city, known to me from the past and who now visits me occasionally, is running around like a frightened chicken, telling pathetic stories about the suffering of his country. If only half of what he reports is true, the situation concerning food, transportation, and morale must indeed be more unfavorable than in Germany.

The American air raid on Paris and Antwerp two days ago caused more than 2000 civilian deaths, among them hundreds of children. This is downright murder, which cannot in the least be excused in terms of military necessity. Not even the excuse of intimidating enemy civilians by terror is valid, because those hit were French and Belgians, thus allied civilians. What will the neutral countries say to all this? Apparently nothing. They are too afraid of their masters, namely the Americans. How very different if the Germans were the culprits. To the subject of German atrocities could then be added welcome, new material for discussion.

Baden-Baden, 8 April 1943

Today I spent with A. in Karlsruhe. The city looks terrible. Entire streets are in ruins. The broken plate glass store windows have been boarded up with wooden planks. Rubble and ruins everywhere, and it still smells of smouldering fires.

Many people are supposed to have perished. No one knows the exact number. One hears rumors regarding the terrible fate of some. Notwithstanding all this, the movie houses are open for business.

Enemy planes were over Western Germany yesterday. No details are available. "The population sustained losses." This is now the typical phrase for such tragedies as reported in military news bulletins.

Baden-Baden, 12 April 1943

Mussolini visited Hitler. They discussed the military situation. Unfortunately two bankrupt partners do not make a solvent business.

The situation in Tunisia is very bad. No news of the Italian fleet. On the other hand, we are holding forth extensively on the radio about our impregnable Atlantic Wall. I fear this will not help us much on the Mediterranean coast.

Today O. came home from school very distressed. His teacher presented the situation to the pupils as it actually is. Desperate.

Baden-Baden, 14 April 1943

There were two early air alerts today. Both times the all-clear sounded after a quarter of an hour. In this town hardly anyone bothers with the sirens, because it is well known from experience that the targets of enemy planes are usually located deep in the interior of the country.

We have published news about a Bolshevist crime we stumbled upon in a forest near Smolensk. The Bolshevists shot over 10,000 prisoners, Polish officers, and then buried them in mass graves. The effect of this publication might have been enormous were it not for German atrocities perpetrated against the Jews.

Ilya Ehrenburg is supposed to have written a book showing the abysmal hatred of the Jews against their torturers. It is said that he especially would like to crush, flatten, and gas all of Europe with its 350 million people. How can there ever be real peace, if Jews, who have been insulted and tortured to the limits of their strength, are the advisers of our enemies? One cannot expect these unfortunates to be just.

And how can we reconcile the world to us if we cannot purge ourselves of these accusations? The Russians, having committed similar atrocities, have incriminated themselves, but that does not excuse what we have done. We? What our leaders have done, one should say. But where is the boundary between us [the common people] and them? How can we prove that *we* have nothing in common with *them* and that *we*, likewise, detest them and have suffered under them like the Jews and the others who have been persecuted? Our propaganda must remain ineffective, because we have not conducted ourselves any better than the Russians.

Baden-Baden, 15 April 1943

At midnight there was an air alarm, and we heard shooting over Karlsruhe and Stuttgart start about a half hour later. The British planes appear to have been numerous, coming in continuous waves. Today the military news bulletin confirmed that Stuttgart had been the target, and that at least 23 planes had been shot down. What do 23 planes and their crews mean compared to the terrible losses in men and matériel which each of these attacks, almost nightly, costs us?

Baden-Baden, 16 April 1943

The Soviet government seems to be rather at a loss concerning the discovery of the mass executions of Polish officers near Smolensk. They declared this to be the discovery of prehistoric mass graves. Until now it was unknown that prehistoric corpses wore Polish uniforms. A more stupid excuse could hardly have been contrived.

Baden-Baden, 21 April 1943

For the past 14 days this month we have had air alarms every day, and by no means only at night. Every time the German Radio Network is off the air it is a sign that somewhere a major attack is occurring. The accounts given by many refugees, who are now appearing here in large numbers from nearby [bombed] cities, explain what that means for those targeted. A woman from Mannheim told A. about the horror of the most recent attack. The destructions surpass all that has been experienced thus far. Even liquid phosphorous has been dropped, causing horrible burn wounds. Because of the large number of high-explosive bombs that hit the city, the loss of human life is very great. There is no protection against these two-ton bombs, at least there was none in Mannheim.

Baden-Baden, 23 April 1943

Notwithstanding the most beautiful weather, a gloomy Good Friday. My former navy colleague from Rio, Captain B. [Bohny], who presently works in Berlin, came to visit me. Nothing he said improved my morale. In Berlin those who are not blinded by, or involved in, propaganda are exceedingly pessimistic. The Tunisian adventure has been written off. Only reports from Turkey still sound optimistic. The Embassy in Ankara apparently cannot see that, even for the Turks, reality is more compelling than pipe dreams; we are cast in the role of the pipe dream, especially in light of the unavoidable loss of Tunisia, our last forward position in the Mediterranean.

Baden-Baden, 25 April 1943

Celebration of Easter without happy tidings. In Tunisia the Americans have attacked in force from the west. Today's military news bulletin sounded very meek.

Baden-Baden, 30 April 1943

Ribbentrop's 50th birthday. The Foreign Ministry, represented by the division heads and led by the Secretary of State, paid him a visit at Fuschl for the purpose of congratulations.

There has rarely been a more irksome farce. I was even later assessed for some kind of silver gift dedicated to the "revered leader" by his officials. Ribbentrop is really a tragic figure, a man without friends and joy, an actor who must compulsively continue to play his part, although the public loathes him and even his own clique betrays him. There was a brief reference to his birthday on the radio.

Laval met with the Führer in the presence of Bastianini. The communiqué was weak and colorless. Again, we have apparently sought in vain for a compromise between our French and Italian policies. Both are hopelessly muddled and thoroughly incompatible. [The official communiqué notes] "The questions pending between Germany and Italy on the one hand and France on the other were examined." Thus we have again tried to apply axle grease to wheels that have already been too hot for too long a time.

There is no ray of hope anywhere. Allied propaganda, particularly the so-called Atlantic Radio Station, never ceases to tell us about the misdeeds of the Nazi regime and to praise democracy. We already know that we are living under the rule of terror, that for us the war will probably be lost, and that human existence fares more pleasantly in a country governed by democracy than under a tyranny. There is thus no need for all this from the Allies.

As far as the German people are concerned, what is entirely missing [from these enemy effusions] and what makes them [the Germans] very mistrustful of the Allies is that they say nothing as to the treatment we—the people—can expect, if we were to lay down our weapons, even against Hitler and the party, and notwithstanding Nazi terror. The man in the street wonders if perhaps what Goebbels maintains is true, namely that the Allies are not only waging war against National Socialism, but are using it as a welcome pretext to eliminate, once and for all, German influence and German competition from this world.

If, today, the British and American governments were to make a declaration over the radio in which they solemnly promise to grant Germany an acceptable peace without Hitler and without the National Socialists, Hitler would be swept away tomorrow, and the German people would be ready for peace.[3]

---

3. Here Prüfer's postwar zeal to defend himself and his people failed to correspond to reality. On the one hand, Nazi opinion surveys (mainly secret police surveillance reports)

Let no one say that the terror of the Nazi regime has made listening to enemy broadcasts impossible and would thus prevent the spread of an Allied proclamation to the German people. One can be certain that, even if only a few hundred Germans were to receive such joyful news from the airwaves, it would sweep through the country like a storm.

Why does such a declaration fail to appear, a declaration that would not only bring life and happiness to thousands and thousands of Germans but also to soldiers and civilians of all other nations? Why, in the name of suffering mankind, does not some responsible person in the Allied camp have the courage to raise this question with Churchill and Roosevelt? Why must the victory for democracy, for which the Allies claim to fight, be more expensive than necessary? Or is this war, perhaps, fought for reasons other than democracy?

---

revealed an unprecedented low by May 1943 in the attitude of Germans towards their regime. The surveys documented their susceptibility to foreign propaganda, their severe criticism of the party and military leadership, and their gradual withdrawal from the cult-like view of Hitler. The Allied bombings of the Reich, on the other hand, had intensified hatred for the enemy and rumors that new German weapons would soon turn the war to Germany's favor. Moreover, no evidence exists to support Prüfer's contention that a coup would have found broad popular support in 1943 or was even expected. Not even the small German resistance that was working secretly to remove Hitler could agree on peace at any price.

nineteen

May 1943

I went to Munich this morning, where I saw my boyhood friend, O. G. [Gulbransson]. One of the most famous European caricaturists, he has aged a little, is somewhat thinner, and is a little depressed; yet, he has lost nothing of his lively humor. His only son, who is an architect, suffered severe shell shock during the last air raid, when he miraculously survived, the only remaining member of a flak crew posted on top of a Munich house.

Munich was not the place to generate much cheer between the two of us. Here, too, one sees but ruins and other traces of air attacks, although to a lesser extent than in Karlsruhe and Stuttgart. It is particularly striking that in the city of beer no alcoholic drinks could be obtained. [Their availability] might have contributed to a better atmosphere. Old artistic Munich, the happy *Bohème* of Schwabing, has ceased to exist.

In the evening I visited the artist, A. B. [Bachmann], in Ambach on Lake Starnberg. He had fled there to a beautiful old inn which, to be sure, is quite primitive but still breathes the spirit of old Bavaria from the Baroque era. My friend's studio in Schwabing, as well as his apartment with his irreplaceable paintings, mementos, and collections of a lifetime, have fallen victim to British bombs. His fate is typical of so many artists and their works.

Now that the original Allied claim to the effect that their planes were only aimed at war targets can no longer be maintained in the face of the destruction of entire cities, Allied propaganda excuses the demolition of

European cultural monuments by pointing out that the Germans began this in Warsaw, Rotterdam, London, and Coventry. Indeed has X a license to commit a murder because Y has committed one? Since German planes are supposed to be responsible for crimes against culture, are the British and Americans permitted to do the same? Works of art do not belong to a people, but to mankind. No one people has the right to destroy them. And even if it is done for reasons of "military expediency"—and that is probably the most repulsive justification because it serves not only as a pretext for the destruction of our cultural heritage, but also for murder—it still causes violence against the creations of divinely inspired [artists]; it is stupid and barbaric and will certainly be condemned by posterity.

All this should be put down in the memorial book of mankind and should be dedicated to the giant midgets of this revolting war!

Baden-Baden, 7 May 1943

Back in Baden-Baden. The Tunisian tragedy continues. The enemy succeeded in penetrating our lines in depth.

Lutze, the S.A. leader, was killed in a car accident while on an excursion; yesterday he was buried with much ceremony.

The career of this man was typical for many Nazi leaders, especially the morally better and relatively harmless ones. Lutze, who came from a lower middle-class family and whose whole character, behavior, and appearance illustrated this, was appointed to his post after Röhm's death; presumably the desire here was to debase and destroy the power of the S.A., even publicly, through the personality of its highest leader.[1] Every man in the party knew that Lutze, neither by virtue of native ability nor by ambition, could compete with Himmler and his S.S., let alone with Hitler himself. He was an insignificant, subservient, subordinate, but nevertheless reliable, man who would never have been able to summon such extravagant ambition as to challenge the demigods who idolize Hitler. He was always overjoyed to be in posession of his villa in Dahlem which, normally, he could never have hoped for even in his wildest dreams. All the brilliance of society life—a large car, riding horses, invitations to diplomatic affairs—was plenty enough to compensate him and his family for the meaningless and purely

---

1. Lutze was hardly as innocent as Prüfer portrayed him here. He intrigued against Röhm in his murder and in the murders of other SA leaders in 1934.

ceremonial power that Himmler had destined him for. His influence was equal to zero. He remained what he had been, a harmless petty bourgeois. There is a certain tragicomical logic about the demise of this man who had to die in an accident on an ordinary pleasure trip with his daughter.

Baden-Baden, 8 May 1943

A thoroughly black day! Biserta and Tunis are lost. There is still fighting, hopeless, of course, south of the city. It is easy to guess what the future will bring. The enemy will force Turkey to surrender its neutrality, and our forces will be driven from the Balkans. Thus we will lose the last source of oil in Rumania.

Again and again one must ask the question: why have we not been able to hold North Africa, not just Tunisia—by that time it was already too late? Did we underestimate the importance of this front, as we did in the first [World] War, or was it no longer possible, for more than a year, to send reinforcements? Stalingrad was a serious and painful defeat, Tunisia will cost us the entire war.

Berlin, 9 May 1943

With much on my mind I departed from Baden-Baden last night. Contrary to expectation, the journey was quiet. We arrived an hour late in Berlin, because somewhere air-raid alarms were under way, a matter of which I was totally unaware.

Berlin, 11 May 1943

I reported back to the Personnel Division. The reception was a little frosty. I somehow had the feeling that, as far as I am concerned, people have a bad conscience.

I had lunch with my navy friends. In view of the bad news from the Mediterranean, the conversation was rather strained. Because the submarine war has also come to a virtual standstill, the navy has good reason to be depressed. The Allies dominate the high seas. Thanks to their new defense weapons.

Berlin, 12 May 1943

Lunch with my old friend W. [Witzleben], who just returned from Bucharest. Nothing he reports from Rumania sounds very encouraging. We no longer enjoy respect or confidence anywhere. Everyone complains about the big shots and even more so about the minor officials. The Führer still enjoys a certain mystical aura. Opinion frequently has it that he does not know what is going on in the lower ranks. W. particularly complained about the extremely brash anti-Semitic activities of our [Nazi] party organizations in Rumania, where they are, in fact, nastier than elsewhere.[2]

Empty routine in the Foreign Ministry. No one mentions Tunisia, oil, or the Eastern front. On the other hand, the internal paper wars are of supreme importance. *Quem deus perdere vult.* . . .

After dinner Schulenburg stayed until midnight. We mutually complained, but could not come up with any solution. Schulenburg told me about his warnings regarding the attack on Russia. Of course, at the time, he did not consider Russian military potential to be as powerful as it has turned out to be; nonetheless, just as the military attaché did,[3] he continually tried to impress on Berlin that in no way should one talk of a mere military promenade to Moscow. But certain civilian advisers and, unfortunately, even a few generals, presented the Russian campaign to Hitler as precisely such [a promenade]—presumably out of servility.

There was no immediate reason for a preventive war in anticipation of a possible Russian plan of attack. Considering the unpredictability and amorality of Soviet policies, one could, in the long run, make no reliable predictions, but in the short run a Russian attack was certainly not imminent. That is proven by the fact that until our invasion, the Russians were still delivering goods to us as stipulated in the economic agreements; indeed, such goods were still delivered on the very day of our invasion. Therefore, even if the Russians had planned a later attack, we would have won precious time for liquidating the war in other areas if we had left the Bol-

---

2. It is uncertain whether Witzleben, who had suffered from poor health since his retirement by Hitler in Mar. 1942 and who lived on his estate near Potsdam, had been in Rumania. Prüfer, who had not approved of the military's role in the attempted assassination of Hitler in July 1944, may have fabricated the information about Witzleben to conceal the fact that he was referring to the former field marshal.

3. Gen. Ernst A. Köstring, attaché until 1941 and once a part of the pro-Russian faction in the German army during the Weimar Republic around the former chief of staff, Hans von Seeckt.

shevists in peace. The severing of relations with Yugoslavia is also proof of the Soviet Union's peaceful intentions.[4] Too late.

Berlin, 13 May 1943

Today I saw the new Secretary of State, Baron Steengracht. Rather in Ribbentrop's shadow than in his sun, this man's career skyrocketed incredibly fast, as is possible only in the Third Reich. Immediately before the war, he played a scarcely noticeable role on the great man's staff, on which, along the way, he was part of the famous "Office of the Commissioner of the Führer for Foreign Policy" [Dienststelle Ribbentrop]. Today he is the second in command at the Foreign Ministry.

In truth, it was in the shadows that Steengracht became great.[5] He never talked about himself, was never one of those on the staff who called attention to himself by intrigues or impertinence. He was a quiet, reserved, well-intentioned man, not particularly ambitious, who controlled himself and compromised, inasmuch as that was possible, considering the way Ribbentrop operates. Thus his new appointment in the Foreign Ministry met no covert resistance from the professionals. Overt opposition has been impossible for a long time anyway.

But even this white crow will not be able to change the course of events. I fail to understand how he could have fallen in with the gang surrounding Ribbentrop.

We are now mobilizing the Mohammedans in Bosnia and Herzegovina, and we are trying to mold them into a Free Corps.[6] At the same time we agitate against Jinnah's Muslim League. How does that make sense? Apparently we have not yet angered sufficient numbers of religious groups.

Last night there was yet another alarm. I had barely enough time to go to

---

4. In a move to conciliate Germany, the Soviet Union withdrew its diplomatic recognition of Yugoslavia, Norway, and Belgium on 9 May 1941. This was three weeks after the Nazi conquest of Yugoslavia and Greece.

5. Prüfer's enthusiasm for Steengracht, a colorless and servile bureaucrat, doubtless resulted from their collaboration in helping remove Luther, a mutual enemy in the AA, and from the aid the new secretary gave Prüfer in securing a leave from the ministry in 1943 to settle in Switzerland.

6. *Freikorps,* volunteer formations. Such units had developed during the German revolution of 1918–19 and contributed significantly to the political violence that characterized the Weimar Republic.

the basement before the shooting started. But it appears that the attack did not penetrate beyond the city's outer districts.

Berlin, 14 May 1943

Rahn, the "victor of Syria," has added another leaf to his laurels in Tunisia. He arrived in Rome, where he was rewarded for his Tunisian deeds with a high decoration. One could vary the old saying: you may not know how to win, but you know how to make use of defeat.

Professor G. [Gudzent] was unable to detect any real improvement in my health. In addition, my liver and heart are considerably enlarged.

Berlin, 17 May 1943

Air-raid alarms every night, but nothing much is happening. One gets used to interrupting his sleep around midnight for some two hours in the basement.

There is much talk about Franco's peace efforts. He will find approval neither in Britain, the U.S., nor in Russia—if, indeed, these rumors are true.

Our defeat in Tunisia has proven to be a genuine catastrophe. Today the British reported taking around 175,000 prisoners. According to a Turkish commentary, the posture of the French, including those in the Vichy government, contributed much to our defeat. How could it be otherwise?

Young N. [Neurath], who has just returned from Tunisia, tells the same tales as all the other combatants from North Africa: complete failure of the Italians, our own arrogance, dilettantism of the civilians, and underestimation of the opponents; these are the reasons for our defeat. Above all, the American preparedness for battle was much greater than we generally had thought.

Berlin, 18 May 1943

Once again I was in the Foreign Ministry, trying to convince Steengracht that I am completely superfluous in the Service. I pointed out that I no longer hold a regular position and that my views are hardly worth more than good suggestions. Furthermore, healthwise I am no longer able to perform regular duties. He finally agreed that I should take a well-needed trip to Switzerland with my wife. I am happy to escape the horrible atmosphere here, even if it is only for two weeks.

In the Foreign Ministry rumor has it that Russia has extended peace feelers via Italy. This sounds very improbable, but it is nevertheless said to be the truth.

Davos, 21 May 1943

Having picked up A. in Baden-Baden, we happily departed for Davos, the place where we met 20 years ago.[7] We arrived in Davos in the late afternoon, indulging ourselves in blissful memories. The place has hardly changed, only—a sign that even here the war is making itself felt—much quieter than in earlier days. The great hotels are closed. The weather is bad, cold and rainy, but to us it is the most beautiful spring. If only I could shake the nightmare of our inevitable return [to Germany]. But how could we remain here without money and without our son, whom we would have to leave at home?

Davos, 24 May 1943

We have been taking walks down old familiar paths and visited the places where we met and where we were so happy twenty years ago, in a happier time of no political rabble-rousing, when one did not suspect an informer and agitator in every person. Even over this fortunate country a heavy shadow has been cast. It is our fault that even here the sun no longer seems to shine so brilliantly on carefree people. Our repulsive propaganda has succeeded in spreading venomous hostility and terrorist spying everywhere, so that, as a German, one no longer dares to say as one pleases and no longer dares to go where one desires.

Today I saw an example of the impossible behavior of the official German and [Nazi] party officials; I heard at the Consulate that a coffee house

---

7. While both received treatment for tuberculosis in a sanatorium.

in Davos, which I particularly liked and was well familiar with in the old days, has been officially declared out of bounds [for Germans] by our own authorities. Germans who wish to enjoy the protection of the Consulate and good will of the party are forbidden to visit this place.

During my stay in Brazil the N.S.D.A.P. no longer played a role. It had not only been prohibited by the Brazilian government, but had actually been dissolved by us and had virtually disappeared.[8] Here the party has unfortunately not been forbidden. At least it might have been ordered to stay silent as, e.g., in Turkey. But it is expressly permitted to act as it pleases. I have seen for the first time the malicious effect which the activity of its organs has on all aspects of the local German colony and its relationship with the host country.

It is simply disgusting to observe the pressure exerted on every German who has not officially renounced the party. Who can dare to take such a step of renouncing the party without risking dire consequences to himself and his family here and in Germany? Only those who no longer have any ties to the Homeland, and people who have neither family, property, nor interests of any sort in Germany. But above all, it requires courage in order to be independent in Switzerland. Only those who have employment permits by reason of long residence [in this country] or those who are of independent means and who, consequently, can afford to live without working [enjoy this freedom]. But the overwhelming majority of Germans in Switzerland had and still have some kind of link with the old Fatherland. Even if people no longer have business ties with Germany as representatives of German firms or something similar, they still have some kind of material interests there. And, in the absence of these, they must take into consideration their relatives or friends [across the border].

If any German who has some connection with the Homeland kicks against the party's spikes, he will unmistakenly be shown the consequences of such behavior. That does not mean that he must join the party, for membership is only obligatory for higher officials, although this is not an official requirement. But every German national must be well-disposed toward the party. If he does not show this by attending party functions, participating in fund-raising drives, or obeying the rules and regulations of local party

---

8. But although banned by the Brazilian authorities in 1938, the party organization there had continued underground. Leading party officials, including Cossel, were attached to the German Embassy in Rio and the consulates to ensure their freedom to guide the party's activities, which involved spreading Nazi propaganda among and spying on the large German-speaking minority in southern Brazil.

officials, he exposes himself to ruthless reprisals from the petty and obsequious party fanatics.[9]

For minor infractions, the reprisals consist especially of a variety of economic ostracisms. If the individual happens to be a businessman, those of his customers who are party members or fellow travelers will boycott him, his business connections in Germany will be disrupted, the unfavorable information about him will be disseminated. If he happens to be a professional, say a physician, teacher, attorney, or academic, he will be openly criticized in Germany and shunned or slandered by the pious party members here in Switzerland. In more serious cases a culprit's passport will be invalidated, thus preventing his return to Germany. If, after all this, the recalcitrant individuals still do not crawl to the cross, they must be prepared for reprisals to extend to their friends and relatives back home.

As a result of this system of merciless terror, a nearly intolerable sense of dread, mutual mistrust, and fear of informers dominates the local German colony here. No one trusts anyone. Each sees in his countryman a possible enemy, spy, or informer.

The aforementioned coffee house is a good example of these realities. My wife and I, of course, immediately went to this place, where we had experienced the most enjoyable and happy hours of our stay in Davos some twenty years ago. The owner of this place and his adult children are dear friends of ours, and it gave us the greatest pleasure to see them again after so long a time. A few days later, we learned at the Consulate that a visit to this coffee house was a crime against party discipline. The reasons for the boycott are so trivial that it is pointless to spell them out. But it is wholly absurd that a foreign agency can impose a boycott in the host country on a duly authorized and legal local commercial establishment.

We did not pay attention to this silly and obnoxious decree and continued to visit our friends as before. I am curious if this "disobedience" will have any consequences for me. The Consul [Diel], being a well-intentioned, if somewhat nervous individual, will probably not denounce me. The party people are likely to do it.

---

9. It should be noted, however, that while the NSDAP in Switzerland, administered through the AO, was well-organized and distributed Nazi propaganda, its influence among local Germans had declined by 1943 because of the defeats inflicted on the Reich in the war. This may have been the reason for the AO's change of its party leader in Switzerland in the fall of 1943.

Davos, 25 May 1943

Today's newspapers are full of editorials on the astonishing news that Stalin has dissolved the Third International, the Comintern. The Soviet government has officially left this organization which, until now, represented the core of Moscow's policy. In the future in Moscow there will only be national Russian policies instead of international Communist policies. This, however, may be a bluff not to be taken seriously. But with this unexpected move on the [political] chessboard, Stalin has deprived the Axis of its main propaganda ploy, the Anti-Comintern pact. The goal of this agreement [the Axis alliance] was to fight against an organization; now that this organization no longer exists, at least on paper, the agreement has lost its meaning and purpose.

One could, of course, come to the conclusion that Stalin has taken this step to make it easier for Germany to conclude a compromise with a non-international Soviet Russia. After all, henceforth no further politically contentious issues should separate us; perhaps Stalin intends to build a golden bridge for a rapprochement.

We do not seem to interpret Stalin's step in this way, because German press responses are very skeptical and negative. The dissolution of the Comintern is interpreted as pure bluff, a maneuver to strengthen the Western powers in the belief of a Russia developing along the lines of democracy and away from internationalism. Is it possible that, once again, we are missing a golden opportunity? We already seem to have committed ourselves to a radical condemnation of the Russian move. Might this not be the right moment for peace feelers by Hitler or, better yet, against him?

Geneva, 27 May 1943

We came to Geneva to visit Abbas Hilmi. I had a long conversation with Consul General K. [Krauel], who is very dissatisfied and disgruntled; I can certainly understand why. A whole group of German officials, he among them, has been recalled from Switzerland. K., who is no party member, does not get along well with the minister [Köcher]. It appears that the latter is jealous instead of being glad that, in him [Krauel], he at least has an experienced and moderate man in his place, a man who is not totally committed to the party, as is the Counselor of Embassy B.; he, too, has been recalled.[10] B. is both a country group leader[11] and rabid National Socialist. At least he gives the impression that he is. I think he is merely an opportunist. Hopefully, his disappearance will ease the situation, especially in regard to Swiss authorities who would do well not to permit a new country group leader to come here. In that event, political peace could be quickly re-established, and the majority of Germans would heave a sigh of relief.

Geneva, 29 May 1943

The Khedive, Abbas Hilmi, my old friend from before the first World War, is very irritated with the German government because last year it forbade him to travel through Germany on his way to Turkey, where he wanted to visit his daughter. We do not refrain from any stupidity. It may be that, as a monarch, the Khedive does not like the current regime in Germany. Who does, after all? But in any case, he is a man who lost his throne in the last war because of us, and out of decency we should not refuse him a small service that cannot cause us serious harm.

Abbas Hilmi is very concerned about his yacht, which the German navy wants to take away from him. It is moored in a harbor on the Riviera. That, too, would be a senseless hardship; of what use is this little boat to us, especially since there is nothing further for us to do in the Mediterranean anyway?

---

10. Freiherr Sigismund von Bibra.
11. *Landesgruppenleiter*, head of a Nazi party organization in a foreign country and subordinate to Bohle and the AO in Berlin. Bibra was transferred in Sept. 1943 to the German Embassy in Madrid.

twenty

June 1943

Geneva, 1 June 1943

We have spent the last few days ambling through the old quarter of Geneva. How beautiful life could be if it were not for this horrible war!

These days there is much talk about an impending German attack on Switzerland from Southern France. That would be utter insanity. God knows we have enough enemies! Our erratic policies are so unpredictable that people believe anything is possible; furthermore, in light of the absurd and secretive behavior of our [Nazi] party organs, every extravagance seems plausible. But unfortunately, our Abwehr people are here in such number and their ineptness is so obvious that even the most innocent bystander must be aware that the fearful stories of German espionage are not just inventions.

Zurich, 3 June 1943

Ascension day. I visited an old acquaintance, the Egyptian statesman, Aziz Izzet Pasha, in the [Hotel] Baur au Lac. This unusually intelligent old man, who always tried to be just to Germany, presented me with an extensive list of our sins: our excesses against political opponents and Jews; our noisy and mendacious propaganda; the nonsense of our "New Order" in Europe, which in reality spells the conquest of Europe; the mistakes of our French policies; our intimidation of the Orientals.[1] I had little to say in response. It is difficult to be the *advocatus diaboli*, particularly if one suspects that the *diabolus* is a stupid devil, and that thus his enemy can make short shrift of him.

The Consul General here [Rausch] has also been recalled. Like K. [Krauel], he is hardly a Nazi, even if he had to run with the pack.

Davos, 5 June 1943

Again back in Davos. These beautiful days will soon be over. We are contemplating with horror our return to the Homeland—a place once so beautiful.

Davos, 6 June 1943

There was an air raid last evening. Even here such things occur. No planes were seen or heard. The Americans or British fly across Switzerland at great heights; this shortens their passage to Italy. No one here talks of neutrality, and the Swiss do not appear to take such violations of neutrality very seriously. Deep in their hearts, they are not neutral but completely on the side of the Allies.[2]

Zurich, 9 June 1943

The new Consul General D. [Dienstmann], an old friend and colleague, has arrived. Today, on my return trip to Germany from Davos, I called on him. He has no illusions as to the difficulties of his position: under suspicion by the Swiss government, informed on and pressured by the party, and without support from Berlin; that is truly no pleasant situation.

---

1. See chap. 8, n. 7.
2. Although Swiss sympathies in the war were significantly on the side of the Allies, Swiss neutrality provided benefits for Germany. Nevertheless, the Nazis planned an invasion of Switzerland and only reluctantly postponed it until after the expected final victory.

The worst is that, here too, just as back home in the Foreign Ministry, the boss can never be sure of his co-workers. He never knows whether someone on his staff has secret connections with an official of the S.D., the Abwehr, or some other dubious outfit, and if so, whether these folk are writing true or false reports about him. But above all, he always has to worry because these clandestine intrigues can compromise him vis-à-vis the Swiss government at any time.

There is hardly any cure for this intolerable situation because this complex system of intrigue is an important and deliberate component of the National Socialist regime. The only radical solution for officials would be to retire from the Service. But "jumping off," as the saying goes, is very difficult for an established official. It smells too much of treason, especially during the war, when the entire country is in danger.

Baden-Baden, 10 June 1943

Back home after an uneventful trip. Here everything is unchanged. Frequent air alarms, but no actual raids. Living conditions deteriorated. This is especially noticeable in hotels. Tonight we dined in an old, first-class hotel which, until recently, was very well provisioned, and where, notwithstanding the war, one could, within certain limits, still eat and, above all, drink well. Now the food is very poor, and wine can only be obtained with difficulty, and even then, only by old customers. This is especially noteworthy in this region, where wine, perhaps not of superior quality, is nonetheless produced in great quantity. It is my impression that much wine is being hidden and diverted to the black market. The physical appearance of this formerly excellent hotel is now dilapidated, although efforts have been made to keep up appearances. Tablecloths are stained and seedy, silverware and china are worn, worse so than a few months ago. This general deterioration is mainly due to the increasing lack of trained personnel. Only old people, disabled soldiers, and unskilled, reluctant foreigners are on the staffs.

Baden-Baden, 15 June 1943

Notwithstanding domestic problems, the last few days have passed all too quickly. In addition, none of us are very healthy. The war news is dismal. The Allies have occupied the Italian islands of Pantelleria and Lampedusa, south of Sicily, almost without a fight, because the Italians provided almost no resistance.

Berlin, 16 June 1943

I am writing in the basement of the Hotel Adlon. It is 2 a.m. and an air attack is in progress. I am dead tired after all the traveling, and I can barely hear the artillery that echoes faintly in the distance. A young man [Sedlmayr] is sitting next to me; I know him from Rio, where he was assigned to the Embassy on a rather dubious and suspect assignment, supposedly for "special economic tasks." As far as I can tell, he represented some industrial cartel that had the approval of the Foreign Ministry. This fellow, at the time, was only 24 years old. He was sent to Brazil during the war, where he was to look after certain German economic interests, i.e., under diplomatic cover. This strange young man is now sitting next to me while the flak is bursting outside. He is visiting Berlin. His office is in Stockholm. How, in these days, he can live abroad, supplied with foreign currency, and exempt from military duty during the war, is one of the many mysteries of contemporary Germany. It is now 2:30, and we can return to our rooms.

Berlin, 18 June 1943

In this burning and perishing world, there are strange instances of calm and inertia. Today, I dined with a colleague [Levetzow] who has been assigned to an insignificant neutral post [Spain]. This man, a grand seigneur of the old school, has come to terms with his appointment, although he is not yet beyond ambition and surely uncertain as to the unimportance of this post. He is actually happy, because the Duke of X. [Alba], of most noble extraction, recently gave a dinner attended by hundreds of guests; "all of Europe" is talking about this event. What a setting for this man, a representative of the Reich! He has forgotten, or has not yet noticed, that the Reich, which he represents, is no longer that of Maria Theresa's. He was born at least 200 years too late. He is so caught up in the social life of bygone times that, like Archimedes in his circle, the soldier came in and killed him.

Sztójay invited me for lunch at the UFA palace for the official celebration of the 75th birthday of the Hungarian Regent, Horthy. He [Sztójay] was solemn and boring. The Turkish Ambassador [Arikan] drove me home. Once again he vehemently assured me of Turkish neutrality. He may [personally] be honest in these protestations. The question is: can his government keep its frivolous promises? I doubt it. It would be suicide for the Turks.

Today, in the hotel lobby, I met a Belgian acquaintance [T'Serclaes]; he is here on some charitable mission. He complained of the inept and obnoxious policies we have recently adopted toward the King of Belgium and the country in general: moderate and conciliatory people [among the German occupation forces] have been recalled and replaced by new and more radical elements. Psychologically our behavior in the question of the Belgian prisoners of war defies understanding. Everywhere, unnecessary rigidity combined with our stupid ideology has lost us such meager sympathies as we still may have enjoyed.

This man, too, claims to know something about alleged Russian desires for a separate peace. Around here such rumors are common.

Berlin, 21 June 1943

I spent the weekend quietly in the country with my friend L. [Langenn] in B. [Bellin]. Here, too, among the landed gentry there is opposition to Hitler, perhaps even more so than among the bourgeoisie. But, by the same token, here too terror does not permit the opposition to develop. The gentry is afraid of local villagers, small peasants and farm workers. These rural proletarians have been wooed and fattened by the party. Thus *they* are the [party's] supporters, *not* the estate owners. The landed gentry and city dwellers who own estates in this region—one of my friend's neighbors is an actor, the other a non-Aryan [i.e., a Jew]—are bitter enemies of the regime. Its adherents are the workers not rooted in the soil, and the small peasants, the Communists of tomorrow.[3] Here, too, the National Socialist and Bol-

---

3. The disenchantment of upper-class Germans with the regime resulted not, as Prüfer implies here in defending his friends, from their disapproval of Hitler and his policies. Instead the unhappiness stemmed from the government's failure to win the war, return the Reich to world-power status, and preserve the elites atop the sociopolitical hierarchy. Regarding the peasants, they were preoccupied overwhelmingly with their own material welfare and rarely looked beyond their villages.

shevist movements have much in common. Both represent the same milieu, the same social strata, and the same methods of agitation.

My friend is the stereotype of the Brandenburg landed nobility: rooted in the sandy soil, religious, austere, and carefully educated. He is a former guards officer, who was imbued with liberal ideas when he lived in England; he has the best patriarchal intentions for his subjects, and is averse to any and all injustice or despotism. He loathes from the depth of his soul the demagoguery of National Socialism, the suppression of free speech, and the absolute domination of the state over the individual. He supports decentralization and local paternal self-government, unhampered by centralized state control. The Hitler regime has undermined this order by pitting asocial and unproductive rural elements against the estate owners. The regime then placed this rabble in positions of control. The lesser party bigwigs in the rural areas are made up of such failures and ambitious upstarts. Sometime in the future, after the collapse of National Socialism, they will turn out to be the vanguard of rural Bolshevism.

There are more than a hundred Russian and Polish prisoners of war on this estate, so-called "foreign workers." They move about freely in the village and do not seem to be dissatisfied with their lot. The driver, who picked me up at the distant train station, was a Pole who, for about an hour and a half, jabbered about agriculture while we were passing through fields and forests. He hardly seemed aware that he was a prisoner.[4]

Berlin, 22 June 1943

Another air raid and some shooting, but the damage was insignificant.

I met a former colleague from Abyssinia who, until recently, was imprisoned by the British. He was set free as part of a prisoner exchange and noted that captivity in Africa was not too unpleasant. British behavior was correct and free of unnecessary hardships.

He denigrated the Italians as soldiers. They surrendered almost without resistance. But to be fair, it should be noted that their lines of supply had been cut and that they were unable to provision themselves locally.[5]

---

4. See chap. 16, n. 4.

5. Prüfer's account in OD, entry for 24 June 1943, shows that this favorable comment about the Italians was fabricated for the time he purported to have written it. Not only had he disliked Italians since their opposition to Germany in World War I, but by 1943, as the conflict in the Mediterranean had turned against the Axis, anti-Italian feeling in Germany had surged forth. Contrast, for example, his view of them in OD, entry for 14 July 1943.

Berlin, 25 June 1943

An acquaintance from Barmen [Kapp] visited me today. He told terrible tales about his home town. British planes caused frightful havoc. He spoke of 18,000 casualties, most of them burned to death in fire storms.

Yesterday the British hit Elberfeld. Losses were "heavy." Army reports have never admitted anything like that before. Our defenses against these massive attacks are weakening. As a result of these reports, people are nervous because they expect renewed attacks on Berlin.

Berlin, 27 June 1943

Unpleasant Sunday. Joyless faces. Worry and fear dominate, and even the paltry pleasures which one can enjoy hereabouts, at the movies and theaters, seem trivial and unnatural. Without saying so, everybody awaits the howl of air-raid sirens. A death dance, as during the plague in the Middle Ages.

My Belgian friend [T'Serclaes] recounted a particularly flagrant case of stupid violence and ignorance on the part of our authorities. Who is responsible? The Belgians tried to obtain the release of their prisoners of war, i.e., those who have more than three children, a total of about 500 men; had we agreed, this might have had a conciliatory effect on the Belgians. Instead we released only those who were fathers of more than five children, a tiny number, and thus we achieved the opposite of what was intended. It is as if we were mocking the Belgians. I have tried in vain to alert the appropriate Foreign Ministry authorities to this calamity.

Berlin, 29 June 1943

Today, the Reuter agency proclaimed that I have been sentenced to 25 years for espionage! In addition, a whole group of former embassy members was sentenced, among others, the assistant to the naval attaché, captain Bohny, and the Legation Counselor, Becker; luckily, like me, they, too, have only been sentenced in *contumacium*. This verdict, which cannot be more annoying, is an outright breach of [international] law, both in the formal and real sense. As an ambassador I am no more under the jurisdiction of Brazil than the [diplomatic] officials subordinate to me. But even if the abrogation of extraterritorality was taken for granted—today any legal anomaly is possible—to indict a diplomat for espionage is totally absurd, because by virtue of his office, a diplomat investigates and reports on everything—incidents, conditions, and moods—in the country to which he has been posted. Usually such information is not common knowledge and would be inaccessible to ordinary mortals. A diplomat is thus always a sort of privileged spy. And precisely because of that he is given legal international immunity, which means that he is under extraterritorial jurisdiction, not subject to the authority of the nation to which he is accredited. If the diplomatic privilege of unrestricted reporting were abrogated, diplomats would become superfluous and could hand their post over to any journalist. All one can demand of them is that they stay away from professional spies, counterintelligence agents, the *deuxième bureau*, the "secret service,"[6] and that they not support these clandestine operatives. Also, reports from those sources should not be forwarded through official diplomatic channels. It must have been very difficult for the Brazilian court to prove that I engaged in espionage, because I never had any professional dealings with those shady figures of the German secret service who, of course, operated in Brazil.[7] The fact that every country maintains secret agents abroad is a truism known to everyone who attends the movies. It is not necessary for diplomats to use these people. For the most part, they are better informed than the pirates of the intelligence services. On the other hand, of course, occasional contact with these people at social and other functions is unavoidable, especially since the agents always seek out diplomatic personnel precisely because they are such an excellent source of information.

Naturally, I immediately lodged a protest against the Brazilian verdict with the Legal Division of our Foreign Ministry. Herr A. [Albrecht], who currently runs this Division after Gaus was moved to Ribbentrop's staff, accepted this outrageous verdict with calm; after all, it does not concern *him.* He said that I, too, should feign indifference, because I am not within reach of the Brazilian authorities. He fails to understand that this verdict defames my character and offends my honor. He also seems indifferent to the fact that, in the likely event that we should lose the war, this business may have very disadvantageous material consequences for me.

Of course I will not allow this matter to rest. Consequently, I also protested to the Secretary of State and asked him for the intervention of Spain, which takes care of our interests [in Brazil]. This he promised to do.

---

6. Original in English and placed in quotes.
7. However, he had collaborated extensively in Brazil with the Abwehr.

twenty-one

July 1943

The former Minister of a neutral power, Herr G. S. [Siddiq], had lunch with me. He spoke insistently in favor of a separate peace with Russia, which he definitely considers possible. Allegedly Moscow is not in the least averse to such a deal. Russia is much more exhausted than we thought, and a new *volte-face* of Stalin would not be unexpected. Mussolini has similar ideas. Since my guest is not only a very bright man, but also an expert on Russian affairs, I believe that his views weigh more heavily than the rumors circulating in the Foreign Ministry. This afternoon I received some confirmation from Ministerial Director Sch. [Schröder] as to the accuracy of Minister G. S.'s opinions, opinions I had just heard at lunch. Sch. favors such plans, and emphasized that Italy urges the liquidation of our ill-fated Russian adventure. Thus far, such diplomatic moves have failed because of Hitler's resistance.

This evening I saw Schulenburg. The conversation turned on the same theme. He, too, believes initiatives with Moscow aiming at a separate peace would in no way be a hopeless venture. He confirmed the Italian efforts along those same lines with Hitler. Ribbentrop is also favorably inclined in the event of Russian peace feelers but, as usual, he failed to act and probably did not even make a serious effort to do so the moment he met resistance [from Hitler]. He is nothing but an obedient servant. For Hitler, anything Russian-Bolshevist is a red flag. Whoever raises such issues risks provocation of one of Hitler's infamous fits of rage. Germany's fate is in the hands of a neurotic.

Berlin, 2 July 1943

Lunch with Planck, the former Secretary of State in the Reich chancellery. Among others, Popitz was also invited. The latter was very pessimistic, particularly in regard to industrial development, which is rapidly declining. The date of our defeat can easily be predicted. Goebbels' phrases cannot undo the damage caused by air raids. This must somehow be aborted, even if this entails accepting inevitable losses. But even Popitz does not have an answer as to how. All of us are lost in a dark forest, unable to find our way out.

Berlin, 4 July 1943

I spent the entire Sunday with Sch. [Schröder] in his house in Dahlem. He thinks as I do about the initiatives here and in Stockholm; this matter is much bruited about in the Foreign Ministry. In Stockholm, a Russian by the name of Alexandrovski [*sic*], apparently a former Russian Minister in Prague, has contacted one of Canaris's men and is supposed to have suggested conclusion of a separate peace with us. The Russians are said to be ready for such a move if it were based on the status quo of 1940, i.e., the division of Poland, annexation of the Baltic states and Bessarabia by Russia, adjusting the Finnish border in their favor, and German agreement to Russian rights to the Straits. By the same token, Germany will renounce all Russian areas.

Allegedly, the Russian emissary is a Jew; because of that, Hitler supposedly has thus far rejected this proposal on the advice of a "Russian expert" in the Foreign Ministry.[1] But the bridges have not yet been burned—so rumor has it.

---

1. The alleged "expert" is unidentified. Alexandrov had arrived in Stockholm in mid-June 1943 en route to London and failed in his efforts to meet Kleist (see chap. 9, n. 1). After Kleist's return to Berlin, at which time he was arrested and interrogated by the SD and the information obtained forwarded to Hitler through the Abwehr, the Germans had mysteriously labelled Alexandrov and Clauss "Jews." This erroneous claim was obviously for Hitler, who had not yet authorized the Stockholm affair; he quickly termed the Stockholm affair "Jewish"-inspired and ordered that it be ignored.

Berlin, 9 [sic] July 1943

Stupidity everywhere. Until now we had a conciliatory and under-standing representative in Brussels, Herr von B. [Bargen]. God knows why, but this man has been recalled, and in his place we sent an S.A. man, per-sonally a good fellow, but a party functionary and, thus, unsuitable for this assignment. That sounds paradoxical for a nation in which state and party are supposedly identical. The hard reality is that abroad an avowed party man is viewed with mistrust. In addition, our new representative in Brussels is a somewhat brusque and crude Bavarian who, for that reason alone, is likely to offend the Belgian Court.

In the press we are reporting Sikorski's plane crash off Gibraltar as though it was a Soviet assassination. This would seem to be a sign that we have abandoned notions of a separate peace with Russia.

There was a mishap in Madrid. Former minister Z. [Zechlin] has "taken off" for unknown quarters. He had been asked to return to Germany. Since there was no good reason for this request, he suspected a trap and preferred to remove himself from all potential hazards by absconding. Because he was a Social Democrat during the Weimar period, his mistrust of Gestapo intentions may not have been entirely unfounded.

Berlin, 7 July 1943

Today I had lunch with Baron O. [Oppenheim], whose nephew re-ported dreadful tales from his hometown, Cologne. The old inner city is supposedly almost completely destroyed. Only the cathedral remains vir-tually intact. Fatalities are reported to be 20,000, the bombed-out homeless are estimated at 300,000. I think that we are paying for Coventry and Lon-don. It is astonishing that no details of these British raids are reported in the newspapers. At best there is only the laconic report of the raid itself. If the intent here is to hide the effects of these attacks from the people, this is a grievous error. The opposite is achieved, because the effects of the attacks become exaggerated through rumor and fear. But above all, no one any longer trusts official communiqués.

Berlin, 9 July 1943

Again the British raided Cologne. There cannot be much left of this city.

Ribbentrop is slightly ill and must remain in bed. Since he continues to "govern" from his sickbed, the general anxiety of his staff and in the Foreign Ministry is more perceptible.

In the Foreign Ministry, to "govern" means inflationary and hectic committee work, which has replaced the work of individual experts. The sovietization of our supposedly authoritarian Ministry has resulted in an unbearable slowdown, a virtual paralysis of the entire system. This is the worse because members of these committees are almost all dilettantes. By way of example, I have noted elsewhere that the three principal members on the Indian committee, the so-called specialists, have never been to India. The Secretary of State, who can certainly not lay claim to expertise in American affairs, is head of the American committee, which has made the removal of Roosevelt—is anybody laughing?—its main task. His deputy is Rahn, the "victor" of Syria and Tunisia, who has never been in the U.S.A. and who knows South America only from a brief economic trip. In these *Gremien*—also a nice new German word—all topics are simply talked to death. No practical results are forthcoming. At best, these activities result in propaganda sheets printed on a massive scale which, for the most part, never reach their intended audience—but this, of course, is no great misfortune. In Fuschl, once again, these policy-makers are chewing on a declaration of independence and eventual unification of the Arab countries. We have discussed this matter ever since I came back to Germany. Because of general doubts and various considerations, this project has never gotten past the "planning stage," as the experts used to say in the day of the League of Nations. Meanwhile, militarily we are no longer in the distant vicinity of the Arab countries. Although our promises of independence for this region are nothing but pious platitudes, we have not even been able to bestir ourselves to make such promises and continue to bow to the Italians in Libya (where they are no longer present), the French in Syria (where de Gaulle and the British now rule), and to the Turks who, sooner or later, will join the enemy.

In Russia, intense fighting has erupted in the region between Bielgorod and Orel, where both Russia and Germany claim to be on the offensive. Probably the Bolshevists had planned a major attack, which we forestalled, realizing in time what they were doing. Now the battle is stalemated, and our troops will be further weakened without a chance of achieving any noticeable successes.

On the propaganda "sector" (another fashionable term) against Russia, we are once again singing the song of Katyn forest. There are other such songs in the same key: Vinnitsa, Odessa, etc. They will surely banish Stockholm's sensitive angel of peace.

A few days ago, I obtained unusual information; it sounds so improbable that I am only noting it: the Anglo-American attack in North Africa did not come as a surprise to the Abwehr. The Führer's entourage, however, told him too late, "in order not to disturb him." It is also said that after he received this report, he did not believe its veracity. Possibly this version is circulated by Canaris in order to detract from his own guilt.

Berlin, 10 July 1943

Yesterday the Allies landed on the southern coast of Sicily. "The battle is in progress," so says the official army report. We have disastrous memories of that expression dating back to the events in North Africa. If the battles were going well, the army reports would certainly not be so quiet.

I heard further details about the Stockholm intermezzo from an official in the office who is familiar with this matter. Apparently it was amply sufficient to discredit the Russian emmisary [Alexandrov], simply because he was introduced by an Abwehr man [Clauss] who was not of pure Aryan ancestry. The Russian himself is not a Jew, notwithstanding earlier claims to the contrary. He actually is supposed to have been with Molotov in Berlin. My source says that we inquired in Moscow via Bulgaria whether the initiative in Stockholm was serious. Of course this was denied. How could one possibly have made the Bulgarians accessories in these matters! There were rumors in the Vatican that in Venice rooms were reserved for the Russian delegation. These were, most likely, pipe-dreams; but they are indicative of how widely the news of a Russian peace initiative had spread.

According to Sch. [Schröder], my efforts to be released with a "permanent vacation" in Switzerland are not entirely hopeless. After all, around here I am only an obstacle.

Berlin, 12 July 1943

It is not unknown that, on the [Foreign] Minister's directive, various committees have been established for all political areas that are supposed to be "handled," i.e., discussed in the Foreign Ministry. These pretty heterogeneous bodies meet regularly and have received instructions that every two weeks they must submit success stories to the Führer—and this is typical—about their propaganda activities. They are supposed to report successes, *à tout prix*. If, as in the case of the Arab committee, such results are meager or fail to materialize? Are the committees supposed to lie? Invent successes? First Ribbentrop sterilized the Foreign Ministry, then he paralyzed its best officials and frequently replaced them with incompetents and dilettantes, and now he finally demands success stories. In any event, the only function of this Ministry, a Ministry in name only, is to dupe Hitler into believing that this organization fufills some useful purpose. One can hardly imagine a more dangerous sham. The reports will be according to expectations. All the committees outdo each other for favorable news.

I have only seen the reports of the Arab committee, of which I am a purely nominal member.[2] Since the members of this particular debating society are mostly decent people of the old school, they tend to abstain from fraud; thus success stories are few and far between. Therefore, this committee is not likely to become very popular with the boss.

Yesterday the Gauleiter in Cologne held a "celebration." Considering the ten thousand casualties of the most recent air attack, this is a somewhat bold, if not, indeed, preposterous undertaking. This is unlikely to increase sympathy for the party leaders of the Rhineland. Everything that happens in Germany now has but one purpose: somehow to make the declining morale of the population appear outwardly resolute and confident for Hitler's benefit. The Gauleiter knows, just like the rest of us, that pain, disappointment, and despair prevail throughout his district and that hardly anyone still hopes for, or believes in, a reasonable end to this great adventure. Those that do, cling by some sort of mystical faith to Hitler's genius, a faith that has been preached to them over and over again, but one they would have given up long ago if they had been thinking straight. They are the sole supporters for their Gauleiter. Only with their help can he present a pretty picture. So he holds a celebration! And thus they feign unshakable faith in "proud sorrow."

Everything is thoroughly hypocritical. Hitler receives whatever success stories Ribbentrop places before him. But even Ribbentrop is ignorant of the truth. A report, which by his order I sent him, was falsified by the "staff" without my knowledge. This I found out only by coincidence, by an inadvertent clerical error; the report was edited so that it would not disturb the serene peace of the Great Man!

---

2. Prüfer was in fact head of the Arab committee.

Berlin, 14 July 1943

Reports from Sicily today sound particularly bad. The Allies are moving inexorably against ever-weakening Italian defenses. Mussolini can no longer overcome the fatigue of his people. Tonight, once again, enemy planes were over Berlin. To sleep is virtually impossible.

Berlin, 18 July 1943

Attaché F. [Ferring], who is here on brief furlough from Leningrad, where he serves as a grenadier, gave me a vivid picture of the situation on that sector of the front. No soldier believes that the city can be taken. There is even less confidence in final victory. He called the mood of the soldiers "gray resignation." The troops are ready to die. To be sure, there is no enthusiasm for rebellion, but by the same token, there is no élan. There is no escape from fate.

Thus, everywhere in Russia we face desperate defensive battles. The Allies are making slow but inevitable progress in Sicily. Why does no one understand that it is high time, more than high time, to end the war by diplomatic means, even if this entails great sacrifices? Weapons are lacking, and our propaganda has long since been discredited.

Berlin, 19 July 1943

Bad news is piling up. The Italians surrendered Girgenti, and today Rome was attacked for the first time from the air. The Italian air force is exhausted, and the fleet is idle in port. Is it inactive because it cannot fight or because it does not want to?

Is it any different at home? A year ago the German army seemed almost invincible. We were racing from victory to victory, and then suddenly there was a drastic change that brought us one defeat after another. The increasing material superiority of the enemy cannot, in and of itself, explain this decline of German resistance. Neither the deterioration of our human and technical resources, nor our miscalculations, particularly in the air war (see the predictions of Göring-Meier), can account for this collapse. Of course, the declining physical strength of the people due to exhaustion and overexertion must be taken into consideration, particularly in view of the food shortages for women; also there is the total paralysis of such modest political authority that National Socialism may still have enjoyed, and which has been replaced by mere propaganda; and finally, there are the corruption and black marketeering, born of hunger and greed. All these factors are involved, but they still do not adequately explain this sudden and terribly rapid demise.

Perhaps the ultimate reason for this dreadful reversal is that the twilight of the gods is now upon the mass of the people who followed Hitler with such blind faith. It has become clear that the wrong road was chosen; that everybody was duped; and that all the unimaginable sacrifices were offered to a false idol, sacrifices which will earn us no reward, only punishment. These realizations have drained our courage, throttled our enthusiasm, and raised doubts as to the justice of our cause.

Most certainly, confidence has been eroded by the excesses of the regime, excesses which have gradually become public knowledge. To the extent to which there is such an awareness.[3] The populace tried to justify them on the grounds that they were directed only against internal adversaries of the system. Given the perception of the New State as just and good, such atrocities appeared to be revolutionary but justifiable suppression of the opposition—no matter how merciless these measures may have been. The Russian-Bolshevist example, which we, as neighbors of the Soviet Union, were able to observe at closer quarters than other European nations, seemed to many to be proof of the old adage that the end justifies the means. But probably even to the most faithful advocates of Hitlerism, the cruel persecution of those, such as the Jews, which the regime strives to exterminate for ideological reasons, must by now seem to be inexcusable. The persecution of these innocent people, who are being annihilated solely because their existence does not conform to the ideal projection of the National Socialist "Weltanschauung," has burdened the conscience of every individual who knew about it and has affected his service to the Fatherland and government that is capable of such horrors. Since coercion and the oath of allegiance exact obedience to the government, people endure, but do not follow voluntarily or with a joyful heart. We are in a crisis of faith and have no one to rescue us. I am convinced that most of our

---

3. This statement, which Prüfer invented along with most of this revised entry, likely referred to the Nazi persecution of the Jews, which he mentioned later in this paragraph. In contrast to his comment here, however, his original diaries (entry for 22 Nov. 1942) show that he had heard about the annihilation of the Jews and believed it to be true. He had also said nothing about the Jews in the original version of this entry; that omission, in fact, revealed that Prüfer supported Hitler and, because of the diplomat's nationalism, found it difficult to criticize Nazi policies.

people desire the removal of Hitler and his system and that they would greet his removal with joy; indeed, they might contribute to his downfall, provided they knew for certain that our enemies had nothing more in store for us. If the Allies were to exploit these very real feelings propagandistically, and if they would offer an acceptable peace on condition that Hitler were eliminated, National Socialism would disappear, notwithstanding all the terror. But as long as the enemy insists on unconditional surrender, thus justifying Goebbels' warnings against capitulation, the nation will keep resisting, reluctantly, but resigned, as long as possible.[4] Determined resistance to the bitter end, which National Socialism preaches, offers some chance, if only a slight one. The Allied terms of surrender offer none.

Once again I have asked to be granted a leave of absence in Switzerland. The Secretary of State, now in Fuschl, appears to be favorably inclined. I hope the decision does not come too late—as usual in such matters; a further delay would prevent me from carrying out my beautiful plan because I would no longer be in physical condition to accomplish my aims. In that event, I would have to abandon my family in this witches' cauldron. This reminds me of a French fable I read as a child: *La chèvre de Monsieur Séguin.* I no longer remember who wrote it. In this fable, a goat desperately tries to save herself and her kid by defending the door of her dilapidated stable against an attacking wolf. The goat—in fables goats indeed talk— says: *Oh, pour vu que je tienne jusqu'à l'aube!* But she is unsuccessful, and the wolf devours her and her offspring. My position and that of my family seems to be similar. *Pour vu que je tienne jusqu'à l'aube!*

Berlin, 20 July 1943

San Lorenzo in Rome suffered greatly during the recent air raid. Apart from that, no monuments seem to have been damaged. The attack was aimed at Porta Tiburtina and Porta Maggiore, primarily working-class districts. The British report said that the pilots had instructions to go easy on monuments and artworks. But what can an average pilot from the United States know about such matters! It is, and remains, unheard of and unnecessary barbarism to bomb a city like Rome.

General N. [Niedenführ] visited me, on leave from the central sector of the Russian front. The bleakest of pictures: general confusion, bureau-

---

4. See p. xii.

cracy, and infighting among the army, S.S., O.T., and civilian authorities. In addition, bad partisan terror far behind the front. Nevertheless, N. does not believe that the Russians will gain serious advantages; nor will we. He stressed that these predictions are only valid now. Russian superiority is increasing; the future can easily be predicted.

The situation in Sicily is extremely serious. Catania is about to fall. The Italians are very exhausted.

Berlin, 21 July 1943

Hitler and Mussolini met the day before yesterday, somewhere in northern Italy. What they decided has not yet been revealed. [The negotiations] are exclusively concerned with military questions of the greatest and, I fear, most disastrous, consequences. The Americans have taken Caltanissetta and are thus in the middle of Sicily. Enna has also been lost. The end seems near.

Tonight, for the first time, the newspapers contain no anti-Russian propaganda. Coincidence or second thoughts?

Berlin, 23 July 1943

The Americans have made further progress along the south and west coasts of Sicily. The news has just arrived that Palermo has been taken. The collapse of Italy can only be a question of a few days. What will our remaining allies and supporters do then? They certainly will not perish heroically with the rest of us.

Seichau, 24 July 1943

We had lunch with our Arab friends; the Secretary of State was also there. We did not talk about the bad news. Only when some of us went for a walk after lunch did we dare to whisper about our apprehensions. Like ostriches, we stick our heads into the sand, for fear of appearing defeatist. This is simply ridiculous.

This evening I traveled to S. in Silesia, to visit my friends R. [Richthofen]. They invited me to "celebrate" my birthday. I arrived here an hour ago, around midnight, after a long journey in an old-fashioned hunting carriage, which met me at the train station. The way led through peacefully sleeping villages, past dreamy fields under an indescribably bright, starry sky. How beautiful this world could be if its inhabitants were less unreasonable.

Seichau, 25 July 1943

We spent the morning in the fields where the harvest is in progress and where we chased a small fox, which the forester shot, from a haystack. There is no trace of war around here. Only occasionally does a plane stray over this region, and even then it is usually one of ours.

Seichau, 26 July 1943

My birthday was celebrated with touching attentiveness: roses on the table and culinary delicacies from an almost forgotten era of peace. The hostess, a famous opera singer before her marriage, treated me to my favorite songs.

There was disturbing news at noon: Mussolini has abdicated. Fascism is finished. The King has taken over the high command, Badoglio is the head of the government, Guariglia, the Ambassador in Ankara, is Foreign Minister. According to Badoglio's proclamation, the war will continue. But in Rome Fascist emblems are being removed, and the city is flying flags as though celebrating a victory. Obviously the intent is to maintain public discipline, in order to conduct peace negotiations without chaos in the background. There can be no doubt that the Fascist dream is over.

The most varied rumors are circulating about Mussolini. According to British reports, he is supposed to have been arrested while attempting to escape to Germany. Other reports say that the king had him apprehended in Rome. The imprisonment of several other prominent Fascists has also been announced. If Mussolini had stepped down voluntarily, in order to spare his people the continuation of a hopeless war, this would indeed have been a great and noble deed. Can we summon similar courage here?

Berlin, 27 July 1943

I returned here early this morning. Everyone is talking about the revolution in Italy. How will this affect the situation in Germany? Our military situation is certainly more than serious. If Italy lays down her arms, the Balkans will be outflanked by the enemy, and sooner or later a great part of the Balkan peninsula, e.g., Albania and the portions of Croatia and Greece occupied by Italy, must automatically fall into its hands. Hungary and Rumania will undoubtedly defend themselves but weakly, if at all. *Facit*: loss of the Balkans. Consequence: the rolling up of our Russian front from the south. And given this situation, we failed to build bridges toward the East!

Berlin, 28 July 1943

This morning I was at the Foreign Ministry in order to ascertain the status of my request for a leave. At 11:00, when I was meeting with Geheimrat [Privy Counselor] P. [Padel] and some other gentlemen, the sirens sounded. We went into the air-raid cellar, where a mob of more than a hundred people had gathered. The cellar is half above ground and has windows facing the Wilhelmstrasse, windows which are poorly protected with iron casements. The old, rather dilapidated house Nr. 75 is located above this "air-raid shelter." A single door leads into the cellar; at best two people can enter at the same time. It is simply scandalous that the Reich authorities, which are charged, at least nominally so, to safeguard our foreign interests, cannot provide better protection. But as absurd as it sounds, there is method in this madness. The Minister does not desire his officials and employees to be better protected against air raids than the ordinary inhabitants of Berlin. *Fiat propaganda, pereat mundus*! If the Foreign Ministry were better protected than ordinary folk, this—so the saying goes—would look like defeatism. One can only ask: why is not everybody well protected? After three years of war there should have been plenty of time to take proper air-raid precautions.

Probably every one of us had such disrespectful thoughts as we sat jammed together in the cellar, awaiting the bomb that would have made short, if not exactly painless, shrift of these authorities. Nothing like this can happen to Ribbentrop, because he is not in Berlin. Why does he not sit in this mousetrap with us to share the fate of his people?

Fortunately the attack was again aimed at the outlying districts; after an hour the all-clear sounded.

Berlin, 30 July 1943

I have received permission to travel to Switzerland and have been released from my duties, which *de facto* no longer existed anyway. I am overjoyed.

For four consecutive days, Hamburg has been bombed most terribly, each time for an hour and a half. Not much is supposed to be left of the old city.

Baden-Baden, 31 July 1943

I left Berlin this morning on an overcrowded train and amid nearly tropical heat. In Halle, the train became even more jammed with refugees from Hamburg. They are in wretched condition and give awful descriptions of the atrocities that took place in that city. The death toll is estimated between 40– and 70,000.

Nothing was available during the journey. Often there was not even water at the train stations. [Railway] personnel were totally inadequate, especially considering the stream of refugees which had fled the destroyed city of Hamburg without luggage and was, in many cases, poorly clad and without food. Everyone was grumbling about the lack of organization. The S.S. people guarding the train were subdued and did not dare say anything. Shortly before reaching Frankfurt, the refugees were transferred for some unknown destination. I arrived in Bad Oos around 11 p.m., rather exhausted from standing in the train; shortly thereafter I reached Baden-Baden.

twenty-two

August 1943

Baden-Baden, 1 August 1943

A very hot Sunday. I am quite tired after yesterday's exhausting and annoying journey, not to speak of the emotional setbacks of the past few weeks. Miss R. [Rohde], my secretary, phoned to say that Berlin is to be evacuated of all civilians who are not absolutely necessary. Thus, even her seventy-year-old parents, for whose sake she had remained in the city, are forced to leave Berlin. Where should they turn for help? No one wants to take in such useless refugees. But who, these days, worries about such small everyday tragedies?

Difficulties have arisen concerning our trip to Switzerland. I will get my German exit visa only if Ribbentrop, who is again unavailable, personally agrees. This is a new regulation preventing anyone from going abroad who, by National Socialist standards, is not entirely trustworthy. Now we will probably have to wait much longer, if there still is a chance to obtain an exit permit.

Again Munich has been attacked. Here, too, we had an alarm; heard detonations in the distance.

Baden-Baden, 6 August 1943

The days pass in tense waiting, which is upsetting. Nearly every night there is an alarm, but the planes have other destinations. We only hear the noise of the engines and flak fire.

Ribbentrop had a discussion with Hitler and Bormann at Headquarters. Why should this be publicized? Simultaneously there was a Cabinet meeting in Rome. Presumably these discussions serve the ultimate break-up of the Axis.

The battle in Sicily continues without the Italians and without hope for us, especially after Catania surrendered. Retreat to the mainland is unavoidable. Of course we will be unable to hold out for long, especially since the local inhabitants there now greet us with open hostility.

Baden-Baden, 8 August 1945 [sic]

The British compared 5 August of this year with the tragic 8 August 1918, when Hindenburg told the Kaiser in Spa that the war could no longer be won. I sincerely doubt whether Ribbentrop has made a similar declaration to the Führer, quite apart from the fact that this is a military matter. In any case, the conduct of our party bigwigs indicates everything other than that they are aware of the real political and military situation. They do not want that known in any case. People like Sauckel, who just gave a major address in Paris, prattle on about victory and perseverance instead of finally trying to negotiate with the enemy. If need be, our government could negotiate in secret, and it would not hurt anything if Sauckel and Co. continued to intoxicate themselves and their followers with their phrases. Unfortunately we lack the "civil courage" to confess to ourselves and to others that it is high time to liquidate this enterprise. It seems to be our fate that forever our laurels of war must wilt all too quickly. We always rattle our sabers—at least in the eyes of the rest of the world. When things are going well, as they did early in this war, when we stormed in with great élan, there are no limits to our goals. Full of hubris we always believe that we can conquer the world, but at the height of our power, and even more so when our strength is failing us, we lack the courage to stop and to negotiate with our foes.

Baden-Baden, 11 August 1943

The Minister has consented to my departure for Switzerland. Our passports have been sent to the Swiss Legation.

I have been acquitted in Rio, on appeal; so were the other members of the Embassy.

The Lorenz church in Nuremberg has been destroyed by bombs. This evening a British radio spokesman noted that one and a half million (1,500,000) kilograms of explosives were dropped on Nuremberg. This city is as far distant from England as are Leipzig and Brandenburg. From those cities to Berlin the difference would only be about 60 kilometers. Draw your own conclusions from that one! When will this insanity end, an insanity in which one is proud of his own destructive mania?

The German Radio Network has been off the air since midnight. It is now 1 o'clock. Which unfortunate city was hit?

Baden-Baden, 12 August 1943

Last night's raid was not the expected heavy raid on Berlin; it was merely a nuisance overflight. On the other hand, this morning our "guests" hit Bonn and Bochum, causing considerable damage. Last night, we had another 90 minutes worth of air alarm.

Baden-Baden, 13 August 1943

No day or night passes without air raids. To the uninitiated, it would seem almost impossible that, under such circumstances, German industry can continue to operate to the same extent as in the past. In many cases, the factories have been relocated in underground facilities. Even so, in the long run this high productivity can probably not be sustained because of the continuous disruption of the transportation and distribution systems, due to air attacks. The worst part is that, under such conditions, supplies and ammunition for the front line troops are bound to run short.

Secretary of State Kepler [*sic*] is here to inspect Baden-Baden and "commandeer" accommodations for the Foreign Ministry. What a foolish idea! Instead of moving out of the way of enemy attacks which, for the time being, are threatening only from the west, we should relocate our government agencies precisely in that direction; in addition, we take the risk that this city, undamaged until now and totally unprotected, will be targeted by the enemy.

The Italian consul general G. [Guida] visited us this evening. He said the coup d'état in Italy had been carefully planned. So well planned, in fact, that on 25 July, the day of Mussolini's forced resignation, most of the former democratic newspapers and organizations were operational, in part under their original managers. Mussolini was captured near Rome. The conduct of the army, which felt increasingly that it was merely fighting for Fascism rather than for Italy, was crucial to the success of the revolution. G., too, is convinced that Italy will desert the pact with Germany. In this connection, he also mentioned Italian rumors about a separate German-Russian peace.

Baden-Baden, 14 August 1943

Once more Rome has been bombed.

For the time being, the commandeering of Baden-Baden for the Foreign Ministry has been set aside, because the Führer did not approve such nonsense.

In Sicily we have given up the Aetna massif; this probably seals the fate of the island. The capitulation of Italy may not be long in coming.

Baden-Baden, 19 August 1943

The air raids continue day by day and night by night. All cities in Southern Germany are systematically bombed. At the same time, there are hardly any reports, only rumors, on what transpires in the bombed areas. It is truly astonishing how the official news and propaganda agencies have succeeded in erecting smokescreens around individual regions, thus, isolating them from each other. All newspapers, of course, are forced to write the same thing; they carry terse factual reports of the attacks, but no details. At best they note that the population sustained losses. They are silent as to the extent of casualties. Given the number of enemy planes deployed and given the explosive power of the bombs, such losses must be very considerable. Nor do we learn how the population takes these losses. According to official press reports, which are confirmed by private sources, they show almost inhuman stoic courage. What else can they do? It is almost incomprehensible how a great and intelligent nation could have fallen so totally into the hands of such a relatively small ruling clique; how it would have lost all powers of self-determination, and almost all comprehension of its own miserable condition. Even here in Baden-Baden we are ignorant of what is happening in our immediate vicinity, such as Karlsruhe or Strassburg. Of course, this can also be blamed on the increasing travel difficulties.

There is general concern about the many foreign workers and prisoners of war; in the event of a general collapse, they could become a very real danger, particularly in northern Germany and in the industrial regions. These folk, millions of them, bitterly hostile to us, and presumably without discipline, could easily turn into a guerrilla force right here at home. Starving and, probably, poorly treated, they will hardly show their former masters much mercy. Although around here, to be sure, I have not heard of any cases of maltreatment. The foreign workers, mostly Frenchmen, naturally have to share our own meager food supply.

Baden-Baden, 31 August 1943

Last week was devoted to preparations for our departure; this in the face of continuous air alarms. Twice Berlin has been severely attacked. In Russia we are on the retreat. Kharkov and Taganrog were lost. Given this deterioration of the war, chances for negotiations become slimmer. Only as long as we hold some trump cards can we expect the enemy to be willing to negotiate. Naturally, once convinced of our defeat, the enemy will refuse to negotiate with us.

There has been a crisis in the government, resulting in further radicalization. Himmler is getting more powerful. Replacing Frick, who was demoted to Reich Protector of Bohemia, Himmler was appointed Minister of the Interior; now he is second to Hitler. Perhaps he is the more powerful of the two. Obviously Hitler is afraid of a development similar to that in Italy and now, in line with the rules of tyranny, he protects himself with his praetorians, the S.S.

This development must lead to an increase in terror and in further suppression of all moderate elements in the [regular] army. Of course, Himmler knows that only the high command can generate a rebellion against the idiocy of resistance at all cost. Therefore, he will do everything to replace the regular army with his Combat SS and put the opposition against the wall. Anywhere else, such meddling of a "Minister of the Interior" in the affairs of the army, in the middle of a war, would cause resistance. Here, the army has apparently accepted its loss of power in silence and without opposition. It is terrible to contemplate how ten years of dictatorship have demoralized the country.

The strictly-controlled unarmed civilian population can hardly be expected to rebel, especially since all able-bodied men are already fighting. It is hard to believe that the generals, and especially those in the Home Army, those who still have some power in the hinterland, keep silent and allow Himmler to take command.

twenty-three

September 1943

Yesterday we turned our backs, God knows for how long, on our poor Fatherland. The last day was rather stormy. After much ado, alarms, and final dispositions, we left for Oos at 9 a.m. with a lot of luggage. Just after we arrived, the sirens sounded, and within minutes a large formation of Flying Fortresses was over us.

Soon we heard rolling detonations from the south, southeast, and southwest. The raid was over at about 11:30. We soon learned that the bombs hit train tracks along the Rhine, in the direction of Basel, our destination. Because the tracks and train stations near Bühl were completely destroyed, our train could not proceed.

Terrible confusion prevailed at the train station in Oos. No connections either to the north, where Mannheim experienced a bad raid last night, or to the south. Finally, around 12:30, a local train comprised of a few cars brought us to Rastatt. Our luggage, except for 10 handbags that we had to carry ourselves, remained unattended on the train platform in Oos. Luckily it was forwarded to Davos.

The train personnel in Rastatt was just as helpless as it was in Oos. It remained for us simply to await what came next. The station was full of people. A local train finally came and after more transfers, brought us along the west bank of the Rhine to Strassburg, which had been bombed a few hours ago. Again, we changed trains and, of course, lugged our bags ourselves helped by only a few obliging young girls from Baden-Baden.

Traveling slowly, we reached Basel in an "express train" that originated in Hamburg, via Colmar and Freiburg. We arrived around 10 p.m. We were treated very kindly by customs and then spent a long night in the hotel. Even here the night was disrupted by sirens, fortunately rather meaningless, and the rumbling of distant raids in Germany.

Today for the first time in a year, we can breathe, think, and talk freely.

Appendix I

The biographical details given relate principally to the period covered in this volume; further information is in the notes.

Abbas Hilmi: ex-Khedive of Egypt exiled in Switzerland

Alfieri, Dino: Italian ambassador in Germany

Arikan, Saffet: Turkish ambassador in Germany

Arslan, Shekib: a Syrian exiled in Switzerland and spokesman for the Arab nationalist cause

Becker, Karl Walther: an official in the Economic Policy Division of the AA

Bohle, Ernst Wilhelm: head of the Foreign Organization (AO) of the NSDAP; chief of the AO in the AA

Bohny, Hermann: a former assistant naval attaché at the German Embassy in Brazil

Boroevich-Heemskerck, Hilva von: member of the family of one of Curt Prüfer's commanders in World War I

Canaris, Wilhelm: chief of the Abwehr and member of the resistance to Hitler

Cossato, Count Conte: counselor at the Italian Embassy in Berlin

Cossel, Hans-Henning von: an official in the AA and former country group leader of the NSDAP in Brazil

Dieckhoff, Hans Heinrich: an official on special assignment in the AA; from 1943 to 1945 German ambassador in Spain

Dumont, Karl Hermann: a counselor in the Economic Policy Division of the AA

Edib-Törelan, Habib: correspondent for the Anatolian news agency

Ehlert, _____: an official in the AA and former employee in the German Embassy in Brazil

Engelhardt, Nanny: sister-in-law of Curt Prüfer

Ernst, Robert: mayor of Strassburg

Ettel, Erwin: German minister in Iran until 1941; liaison of the AA to the Grand Mufti of Jerusalem and Rashid al-Gailani

Felmy, Helmut: commander of German forces in Greece, including the German-Arab training division (DAL)

Glock, Gustav: an official in the AA

Goebbels, Joseph: Gauleiter of the NSDAP in Berlin; Reich minister of Propaganda and People's Enlightenment

Grobba, Fritz: German minister in Iraq until 1939; subsequently on special assignments in the AA, including heading the latter's Arab committee until Dec. 1942

Gudzent: professor of medicine and physician in Berlin

Hassell, Ulrich von: former German ambassador in Italy and member of the resistance to Hitler

Heiden, Erich: an officer in the German army

Hencke, Andor: director after Apr. 1943 of the Political Division in the AA with the title of undersecretary of state

Hentig, Werner Otto von: a Middle Eastern expert on special assignment in the AA

Himmler, Heinrich: Reich leader of the SS and chief of the German police; Reich commissioner for the Consolidation of the German National Community; and after Aug. 1943 minister of the interior

Husayni, Haj Amin al-: Mufti of Jerusalem; Arab leader who fled to Europe in 1941 and allied with the Axis

Inönü, Ismet: general and president of the Turkish Republic

Keppler, Wilhelm: secretary of state for special duties in the AA, in charge of affairs relating to India

Kettenbeil, Karl: a military officer attached to the German Legation in Portugal

Khedive: *see* Abbas Hilmi

Klatten, Werner: director until 1943 of the section in Abt. Deutschland in the AA responsible for production and distribution of literature in and to foreign countries

Köpke, Gerhard: an employee of a major German iron and steel firm and formerly a director of the West European Division in the AA

Kracht, Ulla: sister-in-law of Curt Prüfer

Kroll, Hans: counselor in the German Embassy in Turkey

Langenn-Steinkeller, Helmut von: estate owner in Bellin (Silesia)

Langenn-Steinkeller, Ingrid von: daughter of Helmut von Langenn-Steinkeller

Langmann, Otto: an official in the Information Division of the AA and former German minister in Uruguay

Laval, Pierre: prime minister of Vichy France

Levetzow, Werner von: an official in the AA and former counselor in the German Embassy in Brazil

Luther, Martin: director until 1943 of Abteilung Deutschland in the AA, with the title of undersecretary of state

Melchers, Wilhelm: head of Pol. VII (Middle Eastern section) in the AA

Moltke, Hans Adolf von: German ambassador in Spain in 1943

Mufti (Grand Mufti): *see* Husayni

Niedermayer, Oskar von: commander in Russia of a German army division comprised of foreign and Turkic troops

Oertzen, Hans-Ulrich von: German army officer and member of the resistance to Hitler

Oppenheim, Baron Max von: archaeologist and director of the Tell Halaf Museum and Oppenheim Foundation in Berlin

Oster, Hans: chief of staff in the Abwehr and key organizer of the German resistance

Padel, Wilhelm: a functionary of the ex-Khedive, Abbas Hilmi, in Switzerland

Papen, Franz von: German ambassador in Turkey

Pétain, Henri Philippe: marshal of Vichy France and chief of state

Popitz, Johannes: Prussian minister of finance until his arrest in 1944 resulting from his role in the conspiracy to assassinate Hitler

Prüfer, Anneliese Fehrmann: the wife of Curt Prüfer

Prüfer, Curt Max: ambassador for special duties in the Middle Eastern section of the AA

Prüfer (Prufer), Olaf Herbert Hermann Carl: the son of Curt Prüfer

Rahn, Rudolf: special administrator of the AA in Tunisia

Rashid Ali al-Gailani: Iraq minister president in 1941; subsequently fled to Europe and allied with the Axis

Ribbentrop, Joachim von: German foreign minister, 1938–45

Richthofen, Herbert von: former German minister in Denmark and Belgium

Richthofen, Manfred von: estate owner in eastern Germany

Richthofen, Sigrid von: wife of Manfred von Richthofen

Ritter, Karl: ambassador for special duties in the AA in charge of economic and military affairs

Rohde, Martha: secretary of Curt Prüfer

Sauckel, Fritz: Gauleiter of the NSDAP in Thuringia; from 1942 the Reich plenipotentiary for labor mobilization

Scheliha, Rudolf von: a Silesian noble and official in the AA; executed in 1942 for espionage

Schleemann, Josef: liaison official of the AA with the army high command and overseer of foreign diplomats interned in Baden-Baden

Schlimpert, Martin: an official in the AA and formerly employed at the German Embassy in Brazil

Schröder, Hans: director of the Personnel and Budget Division in the AA

Schulenburg, Friedrich Werner, Count von der: head of Section XIII (Russian affairs) in the Political Division of the AA; until June 1941 the ambassador in the Soviet Union

Siddiq, Ghulam: a former ambassador from Afghanistan exiled in Germany

Sikorski, Wladislaw: general and minister president of the Polish government-in-exile in London; killed in an air crash in 1943

Steengracht von Moyland, Baron Gustav Adolf: member of the German foreign minister's personal staff; secretary of state of the AA during 1943–45

Steffen, Hans: retired German army officer
Stockmann, _____: real estate agent in Baden-Baden
Stohrer, Eberhard von: German ambassador to Spain until Dec. 1942
Stohrer, Marie-Ursel von: wife of Eberhard von Stohrer
Sztójay, Döme: Hungarian minister in Germany
Trottzu Solz, Adam von: an assistant in the AA for the affairs of India
T'Serclaes, Count _____: administrator of Belgian prisoners of war
Weizsäcker, Ernst, Freiherr von: secretary of state of the AA, 1938–43
Witzleben, Erwin von: field marshal in the German army and member of the resistance to Hitler
Woermann, Ernst: director of the Political Division in the AA until 1943, with the title of undersecretary of state

Appendix II

A	Usually signifies Anneliese Prüfer, the wife of Curt Prüfer
AA	*Auswärtiges Amt*; German Foreign Ministry with headquarters in the Wilhelmstrasse in Berlin
Abt.	*Abteilung*; a division or department in the AA
Abt. Deutschland	Division for German Internal Affairs in the AA
Abwehr	Counterintelligence, the Foreign Intelligence Service of the OKW
AO	*Auslands-Organisation*; Foreign Organization of the NSDAP
BB	Baden-Baden
BR	*Botschaftsrat*; counselor of embassy
Büro RAM	Secretariat of the Reich foreign minister
DAL	*Deutsche-Arabische Lehrabteilung*; German-Arab training division
DIS	*Deutsche Informationsstelle*, German Information Office in the Abt. Deutschland
D/Dir/Pers	*Personaldirektor*; Director of the Personnel and Budget Division in the AA
Gestapo	*Geheime Staatspolizei*; Secret state police
GmbH	*Gesellschaft mit beschränkter Haftung*; corporation
LGL	*Landesgruppenleiter*; country group leader of the NSDAP in a foreign country
NSDAP	*Nationalsozialistische Deutsche Arbeiterpartei*; National Socialist German Workers' party, or Nazi party
O	Denotes Olaf Prüfer (spelled Prufer today), the son of Curt Prüfer

OD	Original Diaries
OKW	*Oberkommando der Wehrmacht*; high command of the German armed forces
OMGUS	Office of Military Government for Germany, United States
OPC/KO	Olaf Prufer Collection/Kent, Ohio
OT	*Organisation Todt*; a semi-military unit of the German government responsible for military construction
Pol. VII	*Politische Abteilung* VII; the section for Middle Eastern affairs in the Political Division of the AA
RA	*Rechtsanwalt*, attorney-at-law
RAM	*Reichsaussenminister*; Reich foreign minister
RD	Revised Diaries
RFSS	*Reichsführer SS*; commander-in-chief of the SS
RLM	*Reichsluftfahrtministerium*; Reich Air Ministry
RM	*Reichsminister*; Reich minister
SA	*Sturmabteilung*; storm troopers of the NSDAP
SD	*Sicherheitsdienst*; Security Service
SS	*Schutzstaffel*; Elite Guard of the NSDAP
StS	*Staatssekretär*; secretary of state
UStS	*Unterstaatssekretär*; undersecretary of state
Waffen SS	Combat SS
WHA	*Wissenschaftlicher Hilfsarbeiter*; an auxiliary expert employed on a consultant's basis, a professional assistant appointed for special tasks
zbV	*Zur besonderen Verwendung*; on special assignment

Index

Donald M. McKale is Class of 1941 Memorial Professor of History at Clemson University and the author of *Curt Prüfer: German Diplomat from the Kaiser to Hitler* and *The Swastika Outside Germany*.

Judith M. Melton is Associate Professor of German and Head of the Department of Languages at Clemson University.